Air War D-Day

Volume 2

Assaults From The Sky

Other volumes in this series

Air War D-Day Assaults From The Sky

Air War D-Day

Volume 2

Assaults From The Sky

Martin W. Bowman

Pen & Sword
AVIATION

First Published in Great Britain in 2013 by
Pen & Sword Aviation
an imprint of
Pen & Sword Books Ltd
47 Church Street, Barnsley, South Yorkshire S70 2AS

Copyright © Martin W Bowman, 2013
ISBN 978-1-78159-116-1

Typeset in 10/12pt Palatino
by GMS Enterprises

Printed and bound in England by
CPI Group (UK) Ltd, Croydon, CR0 4YY

Pen & Sword Books Ltd incorporates the Imprints of Pen & Sword
Aviation, Pen & Sword Family History, Pen & Sword Maritime, Pen & Sword
Military, Pen & Sword Discovery, Wharncliffe Local History, Wharncliffe
True Crime, Wharncliffe Transport, Pen & Sword Select, Pen & Sword
Military Classics, Leo Cooper, The Praetorian Press, Remember When,
Seaforth Publishing and Frontline Publishing.

For a complete list of Pen & Sword titles please contact
PEN & SWORD BOOKS LIMITED

47 Church Street, Barnsley, South Yorkshire, S70 2AS, England
E-mail: enquiries@pen-and-sword.co.uk
Website: www.pen-and-sword.co.uk

Contents

Acknowledgements

I am enormously grateful to the following people for their time and effort and kind loan of photos etc, not least to my fellow author, friend and colleague, Graham Simons, for getting the book to press-ready standard and for his detailed work on maps and photographs: My thanks to Ray Alm; Ed 'Cotton' Appleman; James Roland Argo; Peter Arnold; John Avis; Les Barber; Harry Barker; Mike Bailey; Carter Barber; Neil Barber, author of *The Day The Devils Dropped In*; E. W. D. Beeton; Franklin L. Betz; Bill Bidmead; Rusty Bloxom, Historian, Battleship Texas; Lucille Hoback Boggess; Prudent Boiux; August C. Bolino; Dennis Bowen; Tom Bradley; Eric Broadhead; Stan Bruce; K. D. Budgen; Kazik Budzik KW VM; Les Bulmer; Reginald 'Punch' Burge; Donald Burgett; Chaplain Burkhalter; Lol Buxton; Jan Caesar; R. H. 'Chad' Chadwick; Noel Chaffey; Mrs J. Charlesworth; Chris Clancy; Roy Clark RNVR; Ian 'Nobby' Clark; P. Clough; Johnny Cook DFM; Malcolm Cook; Flight Lieutenant Tony Cooper; Lieutenant-Colonel Eric A. Cooper-Key MC; Cyril Crain; Mike Crooks; Jack Culshaw, Editor, *The Kedge Hook*; Bill Davey; S. Davies; Brenda French, Dawlish Museum Society; John de S. Winser; Abel L. Dolim; Geoffrey Duncan; Sam Earl; *Eighth Air Force News*; *Eastern Daily Press*; Chris Ellis; Les 'Tubby' Edwards; W. Evans; Frank R. Feduik; Ron Field; Wolfgang Fischer; Robert Fitzgerald; Eugene Fletcher; Captain Dan Flunder; John Foreman; Wilf Fortune; H. Foster; Lieutenant-Commander R. D. Franks DSO; Jim Gadd; Leo Gariepy; Patricia Gent; Lieutenant Commander Joseph H. Gibbons USNR; Larry Goldstein; Bill Goodwin; Franz Goekel; Lieutenant Denis J. M. Glover DSC RNZNVR; John Gough; Peter H. Gould; George 'Jimmy' Green RNVR; Albert Gregory; Nevil Griffin; Edgar Gurney BEM; R. S. Haig-Brown; Leo Hall, Parachute Regt Assoc.; Günter Halm; Roland 'Ginger' A. Hammersley DFM; Madelaine Hardy; Allan Healy; Andre Heintz; Basil Heaton; Mike Henry DFC, author of *Air Gunner*; Vic Hester; Reverend R. M. Hickey MC; Lenny Hickman; Elizabeth Hillmann; Bill Holden; Mary Hoskins; Ena Howes; Pierre Huet; J. A. C. Hugill; Antonia Hunt; Ben C. Isgrig; Jean Irvine; Orv Iverson; George Jackson; Major R. J. L. Jackson; Robert A. Jacobs; G. E. Jacques; Marjorie Jefferson; Bernard M. Job RAFVR; Wing Commander 'Johnnie' Johnson DSO* DFC*; Percy 'Shock' Kendrick MM; the late Jack Krause; Cyril Larkin; Reg Lilley; John Lincoln, author of *Thank God and the Infantry*; Lieutenant Brian Lingwood RNVR; Wing Commander A. H. D. Livock; Leonard Lomell; P. McElhinney; Ken McFarlane; Don McKeage; Hugh R. McLaren; John McLaughlin; Nigel McTeer: Ron Mailey; Sara Marcum; Ronald Major; Walt Marshall; Rudolph May; Ken Mayo; Alban Meccia; Claude V. Meconis; Leon E. Mendel; Harold Merritt; Bill Millin for kindly allowing me to quote from his book, *Invasion*; Bill Mills; John Milton; Alan Mower; Captain Douglas Munroe; *A Corpsman Remembers D-Day Navy Medicine 85*, No.3 (May-June 1994); Major Tom Normanton; General Gordon E. Ockenden; Raymond Paris; Bill Parker, National Newsletter Editor, Normandy Veterans; Simon Parry; Albert Pattison; Helen Pavlovsky; Charles Pearson; Eric 'Phil' Phillips DFC MiD; T. Platt; Franz Rachmann; Robert J. Rankin; Lee Ratel; Percy Reeve; Jean Lancaster-Rennie; Wilbur Richardson; Helmut Romer; George Rosie; The Royal Norfolk Regiment; Ken Russell; A. W. Sadler; Charles Santarsiero; Erwin Sauer; Frank Scott; Ronald Scott; Jerry Scutts; Major Peter Selerie; Alfred Sewell; Bob Shaffer; Reg Shickle; John R. Slaughter; Ben Smith Jr.; *SOLDIER Magazine*; *Southampton Southern Evening Echo*; Southwick House, HMS *Dryad*, Southwick, Portsmouth; Bill Stafford; Allen W. Stephens; Roy Stevens; Mrs E. Stewart; Henry Tarcza; Henry 'Buck' Taylor; June Telford; E. J. Thompson; Charles Thornton; Robert P. Tibor; Dennis Till; Edward J. Toth; Walt Truax; Jim Tuffell; Russ Tyson; US Combat Art Collection, Navy Yard, Washington DC; Thomas Valence; John Walker; Herbert Walther; Ed Wanner; R. H. G. Weighill; Andrew Whitmarsh, Portsmouth Museum Service; 'Slim' Wileman; Jim Wilkins; E. G. G. Williams; Deryk Wills, author of *Put On Your Boots and Parachutes! The US 82nd Airborne Division*; Jack Woods; Len Woods; Waverly Woodson.

Chapter 1

Planes Overhead Will be Ours

'The 8th Air Force is currently charged with a most solemn obligation in support of the most vital operation ever undertaken by our armed forces.'
General Doolittle, in a message read out to the men at all bases.

'Dick' Johnson a 'Mickey' navigator in the Hundredth Bomb Group, who had been seconded to the 452nd at Deopham Green for the mission, was one who spent all night in briefing with no sleep at all. For the first time to his knowledge there was a password to get to the aircraft. It was 'Pearl Harbor'. When he finally did get to the Fortress one of the guards stuck a Thompson sub-machine gun in his belly and said, 'Halt, Lieutenant Johnson. Who goes there? He made Johnson give the password too. In the 452nd formation, which had taken off at 03:00 Johnson could see the Channel on the scope of his 'Mickey' set. He was astounded. There were so many ships that it seemed like you could scarcely see the water. They could not see the coast so it was planned to bomb blind but it was 07:28½ hours when his ship reached the release point, so they closed their bomb doors and did not drop as the troops were scheduled to go ashore at 07:25 at their location. His pilot had to make all his turns over France to the right, as Allied anti-aircraft gunners had been briefed that any aircraft making a left turn would be considered hostile.

The first mission was primarily concerned with the neutralizing of enemy coastal defences and front-line troops. Subsequent missions would be directed against lines of communication leading to the bridgehead. The Liberators' first mission meanwhile would be in good company, with no fewer than 36 squadrons of Mustangs and Thunderbolts patrolling the area. Initially they would protect the bombers but would later break off and strafe ground targets. It was evident that there could be no delay and that stragglers would be left to their fate. Any aborts were to drop out of the formation before leaving the English coast and then fly back to base at below 14,000 feet. It was a one-way aerial corridor and the traffic flow would be intense. If a plane had to be ditched, only those ships returning to England from the beachhead would stop to pick up crews.

The briefing over, a line of trucks was assembled to take the crews to their waiting aircraft. At 01:30 the slumbering cathedral city of Norwich and the pre-dawn calm of the surrounding countryside were shattered by the roar of hundreds of Twin Wasps and Wright Cyclones being pre-flighted at all points of the compass. Overhead, the moon shone through thick black undercast. By 0200 the Liberators at Flixton were formed in two lines, converging at the head of the runway. This avoided the problem of anyone leaving a revetment, going off the runway and ruining the timetable. Colonel Joe Brogger, the air commander, sat in the cockpit of *Red Ass*, referred to (for public relations purposes) *The Buckeroo* piloted by Lieutenant Charlie Ryan. All aircraft had their navigational lights on, with the yellow-orange assembly ship, *Fearless Freddie*, completing the picturesque spectacle.

Just on 02:20 Captain Smith in the control tower told the crew of the chequered caravan at the edge of the runway to 'Give 'em the green light' and the B-24s thundered down the runway. The first to arrive in the assembly area was Liberty Run, a PFF ship in the 564th Squadron of the 'Sky Scorpions', which Lieutenant L. J. Litwiller of the 'Travelling Circus' and his crew had flown over specially from Hethel the previous afternoon. Robert A. Jacobs the dead-reckoning navigator recalls.

'At this time the 564th Squadron was composed of selected lead crews from 2nd Bomb Division units who were given additional training in PFF techniques, which included bombing through undercast using H2X radar'. Colonel Brogger and the other 446th aircraft in the lead section formed on *Liberty Run* and headed for France. There was solid undercast and they released their bombs on the H2X aircraft's smoke markers. The night before when John A. White wrote that he thought things were going to pop any day soon did not dare ever dream it would be so soon. He was one of the pilots who were briefed for the first raid directly in support of the invasion troops but when his formation arrived over the target area the weather was so bad that he could not see a thing and they brought their bombs back. He wrote: 'Damn, what a disappointment.'

2nd Lieutenant Ben Isgrig, from Arkansas, a bombardier in the 448th Bomb Group.

'Each B-17 was loaded with twelve 500lb and two 1,000lb bombs and we were off at 0600 with 34 aircraft. Two aircraft aborted due to mechanical problems. This was my tenth mission with the 427th Squadron and Colonel Snyder the commander led the low flight. Walter Cronkite flew with Bob Sheets in '*Shoo Shoo Baby*' of our squadron on this mission. We were to bomb a bridge near the invasion coast, but the cloud cover at the target was total, so we were to bomb by PFF (radar). Sixteen aircraft of the lead group dropped 192 500lb GP bombs and 30 1,000lb GP bombs on the target, with unobserved results. Our flight had a radar failure and dropped no bombs. We flew our bombs back to base and made ready for our second mission of the day.

'Our target near the invasion coast was a bridge near Caen that we were unable to bomb because of an equipment failure on the lead aircraft. We saw flak again at a distance but we were not affected. The weather over the French coast was bad with 5/10th cloud cover but we could see bits of the invasion activity. The number of wakes from ships and landing craft covered the entire English Channel for miles. We could see smoke on the French coast from all the artillery. To prevent being fired upon by our own gunners, the fighters and medium bombers had a wide, white stripe painted across one wing and around the fuselage. The heavies didn't bother with this, as we were too high to be seen. We had achieved the desired mastery of the air by this time and the Germans had a bitter joke amongst themselves: 'If you see a camouflaged airplane, it's British. If you see a shiny, unpainted airplane, it's American. If you don't see any airplane at all, it's German.' Much of our mission at this stage of the war was the attrition of experienced German fighter pilots. As they rose up to defend their country, our fighters shot them down. And so, on this day, the destruction of Hitler's Third Reich began in earnest and the outcome is in the history of Earth's greatest war.'

R. 'Dick' Johnson, co-pilot in 2nd Lieutenant Theodore R. 'Bud' Beiser in *Buzz Blond* of the 427th Bomb Squadron, 303rd 'Hell's Angels' Bomb Group at Molesworth.

'It was just getting light as our formation left the English coast and the clouds broke enough for us to see the hundreds of ships in the Channel heading for France. We could plainly see the heavy warships shelling the coast, which was shrouded in smoke. Besides seeing more ships than I had ever seen before, there were also more heavy bombers in the air than I thought possible to put up in one area.'

'I saw battleship firing at gun emplacements. It was quite a sight - quite a show. The flak was light and the mission successful.'

Bob Shaffer, the bombardier in *Naughty Nan* in the 'Travelling Circus' flown by Lieutenant Gomer J. Sneddon of Rock Springs, Wyoming. On 3 March 1944 Sneddon's B-24 crashed on take-off in bad weather at Hardwick killing three of the crew. Sneddon and six others survived.

'The coast itself was covered in clouds. We didn't see our target at all neither did we see flak or fighters.' Some 1,015 heavies bombed coastal installations, while 47 hit transportation choke points in Caen and 21 more hit alternative targets.

Ben Isgrig

'At the briefing Colonel Carl T. Goldenberg, the Group Commander, said: 'Gentlemen, you will be able to tell your children and grandchildren about D-Day. There will be a lot of your friends below you today. Be careful you don't drop on them. If you're down there heading for an invasion, you don't want someone to ruin it by dropping a bomb in your boat.'

Lieutenant Herman C. 'Mitch' Mitchell's crew, a lead crew in the 491st Bomb Group at Metfield in Suffolk where *Miss Stardust* seemed to be Mitch's favourite aircraft and he would ask if she was available for any given mission so he could fly her. But they would lead the third squadron in *Paddy's Wagon*.

'The Channel was churning with boats of all sizes and the air above was black with formations of aircraft supporting the invasion troops. They all had newly painted large black and white stripes on them to designate that they were friendly.'

Charles E. Clague Jr, 21-year old bombardier.

'Our target area was a railroad yard approximately 20 miles south of the Normandy beach and we had explicit orders not to drop the bombs anywhere else if we could not positively identify the target. It was to be a maximum effort by every group in the Air Force. This meant every plane and crew able to fly were to participate. Everything went well. We took off before dawn, rendezvoused with other groups near southern England and started across the Channel just at sunrise. Through scattered clouds, we could see thousands of boats and ships of every description heading south. It was an awe-inspiring sight to see this flotilla, perhaps 50 miles wide, all heading towards the French coast. As we approached the beach, the cloud cover became 10/10 and we couldn't see a thing. We flew by dead reckoning to the target area but failed to find any openings in the overcast. Disappointed, we turned around and headed back towards the base. The sky was as full of planes as the Channel was full of boats. American fighters were everywhere anticipating an all out attack by the German Air Force, which never materialized. We landed at the base and were told by the control tower that all crews were to remain at their planes. Trucks came out to refuel the ships and sandwiches and coffee were distributed. The Colonel, Mitch and I went to headquarters and were instructed that our groups should take-off as soon as we were refuelled to go after the same target. After bolting our lunch, we again took off, formed the group and headed for France. The Channel was still filled with boats but this time the cloud cover had disappeared. As we approached the coast, we could see flashes of gunfire all along the beach. The good visibility stayed with us and we were able to deliver our bombs on the target. We returned to base without losing a single ship.'

'As soon as the plane was parked in our dispersal area we were met by a truck, which took the whole crew back to the briefing room. The flight surgeon met us at the door and gave each man half a tumbler full of whiskey. I had never experienced a pick-up like I received from that booze. We were all terribly tired, as flying on oxygen is quite fatiguing and we had not been to bed in over 24 hours. The flight surgeon kept saying 'Drink 'r down boys, 'cause I need the glasses', which were refilled for the other crews as they entered the building. [1]

23-year old 2nd Lieutenant Howard 'Howie' W. Mesnard, navigator.

Wallace Patterson, 448th BG - in 1st Lieutenant Albert L. Northrup Jr's crew:
'The group was divided into six sections of six ships each and we were No.3 in the first section. Each two sections were assigned separate targets in the same area and there were three different bomb loads: 500lb GP, 100lb GP and Frag. We had 500-pounders and as a target the gun emplacements at Pointe de la Percèe on the coast in the centre of the invasion line stretching from Cherbourg to Le Havre. Fighter support was on the area type and consisted of a continuous movement over the invasion route of 38 groups. The naval bombardment started at 02:00 and we took off at 0230 in the dark with a bright moon. Due to the new system and some previous practice, the formation was neither difficult nor overly dangerous, though we did lose our leader once in the clouds and then picked him up later on. We flew the inland route to Manchester, then south to the Channel. Our target time was 06:00 with an additional allowance of 25 minutes before we were to stop to let the first assault boats and paratroopers land at 06:30.

'At the English coast we observed the landing craft and troopships of presumably the second or third waves massing and heading toward France. Innumerable fighters covered them. As we approached the French coast the clouds shut off our vision of the landing itself but looking obliquely under them we could make out spasmodic flashes of gunfire, though we could not see the source. Over the target and on back well into England we were over ten-tenths cloud cover and had no view of the landing operations. Just after bombs away a terrific explosion rocked the entire formation, leaving a dense cloud of brownish-grey smoke. Though it may have been heavy flak, as we were only 14,500 feet, we are of the opinion that it was a bomb that exploded by some freak accident. On the way back across the Channel we strayed too close to the invasion fleet, which shot some rather accurate flak up at us. We had been warned to stay away or they'd shoot.

'Return to the base was uneventful but due to lack of sleep and rough air most of us were feeling pretty rotten. Back in the hut we listened to the news of the invasion and to

1   'It seemed like it was only shortly after D-Day that our crew completed what was then a combat tour of 30 missions. At this time most of the men returned to the States and received a 30-day leave. After that they were usually assigned to the Training Command as instructors.' All the crew, except Charlie Clague, who worked as a briefing officer, elected to accept the stateside duty. Herman C. Mitchell remained in England where he and Neil R. Fullerton, the radioman, delivered much needed fuel to the troops in France and Germany. Mitch's drinking ultimately led to alcoholism when he returned to the USA and he died aged 46 in 1969.

the messages of Eisenhower and the various prime ministers of their various countries. Then we hit the sack for a while and were roused for a 02:30 briefing to go bomb a railroad overpass and marshalling yards slightly in advance of the invaders. Due to weather, however, the show was scrubbed a few minutes after briefing though we were still on the alert and might be called back at any time. For the first time, each bomb had a crewmember's name on it and the last one had written 'Good Luck to the boys on the ground'. I guess we might claim to be among the first 100 men to invade, though the show was actually little different from what we had been doing for the past few days. [2]

'I took time in the afternoon to fill out my forms saying what I wanted to do when I completed my thirty. I believed that my chances of a 30-day leave at home were pretty good if I survived the next few trips. Then I began to wonder why the boys hadn't come back to the hut; so I made a phone call. By commandeering a jeep I caught the ship on the perimeter two minutes before take-off! I dressed in the ship. Our target was the overpass previously mentioned at Coutances. It was clear over the Channel and invasion coast. The channel was full of boats and planes of all descriptions, headed in both directions. On the coast were a great many fires and near each a crowd of landing craft. In the deeper water were the battleships, shelling spasmodically. I could even make out one of our planes on the ground about a mile from the beach. The target was clear but the bombing was terrible; neither the yard nor the bridge was touched, though the town was totally destroyed. On the way back I had my first view of the islands Jersey and Guernsey. The trip back across England was a nightmare. We were in a bad rainstorm and it was getting dark. Single planes and formations were coming at us from all sides. We flew almost at treetop level and landed nearly in pitch dark. It was the fourth raid for the group today. We had been in the air over twelve hours. We had seen practically no flak and I believed that we had air superiority over the whole of the invaded area.' [3]

'In the evening of June 5th, at about 20:00 hours, we were alerted by the 324th Squadron Commander, Lieutenant Colonel Robert Weitzenfeld and informed in the classic manner, 'This is it'. We knew 'it' meant invasion but we didn't know where 'it' was to take place.

'We took off from Bassingbourn with about 17 other PFF crews flying to various Bomb Groups in the 1st Bombardment Division. Three of us, Clark, Tyson and one other PFF team, which served as deputy lead, headed for the 381st Bomb Group at Ridgewell. We didn't get any sleep and received our final briefing at 01:30 hours. Security was extremely tight. Only pilots, navigators and bombardiers were allowed in the briefing room. All persons briefed were pledged to secrecy until the planes were in the air and the mission was underway. Only then could location of the target be released to the crew.

'In a maximum strength effort, the 381st put up two Groups of 18 planes, with a PFF

2 Altogether, 52 bombers were dispatched on the second strike. Most crews returned with their bombs because their targets were covered by cloud, though 37 bombers did manage to bomb Argentan. Coming back across the Channel from the Cherbourg Peninsula crews in the 1st Task Force of the 1st Bomb Division could see more ships than they could count. Ironically, amid all this activity, the German radio station at Calais was on the air playing a song called *Invasion Day*. The third mission involved bombing the important communication centre at Caen and 56 Liberators managed to bomb through overcast skies. Not all of the Fortress groups made it. Some were briefed for two more raids in the afternoon but the weather was too bad for them to fly.
3 Wallace Patterson flew his 30th and final mission on 18 June.

team leading each Group. Jim Tyson and I led the first Group in an attack on enemy defenders of the 'Gold' invasion beach. The second Group of 18 planes was led by the PFF team of Carl Clark and Clem Abler. Their target was an airport in the St-Lô area.

'The bomb load for our Group on 6 June was twenty 100lb HE demolition bombs in all of the eighteen planes. The load seemed almost puny by comparison with the 2,000lb, 1,000lb and 500lb bombs we had dropped in Normandy and Pas de Calais gun emplacements on 2 June, 3rd, 4th and 5th. Our principal target on 6 June was a gun battery on the beach north of Bayeux. However, our formation consisted of a shallow Vee of Vees with six planes in each Vee. Pilots normally allowed about 50 feet between wing tips. The wingspan of a B-17 is 103 feet 9-3/8 inches. The distance from outside wing tip to outside wing tip of the 18 ship Group formation was over 1,300 feet. There was little likelihood our total of 360 diminutive 100lb bombs scattered along a one quarter mile stretch of beach would wipe out a gun battery. However, we were told the 100lb bombs were supposed to make foxholes for the troops.

'The weather looked bad and we were given strict orders to make certain our bombs didn't fall short. Our assigned target area was the 'Gold' beach and we were flying in support of British and Canadian troops.

'The assembly went off smoothly and on time. Our months of practice and training in formation assembly paid off. We left Beachy Head on time and headed south and west across the English Channel to pick up a 'Gee' line that would guide us in to the target. Mickey operator John Spierling said his radar scope was full of reflections from hundreds of boats in the Channel. Until he said that, I didn't believe it was the real thing. I thought it was just a big practice mission.

'I used the Pembroke-Paris 'Gee' Chart. The 'Gee' box signal was strong and showed no signs of jamming attempts by the Germans. Further, the 'Gee' line on my chart was ideally situated at right angles to the beach line.

'At our 15,000 feet bombing altitude, we had a solid undercast and were forced to use the 'Gee'-H2X procedure practiced at Skegness. I had my eyes glued to the blips of the 'Gee' box keeping us on course. John Spierling gave range and ground speed data to the bombardier who cranked the information into his Norden bombsight. Charlie Eager, our bombardier from the 381st Bomb Group looked for a break in the clouds so he could take over visually. But it never came. Nevertheless, our training paid off. We had confidence the 'Gee' Box course line was reasonably accurate and our practice bombing sessions had proved the 'Mickey' operator and bombardier could hit the beach line with good accuracy. We did what we were trained to do and did it to the best of our ability with full confidence in our equipment and procedures.

'Bombs were dropped at 07:04. Zero hour for landings on the British-Canadian sector 'Gold' Beach below us was 0725 hours. At 'Bombs Away' I left the scope of my 'Gee' Box and came up for air and to look out of my window. But all I could see was a solid undercast and one solitary puff of black smoke in the sky, evidently made by the collision and accidental explosion of two 100lb bombs as they tumbled earthward and collided in mid air. There was no enemy flak over the beaches nor after 'Bombs Away'. Evidently the Germans were saving or using their ammunition on other targets.

'The target of Carl Clark and Clem Obler was an airport near St-Lô. While making his attack at St-Lô, Clem started the approach using 'Gee'. Like our formation, they were not bothered with German flak. As they flew into the target area, Carl brought the formation down to 10,000 feet. They gained contact with the ground and the bombardier took over visually. Clem abandoned the 'Gee' box and leaned over the bombardier watching the 'aiming point' hangar area of the airport with binoculars. Clem describes the action that followed.

'A German truck or weapons carrier came roaring across the tarmac at high speed. I could see the faces of two men clearly as they looked up at us. They came to a screeching halt at the hangar and one man jumped out to open a door. He jumped back into the truck and they drove inside. Just then, our bombs struck the hangar and blew it to pieces. As Clem put it, 'the air war becomes quite personal at lower altitudes.'

'In our formation we didn't see many allied bombers and no enemy aircraft at all. All bomber formations were routed in line astern. After the target, they had to fly a traffic pattern south across the Cherbourg Peninsula, then a right turn flying about 75 miles west and then another right turn flying due north past the Jersey and Guernsey Islands and back to base. It was a thrilling occasion; but for our crew, it was a very easy raid. There was no need for the extra boxes of ammunition we had stashed throughout the plane. We didn't see a single enemy fighter and there was no flak over the target nor along our route.

'Breaking with PFF standard operating procedures, we didn't return to Bassingbourn; but landed at Ridgewell about 1030 hours and were debriefed. The aircraft were again loaded with bombs and serviced to fly another mission. The lead crews of Jim Tyson and Carl Clark were confined to the operations building. Rumours were rampant including one that, 'in the event the invasion went badly, B-17s would be used at low altitudes to drop fragmentation bombs and strafe. The rumours really didn't bother us; but the lack of sleep for more than thirty hours was wearing us down. We made pallets of flak vests and sheep skin lined flight suits. Using partially inflated Mae West life vests for pillows, we went to sleep on the floor of the equipment room. A 381st Squadron Commander awakened us at 1600 hours. The afternoon missions had been scrubbed and we were instructed to return to Bassingbourn.

'A total of 1,622 effective missions were flown by 8th Air Force heavy bombers on 6 June. These bombers dropped a total of 4,852 tons of bombs in support of the troops. Only three heavy bombers were lost on this date. To place things in proper perspective, the 36 B-17s from the 381st involved in these two attacks represented only 2.2% of the 8th Air Force heavy bombers flying out of 36 Bomb Groups in England. Some of the attacks were more successful than ours. Others were less productive. Nevertheless, the 8th Air Force made substantial contributions and greatly assisted our troops fighting below. Of course, our concern for the troops below was real and we worried about dropping short and hitting our allies. I was never able to contact any of the men who hit the beaches north of Bayeux to find out what the results of our bombing amounted to.[4] Apparently, we did our job on D-Day and did it effectively.'

John W. Howland, a navigator in the 91st Bomb Group at Bassingbourn.

4   The only account I have been able to locate was in a book titled *INVASION, They're Coming* by Paul Carell and published by E.P. Dutton & Co., NYC 1963. Carell describes the actions of German soldiers of General Richter's 716th Infantry Division, which was responsible for defence of a coastal sector 21 miles long north of Bayeux. On p.90 Carell describes the experiences of a German soldier named Corporal Behrendsen. 'Behrendsen's machine gun post was half buried in sand. Behrendsen himself had been wounded. The telephone was somewhere underneath the sand and could no longer transmit any orders. But then, what use would the telephone have been since all the wires had been broken by the aerial bombardment anyway. There was no contact left between companies, battalions and regiments of 716th Division - as a fighting unit the 716th Division had been smashed by the murderous aerial and naval bombardment.'

'We were plenty tired after getting no sleep the night before, having been forced to land at a B-26 base following a raid on Paliseau on 5 June. We had flown back to Glatton that night and were unable to get to bed at all before being awakened for the raid on the Cherbourg peninsula. We flew over our target at 16,400 feet and dropped 38 100lb demolition bombs through overcast. The landing troops hit the beach 14 minutes after we dropped our bombs. There were reports that some of our bombs were still exploding as the boys went in. The cloud cover required a blind bombing technique using radar. According to my log we were close to the target; gun positions near Arromanches roughly midway between the Cherbourg peninsula and Le Havre.

'The bomb bay doors of the planes in our formation opened.

'Bombs Away!' the bombardier cried over the intercom.

'The bombs dropped from the bellies of the bombers, disappearing in the clouds to devastate and disrupt the enemy's fighting capabilities far below. I noted in my log: time, 0707 hours; altitude, 14,750 feet; temperature -60C; indicated airspeed, 150 knots; magnetic heading, 344.

'The briefing officer was right. 'There would be meagre flak, if any at all,' he had said.

'There was none. The German guns were busily exchanging fire with the mighty invasion fleet massed in the Bay of the Seine and stretching for miles into the Channel. 'Coming back across the Channel, we could see more ships than you could count. It really was a sight to see the invasion fleet at a port in England ready to set out. They must have been part of the second wave to go over. The boys wanted to go in low for a look but they made us stay up.'

Perry Rudd, 457th Bomb Group - The 'Fireball Outfit'

'On the morning of 6 June I was aroused by the voice of Sergeant Klien, CQ, shouting, 'Breakfast at 01:00; briefing at 02:00', followed by 'You've 'ad it today 'ol boy', meaning I could expect most anything. I quickly dressed, freshened up with a dash of cold water and thence out into the cool June air to combat mess for the usual powdered scrambled eggs. They had cheese mixed with them, which almost camouflaged the awful distaste we had for the ETO food. The meal was topped off with wheat flakes and powdered milk, very tart canned grapefruit juice and very, very strong black coffee.

'Out into the extra cool June night air again for the mile trek to the briefing hut. This sudden trend of early events started to bring our reasoning powers more in focus. GI rumours as to the impending mission had been flying fast and furious in the mess hall. Fred Cascone, tail gunner on my old crew and I talked over three possible conclusions as we walked along. Taking the time of briefing into consideration, the number of ships our squadron was flying and the bomb load for each ship (38 - 100lb Frag.) we boiled our flight plan down to Big 'B' (Berlin), our first shuttle raid to Russia or - Invasion!

'We entered the briefing hut, sat down alongside other combat men on flimsy wooden benches and waited tensely for briefing officers to draw the curtains covering the huge map on the wall. The map has red yarn strung around pins to indicate the mission for the day from our base to enemy territory and return.

'Something big was in the wind! The base photographer was busy with flash bulbs and camera taking shots of us waiting for briefing.

'Here's the briefing officer... tense silence then he speaks: 'This is it, men. This is invasion day!'

'Then he launched into the details of our flight plan. Altitude, weather, rendezvous, zero hour, friendly activity and target, photos of which were flashed on the screen, etc., etc. '11,000 Allied aircraft will be over this morning. Keep on the alert to avoid collisions. There should be little if any flak or enemy fighters. The enemy's heavy 155mm coast gun emplacements will be too busy answering the Navy's challenge to fire at you.' (We hope). '4,000 ships will be in the channel down below you so don't test-fire your guns; you might hurt your own men or hit one of those 11,000 planes filling the sky about you. Remember your POW instructions and special invasion instructions in case you go down. Chaplain Regan is in the back if you wish to see him when you go out. Any questions?'

'Will we use chaff?'

'Only when your pilot receives orders and informs you over the interphone. Any more questions?'

'What's the ETR?'

'About 09:00! Okay men, stations at 0250. That's all.'

'RAF planes are just coming back from their night flight. Their green and red wing lights dot the black sky over our field. I wonder how they made out? All night they have been thundering across the Channel, being the first to start the gigantic invasion machinery to roll like the headwaters of a devastating flood. Now and then the soft full moon filters through the thinning clouds; tiny stars blink down - the weather looks promising.

'Our engines are being revved up now with a deafening roar. How's the oil pressure? RPM? How many pounds mercury indicated on the panel gauge?

'Co-pilot to waist gunner! Check flaps!'

'Flaps down okay.'

'Flap up okay!'

'The ship ahead of us guns forward and disappears from view. Others just ahead of it are already circling the field and starting to climb to altitude. 0450 o'clock, a surge of speed and power as four mighty Wright Cyclones lift 63,000lbs plus 3,800lbs of bombs toward the heavens. We're airborne! A silent prayer to the Powers Above to give us all courage and guide our ship safely.'

Edwin R. Ehret, a radio operator in the 91st Bomb Group at Bassingbourn.

'We airmen in the Eighth and Ninth Air Forces had waited a long time for the D-Day order. It finally reached the 91st Bomb Group on June 6. Our mission was to bomb targets in support of the invasion group forces who were to hit the Normandy beaches at 07.30. Colonel Terry our CO conducted the briefing with all of the Dos and DONTs to follow. It was estimated that from 11,000 to 12,000 aircraft would be in the area and everyone must stay on the briefed course, no aborts. Intelligence predicted limited fighter opposition and light flak in the target area.

'After the briefing, I went to my operations office to help with the details of seeing that the squadron crews were taken care of. I personally was feeling a bit sad that I would not be going on the mission. I was one of the original Group pilots and had waited a long time for this moment. The entire Group got airborne on time without incident. I settled down with a cup of coffee and was shooting the breeze with a Sergeant Birdie, our operations NCO. Within 30 minutes the phone rang. Sergeant Birdie answered and said, 'Major, General Gross wants to talk to you'. Brigadier General

William Gross was commander of the First Combat Wing. I was not accustomed to talking with the General but got on the line immediately. He said, 'Mac do you have a bird flyable that is not on the mission today?' I said, 'Yes sir, we have an old G Model ('Old Faithful') that we use for transition and practice missions. It has no bombs or guns or ammunition.'

'That's OK. Can you get a skeleton crew together? I want to catch up with our combat wing formation and observe the bombings and landings.'

'Yes sir.' I said. 'I'll check on a crew and call you back ASAP.' Frantic phone calls recruited a skeleton crew. I called General Gross and asked him to meet us at the airplane. We had a quick briefing and off we went to catch up with our combat wing. The navigator gave me the headings and we climbed out at full power to 23,000 feet which put us on top of a complete overcast. For as far as we could see, there was a continuous stream of Forts and Libs heading toward the French coast. Finally, about half way across the English Channel, we identified our combat wing.

'We flew alongside the formation until we saw the bomb-bay doors open and soon it was bombs away. There was a fair amount of flak but not a sign of an enemy fighter, nor did we see any of our aircraft go down. A milk run compared to missions flown over Germany prior to D-Day. At this point I expected we would do a 180 turn and return to our base in England. Not so! General Gross said 'Let's go down and observe the landings.'

'I asked the navigator to give me a heading to the landing area on Normandy and he said 'What?' No way was he prepared for this request but said, 'OK, give me a minute or two.' I pulled off the power and started a descent. Soon I had a new heading, with periodic corrections. Down we went through solid overcast in an area that we were forbidden to be in! This was a perfect scenario for a mid-air collision.

'We finally broke out of the overcast at about 700-800 feet above the water in light rain and low clouds but visibility was surprisingly good. What a sight to behold! Ships everywhere. I asked the general, 'What now?' He said, 'Make a right turn.' This would give him a full view of the beach area. During the course of the turn, I began to see black puffs of flak and hear the familiar sounds like rain on a tin roof. The battleship guns on my left were flashing and it was my guess that our Navy was shooting at us! I said to General Gross, 'We don't belong here' and immediately, without waiting for his reply, rammed the throttles and RPM full forward and began a climb back into the overcast while asking the navigator for a heading back to England. We broke out of overcast at about 18,000 feet and continued directly to Bassingbourn without further incident.

'On landing we discovered minor flak damage. I felt we were very lucky to escape with only minor damage and no injuries. General Gross thanked the crew and was gone. I heard later via the grapevine that Major General Williams, our division CO, gave General Gross a verbal reprimand for ordering us to go on an unauthorised mission with no bombs, no guns, no ammunition and no credit for a mission.'

Major James H. McPartlin, 91st Bomb Group at Bassingbourn.

'D-Day started for me at about 02:00. We were awakened to prepare for a bombing mission. Since we were never told the target until briefing, it seemed like any other morning before a mission. After breakfast we headed for the briefing room. Upon arrival we found a major at the door holding a clipboard and checking off the names of all who entered the briefing room. This had never occurred before so we knew something unusual was up. After we were all seated, an officer strode up to the platform behind which was a covered map of the target area. This was the mission map showing the target, the route taken to and from the target as well as the flak concentrations and checkpoints where we could expect to rendezvous with our fighter cover. This was the standard procedure. However, on this day when the cover was removed from the map we saw a red ribbon going into the Normandy area and another coming out on a different heading. Another officer climbed onto the platform in front of the map. His first words were, 'Anyone who divulges any of the information given at this briefing will be shot.' We were then given the details, as they pertained to us, of the D-Day mission. All fighters, fighter-bombers and medium bombers would have white stripes painted around the wings and fuselage. All aircraft must fly the designated routes in and out of the target area. Those that did not would be shot down.

'As the radio-operator for our crew, it was my assignment to pick up the radio codes we were to use that day. Our next stop was the equipment room where we kept our parachute harnesses and parachutes. From there to the armament shack for our .50 calibre machine guns. This was all loaded on a truck, which took us to the aircraft.

'On arrival at the aircraft we stowed our gear. I installed my machine gun in top position of the radio compartment and then tuned my radios to the frequencies being used that day. After finishing these tasks I decided to get out of the plane and have a smoke. I walked a short distance away from the plane, sat down and lit up. I noticed the airplane guard walking back and forth so I offered him a cigarette. He declined the offer. At that time each airplane was guarded by a soldier patrolling back and forth. There was fear of sabotage or German paratroopers dropping on our airfields to destroy the bombers.

'The guard and I began to talk. He said how weary he was of his job and that it seemed he would be doing this forever. There seemed to be no end in sight. He felt that if the invasion would occur soon he would feel his efforts were not in vain. I felt this explosive urge to tell him that today was D-Day but, remembering the officer's words, managed to control this impulse. I decided I better leave before I 'spilled the beans'. I climbed back into the aircraft, went to the radio room and sat down. A few minutes later I thought I heard someone crying softly behind me in the waist. I got up and went back to see what was happening. In the waist I found our engineer and top-turret gunner sitting on the floor quietly sobbing. This was totally out of character for the short hard-drinking, self-centered individual I had come to know. I thought he was crying because he felt we might not make it back, so I said, 'It's OK, Jimmy, we will be fine. You know we always make it back.' His reply stunned me. 'I'm not crying for us, I'm crying for all the poor bastards that are going to die today.' I was so overwhelmed by this unexpected response I turned and walked back to the radio room overcome by my own emotions.'

Sam Stone, '*Sweet 17 Gee*' in the 337th Bomb Squadron, 96th Bomb Group, 8th Air Force at Snetterton Heath, Norfolk.

'The day before D-Day (we did not know at that time) I was a crew chief for a P-51. We were given buckets of paint to paint black and white stripes on the wings and fuselage. We gave the buckets to the flight chef to pass on to another crew. The flight chief said to re-paint the stripes - they were wrong! The black stripes had to be painted white and the white-black.

'That night I was on guard duty from 12 midnight to 8 am. While on duty I witnessed a burst of fire. One of our group pilots crashed into the new control tower. As a crew chief and now told about D Day, I rushed to my plane, went through pre flight procedures topped off the tanks and armorers installed bombs. It was continuous sorties - different pilots flying the same plane. After one mission my plane came back with telephone wires wrapped around the wings.

'It was a long day for all of us.'

Iggy Marinello, 352nd Fighter Group, 8th Fighter Command, Bodney, Norfolk. During takeoff four abreast in poor visibility in the dark with 'oil-drum lighting' Lieutenant Bob Frascotti in P-51 Mustang 'Umbriago' flew into the new, incomplete control tower and he was killed instantly. It was his 89th mission. One Mustang had the volley ball net wrapped around the wing leading edge.

'Mission No. 14 and the day that everyone has been waiting for. They ran four missions today but we didn't have to go on but one of them. We carried 12 x 500lb and hit bridges near Caen, France where the boys were making their landing. The channel was full of Allied boats of all kinds and we could see them just off the French coast making their landings. They had good fighter cover and we had none, but I imagine they needed it. We saw no flak and no fighters. Made two runs on the target and still didn't get our bombs away, but everyone else did. For some reason we didn't get our bomb bay open in time. I hope those boys on the ground had it as easy as we did. Larry Dawson the navigator flew night mission with Devon before Baker's morning mission. 16 to go. 6 hours, 35 minutes.'

Mission diary, Ed 'Cotton' Appleman, engineer-gunner, B-24 Liberator *Duration Baby*, 93rd Bomb Group, 2nd Bomb Division, 8th Air Force, Hardwick in Norfolk.

'I was one of 1,000 Americans interned in Switzerland on June 6. We saw and heard of the invasion from a different perspective in the heart of Nazi-occupied Europe, in an internment camp in the Bernese Oberland. Early that morning I was rousing myself from sleep in a hotel high up in the Alps of Switzerland. We had to fallout for a roll call at the command of our officers and the Swiss commandant. It was a warm spring day and the alpine flowers were blooming on the mountain passes and meadows. Later I went into the village of Adelboden to check on some of my fellow internees who used to gather at the favourite village coffee house on the main street. It was about 11 am when one of my fellow internees flicked on a radio as we sat in the outdoor cafe. We began to hear reports of some kind of a military action in western France but it was not clear what it was. One had to tune to the Yugoslav free radio at that time to get most accurate war reports because Radio Berlin could not be relied on for the true story of what was going on. For hours we listened to these reports not being able to make much of them. This went on for two days and nights until finally on the third day it became apparent that this was no minor military action and indeed it was the long sought invasion of Europe itself.

'Can it really be true' one of my friends said. I and others who were in the 8th Air Force before being shot down had special reasons to feel very close to the airmen, many of them from our own bomb groups, who were at that time leading the assault troops with a bombardment from the air over the beaches of Normandy. Then something wonderful happened that I shall never forget. When this news had gained recognition, the bells of our village church, a small stone church in the middle of the village, began to ring and kept on ringing for hours. Americans, British and many other of the allied national internees began coming from all directions heading for the small village church summoned by the bells. It was quite an impressive sight to see these men; many of them battle hardened veterans of the North African and Italian campaigns, coming together. Others had been in the air war over Germany and many had lost comrades to flak and enemy fighters.'

Forrest S. Clark, a 44th Bomb Group B-24 Liberator gunner who was shot down on 13 April 1944 on a mission to Lechfeld, Germany and forced down at Dübendorf near Zurich.

At Hardwick Bill Francis was one of many who saw the Liberators returning to base. 'All our ships came back without as much as a flak hole. Evidently we caught Jerry with his pants down, for the expected stored up fighter opposition didn't materialize and I can't understand why there was no flak. In Operations a bunch of us were grouped around the radio (wireless), listening to Jerry broadcast and then the British and heard the news of the events so far.

'My crew have been off a regular assigned crew for a month now and some of us have only made one mission during that time. It was because our pilot was made lead pilot and an old crew put with him. We try to kid each other that we don't care as long as we get our 4 hours in a month and say that we are glad we don't have to stick our necks out in this invasion. But I know that if I were not to fly a mission in the next week in the big push, I'd regret it for the rest of my life and the others who spout off feel underneath the same way. So when I learned this morning that our original crew is practically all together again, making it probable that we will fly in the next few days if not today, my hopes mounted and I felt a hell of a lot better.'

That night John A. White reflected on the day's events.
'Our Group flew four missions and rumour has it that two more are to go out tonight. A lot of boys will get in two of them today. We are sweating out the German news broadcasts and midge ['Axis Sally'] now. I'm anxious to hear what they have to say about the thing. Boy! If this goes right, we'll have this thing over with before long. It's got to go right.' Ground crews worked throughout the night of 6 June and all day on the 7th so that two missions could be flown. John White thought he would celebrate his birthday by dropping some bombs on 'Jerry' but the weather was poor and all he could do was sleep and take it easy. Then news arrived from Division that there would be no more tour of duty, temporarily. It was also rumoured that raids for the first few days of the invasion would not count as missions toward the total of thirty. John White wrote: 'I wish they'd make up their mind just what the hell they are going to do with us. The invasion seems to be going OK. Here's hoping.'

Bill Francis in the 93rd 'Travelling Circus' Bomb Group wrote another letter.
'June 7th and the weather typically English with low ceiling and drizzling cold rain. Not very good for the boys on the other coast and worse for us, because we've got to go over and be the Flying Artillery in support of those fellows on the beach heads. All day yesterday there was the steady drone of engines overhead and today it hasn't let up in spite of lousy weather. Four different missions yesterday from our Squadron and we were on the last one. Wasn't bad except for landing. Took off at 5:20; climbed to 16,000 feet, which is fairly low and it was warm upstairs with only -19°. After we got up there was a solid undercast that looked as though a fellow could step out and walk on it. After forming we started crossing the Channel. There

was a steady stream of planes coming back and going over. Nearing the French coast, we could see breaks in the clouds and down below were thousands of ships of all kinds making a steady procession to and from the invasion coast. We were straining our eyes trying to see actual landings but were disappointed. While keeping a weather eye for Jerry and wondering where that stored up German Air Force was hiding, we crossed the coast and on into our target, dropping our bombs squarely and then out again without seeing fighters or flak. I couldn't understand why, but I'm certainly not mad that old Jerry didn't show.

'The worst part of that mission was when we came back with a 500 foot ceiling to drop through in the dark and then trying to find our field. After flying over a dozen different fields in an hour and a half of searching, we finally located ours and landed on a wet runway. That was one of the invasion missions and I only hope the ones to follow are as easy.'

At Deopham Green in Norfolk, Gus Perna and Ralph Reese, the tail gunner and left waist gunner respectively on the crew of B-17 *Smoky Liz* in the 452nd Bomb Group were in the base theatre when Norman Wright, the navigator and James McLellan, the bombardier were called to go to target study at Headquarters. Reese recalls:
'We suspected that something was in the air. We went back to our barracks and were told to report to briefing at once. 'At briefing at 22:30 on 5 June we were told 'this is it'. There would be wave after wave of planes hitting the coast. Our target was coastal defenses at Le Havre. We could not drop any bombs after 07:30, the time the invasion was to start, for the danger of hitting our own troops. Every airfield in England had its lights on at 02:00 - the first time since England had been at war. We carried 38 100lb demolition bombs but there was a solid overcast so we had to bomb using PFF. Bombs were away at 06:59. All planes after the bomb run were to turn to the right, so as to make one way traffic pattern because many planes were in the air. We landed back at our base at 10:30 and our *Smoky Liz* was then loaded with 500lb bombs for another mission within 24 hours.'

'We flew two missions on D-Day, bombing behind the German lines. We did not see a single German fighter or even a burst of flak. Amazing! I could see a battleship out in the Channel. I believe it was the Texas, firing at shore targets. There was a solid mass of ships offshore and we could see the beached landing crafts and others streaking in with their precious burdens. At least we knew we had made a beachhead.'
Ben Smith Jr, 303th Bomb Group at Molesworth.

Tuesday, June 6. Mission #18. We bombed a highway junction back of the invasion beaches flying at only 14,000 feet and using radar for the drop. There was no flak. Above the solid undercast at 10,000 feet. We saw nothing but bombers and escorting fighters.
Diary entry, Lieutenant Abe Dolim, navigator on Joe Hamil's crew, 94th Bomb Group at Bury St. Edmunds.

'It is 0600 - waiting for takeoff; lining up now. 06:20 airborne. Have suspected for several days that it was coming off and last night when they called the first crews at 2300 and we heard so many planes in the air we guessed it, but when they told us in briefing we were very excited. The excitement has gotten into everyone's blood. Joe and everyone can hardly wait to get a view of 'it.' 06:59 - Long just wrote Webster's and Yarborough's names on two of the bombs so they will be in on this anyway. One for Betty, too. 08:20 - looked over London carefully with the binoculars - could not find Piccadilly Circus. English coast ahead. French coast approximately 09:00. Could not see a thing. Undercast solid. I looked up and down the English coast carefully but saw only one boat in motion and quite a few landing craft anchored. We hit the French coast at the spot where the boys were making a beachhead. A few of the crew saw about a hundred landing craft through a break in the clouds. We went on in and bombed the target through the undercast from 14,000 feet. Very little flak and inaccurate. We came around the islands of Guernsey and Jersey. Saw a little flak there against a group of B-24s. Clouds cleared up near the English coast. Picked up two destroyers and several air sea rescue boats quite clearly with the binoculars.

'Joe and I listened to our assigned channel for a while. Heard a Fortress calling in. At first, he was losing 700 feet per minute, at 5,000 feet. Must have lost an engine. Then he called and said that he had lost all four, was at 2,000 feet and losing altitude rapidly. 'Should I use flaps?' he asked very excitedly. Then there was no more. Hope they ditched okay.

'A fighter kept jamming the channel talking to another fighter of ours. Had nine gallons of gas and was trying to get to an airfield. Saw an enormous air depot with more fighters than I've ever seen before. Must have been two or 300. Landed about noon. I slept until 19:00. Ate and went back to bed. Slept until noon the next day, June 7. Ate again and when I came back to the hut had to go to Operations. Raining, cold and bad. Sat around for a while. Came back to pick up the mail. Two from Betty, two from mother, one from Sis, one from R. Baxter and this stationery.'

Harvey T. Brown, Joe Hamil's co-pilot.

'We were to hit the defences in the 'Utah' Beach area, maybe fifteen minutes or so before the landing barges came ashore around 7:00 am. That meant taking off around three o'clock and assembling in the dark, which was very hazardous and there was a lot of apprehension since we had never practiced that kind of thing although we all had experience flying at night. We got off all right and began to form up. The tail gunner had an Aldis lamp, a very bright lamp, which he kept flashing to indicate this is the tail of a B-17 here and don't bump into it. We also flew with wing lights, which would have been of great help to German fighters or anti-aircraft.

'Soon after we took off, the sun was in the sky, although not on the ground. We could see each other and we turned off our lights. Things were normal. We assembled into our thirty-six-ship formation, then the 108-plane combat box of our wing and headed for 'Utah' Beach to bomb the concrete fortifications the Germans had built. I kept looking out and all I could see was our wing, close to 108 planes and I thought now they've really screwed up. Then a minute before we were to bomb, I looked to the right and to the left and out of the high-altitude haze I suddenly saw what looked like the entire Eighth Air Force, maybe 1,500 planes almost in a line abreast like the kick off of a football game. We went on and dropped our bombs. We had expected the Luftwaffe to put up everything they had since once we got our men ashore - we had two million in England waiting to invade - it would be all over. We did not see a single enemy plane or a burst of flak.

'To make sure that nobody mistook who we were when we returned to England, we had a specific course to fly over France and then make a big, wide U-turn. We came over Ste-Mère-Église where a few hours earlier the paratroopers had dropped. As we were passing over Ste-Mère-Église I was thinking of what might be happening to the paratroopers - anyone who came swinging down in a parachute was likely to be shot at. Suddenly, we developed a fire in our control panel. Si, our navigator and Tim our bombardier started tearing away insulation. Bare-handed they pulled some wires loose and stopped the fire. We all thought, 'My god, what a place to have to bail out.' We returned to base without further incident. Actually we were scheduled for a tactical mission later on D-Day. But they had time lines and you couldn't attack a certain area after a specific hour because our guys might now be there. So after we took off we were called back and landed with our bombs.'

19-year old Martin Garren, a co-pilot in the 94th Bomb Group.

'We were off the ground I think around 03:00 and we flew for an hour and a half, two hours in darkness. I sat in the tail. I volunteered because the tail gunner didn't want to do it. I sat there with an Aldis lamp, flashing the letter 'A'-de-da - indicating that this was the 94th Bomb Group. The target's conditions were as we were told. The Germans were not around. We came back and sat on the ground after about seven and a half hours up. I had a bite to eat. We quickly refuelled the aircraft with the bombs and we stayed on the ramp between flights as our B-17s were refuelled and re-armed. While that was going on, I was interviewed by the press.

'All of us flew a second mission and the few that didn't go with us made theirs toward evening just after we returned. The second mission of the day was a little further in because of the action on the beach below. The weather had broken up a bit more; the clouds had more breaks in them. We got a real good look at the action down there. Hundreds and hundreds of boats still coming across the Channel and all those that were lined up along the beach. I saw the battleship Texas firing her big guns across the water to the target areas just beyond the invasion forces and watched the three 1,400lb shells travel to the target and exploded. The crews were very tired after the second mission and the day before we had a long one-and didn't get any sleep for two nights. But we weren't really sleepy. We were all keyed up, wondering what was going to happen.'

Wilbur Richardson, B-17 ball turret gunner, 94th Bomb Group at Rougham near Bury St. Edmunds.

'We were called to the briefing room at 23:00 and Colonel Jerry Mason said, 'This is it'. Our target was 'Omaha' Beach. The first mission was primarily concerned with the neutralizing of enemy coastal defences and front line troops. Subsequent missions would be directed against lines of communication leading to the bridgehead…It was just getting light as our formation left the English coast and the clouds broke enough for us to see the hundreds of ships in the Channel heading for France. We could plainly see the heavy warships shelling the coast, which was shrouded in smoke. Besides seeing more ships than I had ever seen before, there were also more heavy bombers in the air than I thought possible to put up in one area. 'The coast itself was covered in clouds. We didn't see our target at all; neither did we see flak or fighters.'

Ben Isgrig, 448th Bomb Group, 2nd Bomb Division, 8th Air Force at Seething, Norfolk.

'…you are in support of ground troops…Colonel Terry had said.

We were all in it together now. Blood is the same whether it spills on aluminium or Normandy mud. It takes guts whether you fly a million-dollar airplane or wade in slow with a fifty-dollar rifle. But the time element is different. And we get all the breaks there. If a German takes a pot-shot and misses a Yank on the ground, he may get another shot and another. But the last guy that shot at us went by in a Focke-Wulf and he was four miles deep and below before I took a deep breath. The flak-batteries are shooting at whole formations. There's nothing personal in it.

Maybe some of the air-power fanatics will scream that the big brains didn't give us a chance to win it our way. Maybe we could have. Maybe not.

There aren't many guys around here who mind sharing this war.

The only thing that matters is to win and win in a way, so there is never another one…

When we got home the truck didn't come for a while, so I went back behind the tail-wheel and lay down in the grass.

It had been the milk run of all milk runs, no flak, no fighters, no weaving around for position on the bomb-run… just straight in, turn right and straight home again, alone in our blue-white world of sunshine.

The flak-guns were all set low, waiting for tanks to lurch through the hedges and jeeps to wander down the lanes.

After the truck came we got dressed fast so we could get to a radio.

We spent an empty day waiting around the radio in Fletch's room, thinking about that long shot through the clouds and the curve of landing-craft.

One look was all I got.

I looked out the window, south toward France and tried to imagine what it was like. I'd been to Paris, Avord, Metz, Nancy, Le Havre, St. Dizier, Cherbourg, Calais and all the places between. I could tell how green the fields look in Normandy. I could see no sign of a maid when we went over Orleans. I know about the sun patterns on the Seine and the flowers in the fields, the way the Alps grow up out of the mist, east of Chalon.

I could tell, too, about the diseased sky over Paris, the flak-blotches over all the towns and all the ports.

…I'd seen Sharpe in bloody shorts, wrenching his neck to see the wound on his left cheek. I'd seen what a knee looked like with the kneecap clipped away and a waist-gunner with his brains all over the Alclad and his legs shot off just below his flak-suit. That guy was just as dead as any of those in the surf today. A dead one lies just as still in the sky as in a mud-hole.

But most of the time you don't live with death in a Fort the way they must in a ditch. The smells don't get to you and neither do the sounds and every night as long as the luck holds out, your sack is in the same place, ready and waiting, soft and dry.

I thought about those guys in the grass, moving down the roads, crawling through the brush, ready and waiting and I hoped they made it okay…'

D-Day by First Lieutenant Bert Stiles, 401st Bomb Squadron, 91st Bomb Group, 8th Air Force at Bassingbourn. Taken from the classic, *Serenade to the Big Bird*. Staff Sergeant Edward L. Sharpe was the 21-year-old tail gunner from Hot Springs, Arkansas. Stiles, from Sioux City, Iowa, completed his bomber tour but instead of returning to America on leave due to him, he asked to be transferred to fighters and he moved to the 339th Fighter Group and to P-51 Mustangs. At age 23 he was shot

down and killed on 26 November 1944 gaining his only victory as a fighter pilot while escorting bombers to Hanover.

'As we passed over the southern coast of England and headed south over the Channel, I began straining my eyes to see some of the invasion fleet our briefing had disclosed. A low undercast in patches obscured most of the water, but whenever open spaces permitted, I could see landing craft and large ships moving south and southeast on a fairly rough sea. Also below us, just above the clouds, I saw B-26 formations assembling. Didn't see a single friendly fighter, though we were expecting 35 squadrons as cover. They were probably at a low altitude, below the clouds, actively aiding the first assault on the coast. We didn't need them.

'I know each man on the crew prayed for the success of whatever those in the landing barges below us had to do. Their job was infinitely more dangerous than ours. We were scared a bit, yes, because we didn't know exactly what kind of air opposition Jerry would throw at us. Frankly, I expected to see a sky full of fighters and flak, all confusion. But those boys in the barges knew they'd meet steel and concrete and a tough fight!

'It was daylight, with the sun shining above the clouds in the east, as we turned right to head 270 degrees for 90 miles until we were west of the Cherbourg peninsula. Several bursts of flak came up. A group to our right passed too close to either Cherbourg or the islands just west of it. A ball of flak, like that I'd seen over Brunswick once, came up at them.

'Our let down over England was gradual. Clouds broke up and when we arrived back at our base area, only small fair weather cumulus and haze existed. The sky was a trifle overloaded, but we managed to cut our way through the snag and land safely. 'I was so sleepy on the trip back that I contemplated taking a pill to keep awake. Glad I didn't because we were allowed to go to bed immediately after landing. We'd be called if we were needed, they told us.

'An S-2 man, Hodges, met us at the plane for interrogation. We asked for news, but all he could say was, 'The invasion is on.'

'Back at the barracks, Smith had appropriated our radio and was listening to newscasts. Our troops were 10 miles inland already.

'I wrote another letter to Mary, adjusted my gun and went to bed. Someone said Nazi paratroops had landed near us.

Claude V. Meconis, 785th Bomb Squadron B-24 Liberator co-pilot, 466th Bomb Group, US 8th Air Force.

'One of the Bomb Groups of Marauders destined for 'Utah' Beach was briefed by its colonel, Wilson R. Wood and his briefing made such a deep impression on his crews that many of them never forgot what he said. Colonel Wood was rather an impressive person at any time, partly perhaps because he was tall and remarkably handsome, partly because he was a Texan and had the distinctive charm of a southerner and partly because he was only just twenty-five. He himself had known of his group's invasion mission for nearly a fortnight and he had not been allowed to fly since he had been told it. That morning in the briefing-hut on his airfield in Essex, north-east of London, he stood up as usual and began to speak in his unemphatic sleepy Texan voice.

'This morning's mission,' he said, 'is the most important mission you've ever flown. Maybe the most important mission anyone has ever flown. This is the invasion. Our job is to bomb the beach and right after our bombs go down, thousands of Americans just like us will be landing there from the sea.'

'This introduction had his crews on the edge of their seats. 'I don't care if any of your aircraft are not a hundred per cent.' he went on. 'You'll fly them this morning and you'll get over that beach whatever happens and you'll take any risk to get right on your targets and give those boys in the boats every bit of help you can.'

'After that, he gave the crews his usual meticulous details of timing, targets, routes and tactics. The targets were seven of the centres of defence on the narrow strip of dunes. The timing was more critical than usual, because the whole operation had to start after dawn and end by the clock immediately before the landing craft reached the shore. When Wood sent his men out to their aircraft they were certainly imbued with his own conviction that the safety of a few aircraft and even the lives of a few crews were of small importance beside the help they could give to their fellow-countrymen in the boats. In this spirit, they took off at 4 am.

'Wood led his own group very low across the Thames below London, over Kent and Sussex and out across the Channel, flying all the way below the cloud base. As usual when he was flying, he was happy. One might say that he was a born airman. His father was an engineer, his home was four hundred acres of virgin land in Texas and from his earliest boyhood in the era of Lindbergh, flying had been his dream and his delight. He had joined the air force as soon as he left his university, when he was twenty and had risen from enlisted man to colonel in five years simply because he was a natural leader and had a single-minded love of aircraft. Like most American bomber pilots, he did not particularly hate Germans, or particularly like dropping bombs; but he would have said that the only way out of a war was to fight your way out of it. Somehow, he had managed to combine his love of flying with being happily married. It was typical that when he was made a colonel, four months before the invasion, he sent his wife a cable saying 'Promoted - Wilson' and forgot in his excitement to send her his love; but she was sufficiently sure of it to forgive him.

'Now he was in the middle of a tour of fifty combat missions; and he felt that this morning, whatever the future might bring, was a climax in his flying career. Over the Channel, this feeling was strengthened when he saw the countless white wakes of ships all pointing like arrows towards the coast of France.'

Dawn Of D-Day. [5]

'Six thousand feet below, troops surged over the beaches of France and against Hitler's Atlantic Wall and as the first black dots moved over the white sand a gunner said over the interphone : 'Jesus Christ! At last.'

'On the dirty dark green of the Channel waters, battleships, cruisers, destroyers and more man-carrying craft than you could count rolled steadily toward the green fields and the white towns the Nazis had taken from France. Through a smoke screen the wraith-like shapes of warships loomed a moment, chameleoned into blobs of flame as another broadside roared off to find some Wehrmacht strongpoint beyond the coast. This was the invasion.

North and South, all across the Channel and deep into the reaches beyond the concrete-bound coast of the Continent, some 7,000 American and Allied warplanes flew

5   By David Howarth (The Companion Book Club 1959).

in the greatest aerial armada in history. They drove the Luftwaffe from the skies and the German gunners and infantry from their camouflaged strongpoints beneath. Marauders and Havocs, Fortresses and Liberators, Mustangs, Thunderbolts, Lightnings and all the other myriad craft of the RAF filled the sky until there was no room for more.

From a Marauder medium bomber of Col. Wilson R. Wood's Ninth Air Force group piloted by 1/Lt. Richard E. Robinson of Pittsfield, Ill. 'I saw the first. Americans go ashore. Just as they went into the low surf our ship and with it thousands of other bombers and fighters carried out the job toward which Eighth and Ninth Air Force airmen have been aiming since the first Fortress opened its bomb bay, above Rouen on August 17 1942. We poured onto every known German strongpoint in the Cherbourg peninsula area in front of the assault craft the heaviest concentrated bombing any spot in the world ever got.

Fountains of smoke and flame and Nazi-poured concrete leaped up along the ridges behind the beaches.

The airmen had been told that on them would rest the task of making the foot soldier's job, less bloody. They accepted that task and in its execution bombed from half the altitude they knew could give them a fighting chance of getting home so that their explosives would not miss. To do that job they had gone through a nightmare of flak before they came to the targets.

For long months the bombers and the fighters have woven a pattern of craters across the ramparts of the Atlantic Wall. The pattern was cut for invasion. On Monday, I flew in the co-pilot's spot of a Marauder piloted by Major Paul Stach, of Rosenberg, Texas to watch the last attack of the many which had come to be called 'the pre-invasion blitz.'

The bomber men went back to base. They ate and went to bed. At one o'clock in the morning they were called. Sleepy, worn with the strain of two hauls a day almost every day for two months; they walked through the wet night to the briefing. In a plain, undramatic Texas voice, Wilson Wood told them: 'Thirty-three seconds after your bombs hit the target, hundreds of thousands of American boys just as you are going ashore in France. This is the invasion.' He talked some more and ended; 'Lets kick the hell out of everything Nazi that's left.'

Then they cheered and went out to work.

The clouds broke over the Channel and suddenly there were more ships than you could see, with the white wakes of them streaming back to the English coast and the dark green of the Channel flat before them to the coast of Europe.

The flak began to come up, but for once the bomber men weren't watching it because through the murk above the coast there burst the angry red of warship broadsides and inland came the answering crimson a few moments later as the shells hit home.

At half the height they've used for bombing the Marauders swept in.

The heavy flak burst around the formations and tracer from machine guns streaked up past the wings; that's how low they flew.

We went away from the flak and began the long journey home and talked too much over the interphone. Because this had been the day.

First Eyewitness Story by **Bud Hutton** *Stars and Stripes* **Staff Writer who flew with the 323rd Bomb Group at Earl's Colne, Essex. On D-Day 'Wood's Rocket Raiders' flew three 18-plane formations instead of the usual 36 to bomb targets near the beach-head.**

'We awakened at two o'clock in the morning on 6 June. This was my 21st mission and take-off was at 0420. It was still dark. A steady rain was falling and we could hardly see to taxi, much less fly. But there was no holding back and we poured on the coals, taking off at twenty-second intervals between shifts. By the time we cleared the end of the runway, we could barely see the lights of the airplane ahead of us. We climbed on instruments and when we broke out on top of the cloudbank, we could see B-26s and all kinds of other airplanes circling around. It was really a beautiful sight.

'By following prearranged signals, we tacked onto our squadron leader and subsequently were on our way across the Channel. We were part of the spearhead of the invasion, entering the coast of France near Cherbourg over 'Utah' Beach. Our targets were coastal guns and blockhouses along the beach, which we were to hit in collaboration with shelling by naval vessels. We were among the very first aircraft to hit the invasion target.

'As we moved in toward the beaches, we could see an armada of invasion vessels in the Channel below us, their courses converging toward the several invasion beaches. I had the surging feeling that I was sitting in on the greatest show ever staged - one that would make world history. As we flew nearer to the target, that feeling increased to exhilaration and excitement, for it was truly a magnificent operation. We saw hundreds upon hundreds of ships below, moving toward the coast of France and when we approached the target area, we could see the big naval guns shelling the coast. The Germans were not idle, however, as they threw heavy barrages at the landing craft. I saw one large ship going down but still throwing shells at the coast. We saw hundreds of discarded parachutes that had been thrown off by paratroopers who had landed simultaneously with the other attacks. These were quite a ways inland from the beachhead. I saw one B-26 Marauder explode in midair near the target area.

'We went through the heaviest concentration on antiaircraft fire I had yet seen. Tracers and flak explosions were so thick that it looked impossible to get through without being hit, especially knowing that for every tracer there were six other rounds. The barrage literally filled the air all around us and the flak explosions made the air alive with fire.

'On the beachhead, there was a tremendous wall of smoke all along the shore where the bombs and the shells were exploding. The landing craft were moving up as we turned off the target area after dropping our bombs. Every move was timed to the split second. We went in at 4,500 feet on this first mission. Our bombs went away at 0630, the precise time planned.

Lieutenant Allen W. Stephens, a co-pilot in the 397th Bomb Group at Rivenhall, Essex. Between May 12-24 the 397th attacked seven German coastal defence targets and continued to do so in the first three days in June, culminating on D-Day 6 June with a 'maximum effort' mission in support of the landings in Normandy. Crews were roused at 02.00hrs and briefing quickly followed. The Marauders had to be over the targets at precisely 06:09 - 21 minutes before the first landing-craft grounded on the beaches. A record number of 53 group aircraft took-off from Rivenhall in the early hours and joined other Marauder and Havoc squadrons, to provide a total of 276 bombers. They had all been briefed to attack seven defensive positions off 'Utah' Beach a few minutes before the US 4th Infantry Division stormed ashore at 06:30. The 397th Bomb Group B-26s dropped to 3,500 feet to try to see the objective and when the position came into view the group bombed at the set time before the first troops waded ashore. Following a hectic few minutes in one of the most crowded pieces of sky on that memorable morning, their mission accomplished, the groups turned for home. Landing back in England some of the

crews of the 397th prepared to fly their second mission of the day, this time against coastal defences at Trouville, on the other end of the invasion beaches.

On D-Day the 422nd Bomb Group at Andrews' Field, commanded by Colonel Glen C. Nye and known as 'Nye's Annihilators', was one of the key units in the opening bombardment and the 322nd Bomb Group dispatched three boxes of 16 B-26s each, including a pathfinder for each box during the early morning hours. Only two Marauders of the first box succeeded in dropping their bombs on a battery at Ouistreham. In the second box, seven were abortive due to weather while nine bombed the second gun position at Ouistreham through 7 to 9/10ths clouds. The third box hit the Montfarville gun positions with excellent results. There was no enemy air opposition and no flak damage was sustained. *Pickled-Dilly* flew with a crew of only three men. The pilot, 1st Lieutenant William L. Adams did his own radio and navigation work as well as flying the Marauder, co-pilot 1st Lieutenant Carl O. Steen took over the bombardier's duties while the bombardier, Staff Sergeant C. W. Holland went back and handled the tail guns. *Pickled-Dilly* put its bombs right on the target. *Pickled-Dilly* would complete 105 combat missions before being lost on its 106th mission on the night of 7/8 July on the raid on the Noball headquarters at Château de Ribeaucourt.
    US 9th Air Force Bases in Essex 1943-44. [6]

'…This was what we had been waiting for. Our mission was to lead the 446th Bomb Group to bomb the invasion beaches of Normandy immediately prior to the ground assault. We had been selected to be the first heavy bomb group to cross the French coast on the day. We took off at 02:20, climbed to 10,000 feet and circled in our prescribed forming area firing specific flares as the 446th aircraft assembled in formation behind us. The mission went precisely as planned except for an undercast, which necessitated bombing by radar. As we approached the French coast, the radar navigator called me over to look at his PPI scope. It clearly showed the vast armada of the invasion fleet standing just off the coast of Normandy - a thrilling sight even on radar. Bombs were away at precisely 06:00! We led our aircraft back to Bungay via Portland Bill and returned to Hethel. Much to our surprise, no flak or German fighters were observed. Our fighter cover was everywhere.
    'As we started to undress to get some rest, we were again told to get over to Bungay for another mission. During the course of the briefing the flight surgeon gave each aircrew member a pill with instruction to take it only 'when you feel you can no longer keep awake.' We had been up since 02:30, 5 June and it was now the afternoon of 6 June, some 36 hours later we were running on reserve energy.'
    Lieutenant Robert A. Jacobs, 564th Bomb Squadron, 389th Bomb Group DR (Dead Reckoning) navigator, in the first Liberator, *Liberty Run*, over the beaches.

'We took off at 14:00 hours. The flak was light and the mission successful. I flew as lead bombardier in *Naughty Nan* piloted by Lieutenant Sneddon. There was a full moon and I have never seen as many ships of all descriptions as there were crossing the Channel. I saw battleships firing at gun emplacements. It was quite a sight - quite a show. The flak was light and the mission successful.'
    Bob Shaffer, bombardier, *Naughty Nan*, 93rd Bomb Group, 8th Air Force

6   by Martin W. Bowman (Pen & 'Sword' 2010).

Chapter 2

Never A Sign Of The Luftwaffe

'The D-Day missions were disappointing. No results of our action could be seen and we had not been able to do what we had in our potentiality to do to further the great undertaking. Nevertheless, the presence of nearly every flyable plane in England, the gigantic and continual roar of their engines and the bombs hurtling down through the overcast, must have given the Germans pause, aware of the destruction capable of being sent him from on high and given our own men a sense of security in the airpower overhead.'
Allan Healy, 467th Bomb Group, 2nd Bomb Division, 8th Air Force at Rackheath near Norwich, Norfolk.

'We were called well before dawn and driving across the darkened airfield to the Ford mess for an early breakfast we heard the roar of powerful engines as the first formations of day fighters made their way to Normandy to relieve the night patrols. After a hurried meal we strapped ourselves into the cockpits of our Spitfires. I took the three squadrons across the Channel, over a choppy grey sea, to patrol the line of beaches being assaulted by British and Canadian troops. Throughout the previous night Lancasters of Bomber Command, followed by American heavies, had dropped vast quantities of high-explosive on the enemy's coastal defences. Airborne troops had parachuted into the area to prepare landing-zones for glider reinforcements and to secure the flanks of the bridgehead by assaulting enemy strongpoint from the rear. Already the Normandy coast-line from the Orne River to Carentan at the base of the Cherbourg Peninsula was ablaze, as the spearheads of our invading forces fought to secure a foothold. I thought of these things as we sped across the Channel. Surely, by this time, the German High Command would have diagnosed the Allied intention to invade Normandy. Even at this moment, fighter squadron of the Luftwaffe might be in the air on the flight from Germany to reinforce their depleted forces in France. The Luftwaffe possessed plenty of airfields within striking distance of the assault area. They had always been a flexible organization and capable of rapid reinforcement. Perhaps the scale of fighting would be similar to the stirring air battles fought over Dieppe. Tense and eager in our cockpits, anticipating bitter opposition, we made an accurate landfall on the Normandy coast.

'From the pilot's viewpoint, flying conditions were quite reasonable - better than we expected after the gloomy forecasts of the previous two or three days. The cloud base was at about 2,000 feet and the visibility between five and six miles. Calling the wing leader of the formation we were about to relieve, I told him that we were already on our appointed patrol line. Had he seen anything of enemy fighters? 'Not a bloody thing,' he replied, 'although the flak is pretty hot if you fly a few hundred yards inland.'

'Amongst the mass of shipping below us was a fighter direction ship. I called the RAF controller on my radio and asked if he had any plots of enemy formations on his table. The controller came back with the guarded reply that for the moment he had no positive information for me.

'We swept parallel to the coast beneath a leaden grey sky and I positioned the wing two or three hundred yards off-shore so that we should not present easy targets to the enemy gunners. Our patrol line ended over the fishing village of Port-en-Bessin, while farther to the west, beyond our area of responsibility lay the two American assault beaches 'Omaha' and 'Utah'. When we carried out a wide, easy turn to retrace our flight path, a wing of American Thunderbolts harried our progress and for a few uneasy moments we circled warily round each other. Formations of different types of Allied aircraft had attacked each other during the preceding months, but in this instance recognition was soon affected and we continued our flight to the south of the Orne. For the present there was little doubt that we were the undisputed masters of this little portion of the Normandy sky, so for the first time that morning I was able to turn some of my attention to the scene below.

'Off-shore the sea was littered with ships of all sizes and descriptions and small landing-craft ploughed their way through the breakers to discharge their contents at the water's edge. We could see a fair number of capsized vessels and afterwards learnt that the various obstacles erected by the Germans below the high-water mark were considerably more formidable than had been expected. Not content with the erection of these steel obstacles, the Germans had attached underwater mines to them and so added to the hazards of our landing-craft. Further out in the bay, cruisers and destroyers manoeuvred to lie broadside on to the assault beaches: we could see the flashes from their guns as they engaged the enemy defences well inland. As I watched the naval bombardment I realized that we flew constantly in air space between the naval gunners and their targets. No doubt the shells were well above our height of 2,000 feet, I made quite certain that we did not exceed this altitude.

'Swimming tanks, a recent innovation, were launched their parent ships well out to sea. From the air it seemed as if these amphibious tanks had a fairly long and rough journey before they reached the beaches. During the last of their journey the tanks opened fire against adjacent enemy positions and this must have come as a considerable surprise to the defenders. Here and there the enemy appeared to be putting up a stiff resistance: we saw frequent bursts of machine-gun fire directed against our troops and equipment on the beaches. Small parties of men could be seen making their way to the beach huts and houses on the sea front, many of which were on fire. But the greatest danger to us pilots lay from the mass of Allied aircraft which roamed restlessly to and fro over the assault areas. Medium bombers, light bombers, fighter-bombers, fighters, reconnaissance, artillery and naval aircraft swamped the limited air space below the cloud and on two occasions we had to swerve violently to avoid head-on collisions. Towards the end of our allotted patrol the controller asked me to investigate bogey aircraft flying down the Orne from Caen, but these turned out to be a formation of Typhoons, so we resumed our cruise above the beaches.

'Four times that day we made our way across the Channel and never a sign of the Luftwaffe! We arrived back at Ford from our last patrol as dusk was falling and had to wait for a few minutes for the night fighters to take off and maintain the vigil over the beach-head. Tired and drained, I drove to the mess for the evening meal. All my pilots were there. All had flown on this day and some had participated in all the missions. They were very quiet; it was apparent that they were bitterly disappointed with the Luftwaffe's failure to put in an appearance on this day, which was one of the most momentous in our long history of war. We had geared ourselves for a day of intense air fighting and the actual result had been something of an anti-climax. I could not let them go to bed in this mood of apathy and frustration and I gathered them together for a short 'pep' talk. Although we had not succeeded in bringing the enemy to combat, I said, it was still a brilliant triumph for the Allied Air Forces as it marked our complete dominance over the Luftwaffe - an ideal we had striven to attain for more than three years. I glanced at my audience. Lounging in chairs, propped up against the walls, rather dirty and many of them unshaven, they received this somewhat pompous statement with the cool indifference it merited. I tried another approach.

'We know that the Luftwaffe squadrons in this area are not very strong. In fact, the latest order of battle estimates that they have only about 200 fighters and less than 100 fighter-bombers. But they still possess many crack squadrons of fighters based in Germany. You can bet your last dollar that some of these outfits will move into Normandy immediately, if they haven't already done so. You'll have all the fighting you want within the next few weeks and perhaps more! Don't forget that we shall soon have our own airfield in Normandy and then we shall really get at them. And now we'll force a beer down before we turn in.'

'We repaired to the bar, where we partook of no more nor less than one pint each and on this note called it a day.'

Spitfire IXb pilot Wing Commander 'Johnnie' Johnson DSO* DFC*, Wing Leader, 144 Wing RCAF at Ford. Johnnie finished the war as the top scoring British fighter pilot with 34 confirmed victories.

AT AN AMERICAN AIRFIELD
Tuesday.

As General Eisenhower was broadcasting his invasion message to the world to-day two American Lightnings touched down on an English meadow. They were the first of a photo reconnaissance unit back from the beaches of Northern France and in a few minutes more than a thousand negatives, most of them taken at short range, were in .the dark rooms.

The pilots were Lt.-Col. C. A. Shoop, of Beverly Hills, commanding officer of the unit and 23-year-old Major Norris E. Hartwell, jun., of Cheyenne, Wyoming, who told me how for two hours they cruised up and down the extensive battlefields, in and out of cloud, sometimes as low as 500 feet, taking photos all the time.

'The Channel' said Col. Shoop, 'was like a regatta - all sorts and sizes of ships and landing craft milling around, darting to beaches, disembarking troops and away again, We got over about 7 o'clock and by then the troops were ashore and had established beach-heads covered by fighters and fire from the Navy.

At that time there was only one fire burning, but before we left it looked as if every town and village over a wide area was ablaze. Smoke billowed out to sea.

'As for ships, the Channel seemed full of them. Convoys were going across in steady streams, protected by fighters that had no fighting to do and all up and down the French coast big warships were pouring in terrific fire. Some of them stood as close inshore as was possible with safety, their smaller guns firing point-blank at the enemy positions close at hand and their heavies smashing the areas behind the beaches.

'The enemy at that time were returning the fire strongly both at the ships and on the beaches, but they could not stop the landings. Our craft defied the obstacles in the water and it was magnificent to see the troops swarm through the sea.

'Then they calmly formed up in companies on the beaches and brought s their vehicles ashore. There seemed to be few casualties on the beaches.'

'At one point we saw gliders and parachutes on the ground and the smell of burning oil made me think that maybe they had been doing good work at some oil refineries. 'Everywhere it was a great show,' he said, his oil-smeared face wreathed in smiles. 'Our aircraft were everywhere and if the Luftwaffe did not show up their ground defences did. It made the two hours we were over there seem like a week.

'The weather was bad for us and we had to come down low at times to get through clouds. Then we met the smoke from the burning buildings. However, we managed to stick close to each other except for one awful moment over an airfield some miles inland. They let fly at us with a hell, of a bunch of machine-gun fire. That scattered us, but it didn't stop us. We got the first pictures safely home. Now we're going back for more.'

'The amazing change which came later in the day when Allied warships, unmolested, battered the French coast and reconnaissance aircraft flew at incredibly low levels without even being fired at were described to me by two pilots who 'hopped across' to the invasion beaches before lunch and spent a little over an hour collecting about 1000 photographs.

Capt. Jack Campbell and Lt. John T. Cameron of Los Angeles said that when crossed to the other side they could see a tremendous lot of naval gunfire. 'Every time you looked at a ship,' said Capt. Campbell, 'it seemed to blaze shellfire.

Capt. Campbell said: 'Hitler's West Wall is in parts 'gone west' wall. The bombardment has blown hell out of the German fortifications and we could see great concrete slabs lying all over the place.'

Lieut. Cameron said that the mines blown up in shallow water had torn great holes in the red clay which were clearly visible from the air. 'Believe me,' he said, 'this isn't Dieppe. At the most we went 40 miles inland and we saw no enemy troops at all.'

Major Walter L. Weitner, of Yonkers, New York, whose job was to observe rail tracks, flew 200 miles inland, but apart from a burst from a machine-gunner he met no opposition. The towns seemed deserted. 'Even the defences had stopped firing back at the ships, so far as I could see and there they were, destroyers and light cruisers, sitting off the coast and blazing away for all they were worth and not a shot back at them.

Seen From The Air: 'Channel Like a Regatta' by Press Association Special Reporter. **The American airfield mentioned in this newspaper report was Mount Farm, Oxfordshire, (a satellite of RAF Benson, home of the RAF's Photo Reconnaissance Unit) and the Lightnings were F-5Cs of the 7th Photo Group (R) assigned to the 8th Air Force. Prior to D-Day sorties were normally carried out at 25,000 feet, the optimum level for F-5 operations. Beginning on 31 May, the F-5s, each with two or three cameras in the nose of each Lightning flew sorties along the French coast to obtain detailed photographs of assault obstacles and defences at the proposed landing beaches. Sometimes this work was carried out at 15 feet.**

Lieutenant Colonel Clarence A. Shoop, a Lockheed test pilot, had been flying with the 55th Fighter Group while in England reviewing and making modifications to Lockheed's P-38 aircraft. He was given orders to report to 8th Air Force HQ on 5 June where he learned that he was to take over the 7th Photo Group from Lieutenant Colonel Norris E. Hartwell and who now became the Deputy Group Commander.

'...Colonel Shoop had a bang-up beginning at his new command. He got up at 04:45, had some coffee and went straight over to Operations. As word spread that this was the big day, the base erupted in activity. Briefings for missions and planning at Operations and Intelligence set the tone for the day. Everyone who could get in the air wanted a sortie over the beaches. On the flight lines and in the dispersal areas, the strangely striped aircraft waited. New to photo recon, Shoop had to be briefed on the operation of the cameras. He and Hartwell took off at 06:00 as planned. Spotting a P-38 Fighter Group heading for the Channel, they tagged along. As soon as they crossed out over the coast they could see the Channel full of ships. Hartwell thought, 'They were so close you could have walked almost from shore to shore on their decks.'

When they got to mid-Channel the fighters began circling a convoy and Shoop and Hartwell broke off to go over the beaches. Below them there were ships burning and geysers of water around from enemy shelling. They could see that the overcast was too low for photos from high altitude. Flying back out over the Channel, the pilots dropped their two black and white striped F-5s down to 1,000 feet and flew in under the cloud layer where they ran into light rain at the coast near Le Havre. Their flight plan called for each pilot to fly along just behind the beachhead in several different areas. They flew down the coast to the point where they planned to turn inland. The weather worsened as they flew over their targets. Shoop thought that the ceiling seemed to be getting lower and the light was not good for pictures. They turned back to the coast. 'Suddenly little red golf balls started floating by my wings - light calibre flak. I yelled at Hartwell and he turned one way and I turned the other. The air was pretty full of lead for a few seconds. I snapped a few pictures and discovered later that we had flown over Caen/Carpiquet Airport. I had turned right, which took me directly over the city of Caen and more flak came up but I got a few pictures of it while I was dodging.'

They expected heavy flak but what there was according to Hartwell, 'Was enthusiastic but wild. We had a grandstand seat for the show.' Hartwell went down near Cherbourg then returned to the beaches. 'There were Allied fighters everywhere, all sporting the black and white invasion stripes, but no enemy fighters.' Hartwell could see troops moving inland and concentrations of tanks and vehicles in assembly areas. Behind the beaches, fires burned in the villages.

Rejoining their formation, they swept low along the beaches under the low clouds until Hartwell and Shoop found themselves too close to crossfire from the ships and shore batteries and got out of there in a hurry. They had exhausted their film anyway. As they turned back toward England they could see thousands of boats of all sizes scurrying back and forth with large naval ships hammering away at the shore defenses. They landed at Mount Farm shortly after 0900.

Camera Repair unloaded the magazines and the Photo Lab rushed to see what they had. The tree top flights over French villages produced pictures where you could read signs on buildings. The camera caught people startled by the low flying planes in various poses of astonishment. Hartwell's film magazines included pictures of an old lady kneeling in prayer in her garden.'

'Eyes of The Eighth: A Story of the 7th Photographic Reconnaissance Group 1942-1945 **by Patricia Fussell Keen (CAVU Publishers L.I.C 1996). On D-Day, the 7th Group flew 29 successful sorties. One pilot failed to return Colonel Shoop was awarded the Distinguished Flying Cross. The 7th Photo Group was awarded a Distinguished Unit Citation for flying 44 photo sorties 31 May-30 June in support of the Normandy invasion.**

'Today the invasion of France started! We took off for two separate missions. The first target was an intersection of roads outside St. Lo. Cloud cover was so dense we returned to base both times. There was a real danger of hitting our own troops if we had bombed. There were a total of 24,000 Allied aircraft in the air that day; we were disappointed we couldn't contribute to the effort.'

Diary entry, 2nd Lieutenant Paul Valachovic.

'Here are the stories told by men who watched the landings.

Fighter pilots returning from over the landing. Areas report that Allied infantry scrambled ashore at 7 am, in two areas of the French coast, apparently without heavy opposition, says Robert Richards, British United, Press war correspondent at a US Fighter Base.

'One of the pilots, an American Colonel, William Curry, told me: I saw the first troops wading ashore about 7 am from light landing craft. From the height at which I was flying they did not appear to be meeting heavy opposition and were covered by extensive and heavy naval bombardment from our warships.

'Flying Fortresses were also bombing the beach which appeared to be marshy instead of sandy.

'Major John Locke of Texas, who led a squadron of Thunderbolts, said: 'I have never seen so many ships in all my life. Flying over the harbour at one port I counted great numbers of cruisers, destroyers, corvettes and other, craft. The constant flashes from their guns indicated that the beach was getting a heavy pounding.'

'Behind this advance brigade, stretching in a never-ending stream across the Channel came line after line of LCTs (landing craft, tanks) escorted by corvettes and PT boats. 'We were never attacked by enemy airplanes although the flak was terrific.'

'Second Lieut. Benson from Iowa said: 'The Channel waters were fairly calm and the boats bounced along smoothly. They were constantly patrolled by warships and many were towing barrage balloons.'

'Colonel William Schwartz added: 'When I arrived over the beach our battleships brought all their fire to bear on the shore.'

Stories of The Men Who Watched, **London** *Evening Standard,* **Tuesday June 6 1944. Colonel William H. Schwartz Jr commanded the 373rd Fighter Group, Ninth Fighter Command, at Woodchurch in Kent. Major John Locke was promoted to colonel and took command of the 368th Fighter Group in November 1945.**

'I am writing in the cabin of a British Merchant Navy troopship - a few minutes before she sails for Europe with a jam-packed cargo of the men who are going to beat Hitler. The troops are aboard. They have been sorted out, accommodated and fed. They are lining the decks, chewing or smoking, taking their last look for some time at England. And over their heads to-day flies the Red Duster.

'This is a ten-thousand ton; 32-year-old, professional 'trooper.'

She has trooped since the last war, carried tens of thousands of troops all over the world, in peace-time as in war. To-day she is carrying her normal complement.

'She's a good old lady,' said an officer who popped his head into this cabin a few moments ago.

Like the troops who have been filling up gangways at British ports all over the country, I reached this ship without knowing her name, where she lay, her ultimate destination. I received telephoned instruction to report to a London address early one morning. The address was the Admiralty.

With only two other Merchant Navy correspondents I reported. We were the first three assigned. We have embarked in our respective ships. Right now, we are sealed.

The only communication I can have with what is now genuinely the 'outside world' is this story - which I may hand in a sealed bag to the Security Officer as he takes his last leave of the ship.

I am assigned to a cabin with a captain in the Military Police and a lieutenant from a famous division which fought in the desert, whom I haven't yet met.

Warning has just come that sailing time is approaching. The purser, Ronald Godley, from Gosforth; Newcastle-on-Tyne, who lent me his cabin to type these few lines, has handed over his last mail from the ship. In the few minutes that I have so far had to meet the men who are sailing this ship, I would pick him as typical of the some 50,000 merchant seamen who have volunteered to sail at this job.

Ronald Godley has been away from his home, wife and two children for two years and nine months. He could have taken leave to see them. But he would have missed the Invasion.

We are about to sail. It might be a month before D-Day. We do not know yet.

The gangways are coming up. And the Merchant Navy - God bless them have just offered me a gin.'

With D-Day Troops Under 'Red Duster' From Peter Duffield, *Evening Standard* Merchant Navy Reporter at a British Embarkation port. Peter Duffield had been *Evening Standard* War Reporter in Cairo, Palestine and Turkey and covered the war in the desert, flown with the desert air forces and visited Malta. He had flown back recently from Cairo in 19½ hours.

'On the eve of the great invasion I have been told some of the Navy's secrets. The facts in many, ways surpass fancy and I will set them forth baldly. Properly digested, they tell the story of the devastating power and gigantic proportions of the Allied naval effort better than any terms that I might use.

On D-Day - and this will not be read until it has dawned - a great naval bombardment will smash the chosen sectors of the enemy occupied coast.

Hundreds of guns, ranging from 4in to 16in - largest of all naval guns - will batter the Nazi West Wall. From warships alone thousands of tons of high explosives will go down on the enemy coastal batteries and beaches in ten minutes.

The scene in this port - and I know that it is repeated in many other ports around our shores - is almost beyond description. There are ships of every conceivable type; those specially built for the invasion out-numbering the vessels of more orthodox design.

When I made a journey of several miles in open waters outside the port I found more and more ships. At no time did we come to a place where the field of vessels appeared to thin out.

Most of them are already loaded, although Zero hour is still a well-kept secret. Among the special invasion fleet vessels are L.C.I.s (Landing Craft, Infantry), L.C.T.s (Landing Craft, Tanks), which can take getting on for a hundred tanks, Rhino-ferry craft, which are sectional vessels like huge nautical caterpillars, L.C.F.s (Landing Craft, Flak), L.C.S.s (Landing Craft, Support) and still the list is not complete.

Nothing has impressed me more that the calm deliberation with which everything is being done. The long period of preparation and the thorough rehearsals have eliminated the need for any last-minute rush.

'There is an inevitability about the final preparations for this operation which far surpasses anything of the kind that I have previously experienced.

It does not seem out of keeping with the general situation in this ship, for instance, that on the eve of the mightiest conflict of the war, a party of men should gather round the piano to try out the new theme song:

All over the place
The ship goes,
To fight all our foes,
To deal out knock-out blows –
That Jerry well knows,
All over the place.

Both Navy and Army are in magnificent fettle. Sure of themselves, sure of the outcome of the great adventure, they are ever conscious of what they must owe in the end to two her wonderful services, the R.A.F. and U.S. Air Forces - and the Merchant Navy.

The L.C.T.s are snaking their way through the maze of bigger vessels and they are making for the open sea. Over some of them camouflage nets are spread, but seen from sea level the gun barrels push the netting up into innumerable hillocks.

There is no movement yet among the bigger ships and a few hundred landing craft of all sizes can disappear out of this armada and not be noticed.

But they are all full of fighting men going to battle, with the men of the Eighth and Fifth Armies and the fall of Rome ringing in their ears.

There are great hazards to be overcome and, we go dependent first upon God's providence. Given that, the first faith that all these fighting men have in their armoury will surely see them through.

But the movement of ships, which will take hours to come to its world-shaking peak, goes on.

Aircraft drone watchfully overhead, a little smoke comes from the funnels of the big ships - our 'finest hour' is close upon us.'

Secrets of the Invasion Navy: We Sail in a ship That is Just One of Thousands. From Gordon Holman, *Evening Standard* naval Correspondent at a British port. June 6 1944. Holman had been 14 years a Naval Correspondent. At the outbreak of war he served as a war correspondent in France with the BEF. He was at Lofoten. He won the Croix de Guerre and was mentioned in despatches in the great combined raid on St. Nazaire.

'In mid-afternoon I led Blue Section during the third patrol of the day, the other Section pilots being Maurice Mayston, Keith Macdonald and Eddie Atkins. South of 'Omaha' Beach, below a shallow, broken layer of cumulus, I glimpsed a Ju 88 above cloud, diving away fast to the south. Climbing at full throttle I saw the enemy aircraft enter a large isolated cloud above the main layer and when it reappeared on the other side I was closing in rapidly. Our aircraft were equipped with the gyro gun sight which eliminated the snap calculations or guesswork required to hit a target aircraft - especially one in a reasonably straight flight path; and it also enabled the guns to be used accurately at a far greater range than before. I was well aware, however, that most pilots were sceptical of the new instrument and preferred to use the conventional type of sight, which was still incorporated on the screen of the new sight. Normally one would open fire only at ranges below 250 yards; but I adjusted the gyro sight on to the target at 500 yards with a deflection angle of 45 degrees, positioned the aiming dot on the right-hand engine of the enemy aircraft and fired a three-second burst. The engine disintegrated, fire broke out, two crewmembers bailed out and the aircraft dived steeply to crash on a roadway, blowing apart on impact.

'As I turned back towards the beachhead I sighted a second Ju 88 heading south and made an almost identical attack, which stopped the right-hand engine. This aircraft then went into a steep, jinking dive with the rear gunner firing at the other members of my Section who all attacked, until the Ju 88 flattened out and crash-landed at high speed. One of its propellers broke free, to spin and bound far away across the fields and hedges like a giant Catherine wheel. As we reached the beachhead, radio chatter indicated that other pilots (349 (Belgian) Squadron) were dealing with another German bomber, so this belated effort appeared to have been a costly exercise for the Luftwaffe.

'By now, two lines of ships were ranged towards the beaches, with two more lines of unloaded ships heading back. As we flew back over the in-bound lanes, the two lines of ships advancing up and down Channel to the turning point for Normandy stretched right back to the visible horizon. The Squadron's fourth patrol at dusk was uneventful. And so ended D-Day. Intelligence reports confirmed that the Army was ashore in strength, there was no doubt that the invasion had succeeded and an overwhelming mood of relief had replaced the tension of the preceding days.

'Supreme Headquarters nominated the first Ju 88 I had destroyed as the first enemy aircraft to be shot down since the invasion began, putting 485 (NZ) Spitfire Squadron at the top of the scoreboard for D-Day. Some days before the invasion I had casually suggested we should run a sweepstake for the first pilot to shoot down an enemy aircraft after the invasion began and I duly collected a few shillings from the pool. When we later had time to unwind and celebrate, my modest winnings were well short of the cost of that party. (By coincidence Flying Officer R. E. Lelong (later Flight Lieutenant DFC*) from Auckland destroyed a Me 410 on the eve of D-Day when flying a night intruder patrol with 605 (Mosquito) Squadron over the German aerodrome at Evreux).'

New Zealand Flight Lieutenant John Houlton, pilot, Spitfire IXb MK950, 485 Squadron RNZAF, 135 Wing, 2nd TAF at Selsey, describing how he destroyed the first enemy plane on D-Day. On 8 June he destroyed a Bf 109 and he shot down another Bf 109 on 12 June to take his overall score to four destroyed, 2 shared destroyed and four damaged. (Houlton finished the war with five confirmed victories). In all, Spitfires of 485 Squadron shot down two Ju 88s over 'Omaha' Beach on 6 June and in the following week shot down another seven Luftwaffe fighters, including four rocket-firing FW 190s. 2nd TAF and ADGB flew around 90,000 sorties in June, by far the greatest monthly effort ever recorded in the history of aerial warfare. About a quarter of this effort was directly above the Allied beachheads.

The Hawker Typhoon was a seven ton brute. Its huge Napier Sabre engine presented a number of problems for those who had to service and maintain it and quite a proportion of its pilots would confess to being apprehensive about its reliability. Once started, none doubted its power. In due course most of the early problems were solved and the 'Tiffie' earned a great reputation as a close support fighter-bomber. This role it fulfilled with great effect over Normandy in 1944 when

it equipped no less than 26 squadrons of the 2nd Tactical Air Force. Their effectiveness was increased by what became known as the 'Cab Rank' system whereby formations of Typhoons maintained standing patrols over the battle front ready for immediate action. Being a pilot with a tactical support Typhoon squadron was, however, a most hazardous occupation and a high price was paid for the success that marked these operations.

'It was just getting light when we were awakened by the duty orderly. I had only taken off my flying boots and battledress jacket so it did not take long to dress. After sloshing some cold water on my face I went with Norman Pye to the mess tent for a mug of tea and bread and marmalade. My appetite was non-existent with the apprehensive excitement of the day to come. We were all imbued as never before with a determination to press home our attacks and keep flying to the utmost of our abilities, to give every possible aid to the army as we knew that they were in for a very sticky time.

'We went to the Operations tent in the Commer and were briefed to attack the headquarters of the German 84th Corps at the Château La Meauffe near St Lô. The attack was to be made at 0800 hours so we had some time to wait until take-off. Waiting like this was always the most difficult part of an operation. We did not know what to expect from the Luftwaffe and imagined they would be out in force over Normandy by the time we arrived.

'At last the time came to go to our aircraft. At 0715 hours the twelve Typhoons started up and commenced taxiing to the runway. 609 Squadron were getting ready as they were to follow ten minutes after us.

'The sky was overcast with cloud at about 5,000 feet and it looked as if rain could follow. The CO and I took off side-by-side, followed rapidly by the other ten aircraft. I was flying in JR366.

'Soon after we were airborne there was a tremendous sight. As far as we could see out to sea there were lines of ships of all shapes and sizes, moving steadily and purposefully towards France. The lines continued without a break for the hundred miles to the Normandy coast. The sight was inspiring and comforting; for years we had flown across a deserted Channel where the necessity of a crash landing or baling out, through flak damage or engine failure, could be a very lonely business. Now we knew that help would always be on hand.

'We flew to one side of the stream of ships, keeping below the clouds which became heavier and lower as we approached France. When a few miles from the coast we could see the battleships and cruisers of the Royal Navy with constant flashes coming from their guns as they bombarded German strong points inland. Closer in, rocket launching ships were sending up their shoals of projectiles. We could see assault boats and LCTs making their way to the beaches, with black smoke and flashes of either exploding shells or German guns firing. Soldiers could be seen moving up the beach and then we were over them and flying inland.

'The cloud became lower forcing us down to 2,000 feet, making an easy target for any light flak. However, everything appeared quiet as we sped towards the target; the CO was map reading while the rest of us kept a sharp look out for the hordes of German fighters which we expected to encounter. Nothing happened - no flak - no fighters and nothing appeared to be moving on the ground. Suddenly Dave Davies voice came on the radio, 'Baltic aircraft - target coming up eleven o'clock - echelon starboard for low level attack'. I looked down and there, about three miles away, was the large château surrounded by trees with a long circular drive leading to it with a spacious lawn in the middle. It made a splendid target, large enough for all of us to hit.

'I veered my aircraft further away from the leader to give more room for aiming, selected the eight rocket salvo on the firing switch, checking that the gun button was on 'fire'. The rest of the squadron had now spread out behind in echelon and we were all set. 'Going down Baltic squadron', called the CO dipping his port wing to commence a shallow dive, with me about 100 yards behind. We came over the tops of the trees and I saw the flash from underneath his wings as he fired his rockets and then he pulled his aircraft up and to port. I started firing my cannons and saw his rockets explode on the front of the building. Now less than 300 yards away, travelling at over 400 mph, I fired my rocket salvo and heaved the aircraft into a steep left hand climbing turn to avoid any flying debris and to follow the CO. By the time I had pulled around and could see the château again our fourth aircraft was just firing his rockets. They hit the drive just in front of the building which by then had flames and smoke pouring out of it. With the rest of our aircraft on their way in, more and more rockets exploded on the walls and the smoke and flames rose higher. One could not imagine that any 84 Corps staff inside could have survived.

'We all arrived safely back at Thorney Island except that my propeller started throwing oil on the windscreen which decreased visibility making landing difficult.

'We reported on the results of our attack to the Operations tent. It was now about 0900 hours so we went to the mess tent to see if any breakfast was available, which was not much.

'The pilots from the other squadrons who had been over Normandy said they had not seen any German fighters and although the firing on the ground appeared fierce, the flak was light compared with our experiences of recent weeks.

'Just after midday we were called to Operations again and given the task of an armed reconnaissance in the Bayeux-Caen area looking for and destroying anything on the roads. This time I flew Typhoon MN585.

'Once again we followed the lines of ships across the Channel, navigating was no longer necessary. Everything seemed much as before except there was more smoke and more figures on the beaches. Bayeux was only a few miles inland and as the clouds were now higher we flew at about 6,000 feet spread out in two sections of four aircraft. While No 1 and No 3 in each section looked at the ground, the No 2 and No 4 scanned the sky for enemy aircraft. We had expected to see enemy reinforcements pouring along the roads, but nothing was visible. Flying lower we crossed and re-crossed the area, staring at every bush and tree hoping a Tiger tank would emerge.

'Eventually we reached the fork in the road west of Caen, near Carpiquet airfield. Here, Yellow 1 called up that he could see vehicles and tanks on the road alongside the airfield. Turning right we followed Yellow section down into the attack; as we did so all hell was let loose as flak from the guns around the airfield came hosing up towards us. We replied by hammering back with our 20 mm cannons at anything that looked as though it might be a gun position.

'We saw the rockets from Yellow section exploding among the vehicles along the hedge. Levelling out the angle of dive I got my sight down this line of vehicles and fired my rockets in pairs as I flew down the road. When the rockets had gone, I fired my cannons again. I pulled up and joined the Typhoons in front. We climbed turning to starboard away from Carpiquet. 'OK Baltic aircraft' came the CO's voice, 'prepare to go down again and use up the rest of your ammunition'.

'This time we dived down the road the other way, from east to west. It didn't seem to confuse the flak gunners because as soon as we came in range of their guns they started firing. Clouds of white puffs and tracers filled the air and explosions could be heard above the engine noise when they were close.

'I followed the CO down and raked the line of vehicles with my remaining cannon shells. We pulled up over the outskirts of Caen to be greeted with more flak from the guns around the town. 'Reform Baltic' came over the radio and at full throttle we all joined together - still eight aircraft I was pleased to see. Having been airborne for 80 minutes we were getting low on fuel, but still had another 25 minutes flying to get back. Our full throttle flying would have increased fuel consumption considerably. We made our way to the crossing out point and returned alongside the shipping lane to Thorney.

'After debriefing we found that lunch was finished but something cold was found for us. At 1700 hours we were back at Operations and told to go to the Bayeux-Caen area again to seek out and destroy more enemy vehicles. Again we flew across the Channel and crossed the beaches towards Bayeux. This town, falling to the British 50th Division the following day, was the first French town to be liberated and one of the few towns and villages in Normandy to escape heavy damage.

'Heading down the road towards Caen and Carpiquet, the CO turned south crossing the railway line towards Tilly-sur-Seulles. The country around this part of Normandy is heavily wooded with sunken roads and tracks concealed from the air by trees and shrubbery. Called 'bocage', the French for grove, it was, of course, ideal for the concealment of troops and transport.

'We continued in spread out formation looking for vehicles, but none were seen and we turned east, then north and, just as we were beginning to think nothing would be seen, the CO called 'Tanks at nine o'clock, follow me'.

'We dived and I saw cannon fire and rockets striking amongst some vehicles partially hidden under trees at the side of the road. There must have been others in the woods for flak started up, light stuff from mobile multi-barrelled guns. White puffs appeared everywhere. I got my sight on two tanks that were close together and fired a salvo at them. As I pulled up there was a loud bang on the aircraft behind the cockpit. I tried the controls to find they were working OK and instruments remained normal. Calling the CO I told him my aircraft had been hit. 'OK' came the reply 'reform we are returning'.

'Circling the area, gaining height, we saw smoke coming up from the two tanks and several other vehicles; they all looked as if they wouldn't move again. The flak died away as we climbed and made our way to the crossing out point.

'The landings were still continuing with craft busy ferrying. Smoke was billowing from land and sea. Gun flashes from ships and explosions continued with unabated fury. The beaches now seemed to be covered by either people or debris. 'The noise and the people', said some humorist over the radio. At least, I thought, we are going back for a rest until tomorrow morning and not having to sweat it out down there all night.

'Once again our fuel was low and I was feeling anxious about the extent of the flak damage. In spite of the comforting sight of the ships it seemed a long way across the sea to Thorney Island. We reached there with very little fuel, having been airborne nearly two hours. When I got out of the cockpit I could see the result of the loud bang. A 20 mm shell had hit the tail fin just in front of the rudder making a six inch hole.

'It had been a tiring day; we had carried out three sorties totalling over five hours flying. We had destroyed a château, tanks, other AFVs and transport. I had been hit by flak and got away with it once again. We felt we had done our best for the army and should be out tomorrow to give them more close support.

'When we had finished the debriefing it was dusk; the evening meal was over of course, so we had something cold again. We were released until dawn. Since getting up we had been on the go for eighteen hours. It had been a long day.'

Wings of Chance **by Denis Sweeting, 198 Squadron at Thorney Island.**

'The night was still dark and stormy at 4.30am. The wind and rain lashed the tent as I climbed, steel-helmeted, out of my canvas bed, donned my battledress and proceeded to the met briefing with 30 other pilots. The previous evening the mess had bristled with expectation, but a storm had raged unabated for the past 24 hours. The forecast was still bad and I was sceptical as to whether or not we would go this time. The wind was howling and the rain beat down as two squadrons of Typhoon fighter bombers, fully armed, taxied out for take-off. At 6.15am I was airborne. We formed up in tight formation and coasted out at 900 feet in poor weather conditions, heading for our target at Bayeux, a small town just inside the Normandy coast. Immediately the wheels of my aircraft left the ground I was confronted by an almost unbelievable panorama of ships of all shapes and sizes, grouped closely together as far as the eye could see. The armada-like stream of naval traffic in the Solent and across the Channel was maintained over the whole hundred miles to the French coast. The Isle of Wight was surrounded and appeared as if it was being towed out to sea. What a spectacle it was! Flying low over this continuous stream of ships, the sea looked bad to us and I spared a thought for those on board.

'Approaching the French coast we saw the morning sky alight with rocket salvos, a bombardment from the mightiest naval armada ever assembled in the history of warfare. We could feel the drama that was unfolding that day. The long-awaited invasion of the continent had begun. The Allies had set sail to storm the Nazi fortress of Europe. The great day of decision had arrived. 'You are about to embark upon a great crusade,' said General Eisenhower. The massive number of shells exploding on the blazing beaches seemed remote and unreal as we crossed inbound at 6.40am at about 500 feet, the maximum cloud base and visibility would allow. We cruised quickly up to the target, a German High Command headquarters. Buzzing around at 300 mph, bombing and strafing at will, the Château was soon a place of ruins. There was little opposition and only a small amount of concentrated light flak was noticeable.

'We departed after 20 minutes, our mission for that morning successfully completed. The Château was a smouldering waste. But action was not yet over. On coasting out homeward at 1,500 feet, due to the vagaries of the weather the cloud base lifted a little. I was astonished and annoyed to witness more flak whizzing past me in all directions, especially as it appeared to be arriving from our own troops on the beachhead. Having stormed the beaches, they had managed to get some guns ashore and as we did look like a German FW 190 fighter aircraft in the gloom of the morning, maybe excuses can be made for trigger-happy soldiers. But it was cold comfort for us being fired upon, even under those circumstances. Fortunately not one of our aircraft was hit. No-one became a victim of our own forces in this instance, but certain misunderstandings did occur later.

'Once again we headed north in loose battle formation, feeling relaxed and confident, viewing the vast array of ships still sailing onward towards the beachhead. Thinking about and imagining the thoughts of the men aboard, I wondered how and when it would all end.

'All our wing aircraft landed safely back at our tented base, quickly refuelled and were again available for the next assault on the beachhead wherever it might be. It wasn't long before the squadron was airborne again and that time they weren't so fortunate. Luckily I wasn't with them.'

Typhoon Tale by James Kyle DFM who flew 170 combat sorties in WWII.

'It was learnt that a couple of Tiger tanks along with approximately 100 infantry had been bypassed by our forward troops and were dug in, in a wood a few hundred yards up the road. The three tanks attached to our HQ had got up, but two of them were 'brewed up' [hit by enemy guns and immobilised]. Apart from our own personal arms, we had nothing! We expected them to attack us that night, so every man slept with his weapon and ammunition, ready for a do! I didn't mind the infantry, but tanks! You can't knock them out with personal arms fire. Went to bed resigned to the fact that we would be for it! Woke up surprised to find we were OK! An hour later, twelve rocket-firing Typhoons came over; the first time we had seen them in action! What a sight, what a terror. They got those tanks alright.'

Sergeant Mackenzie, Royal Signals.

'On 5 June 1944 at Hartford Bridge there began to develop, by mid-afternoon, some sort of a 'flap'. We had been up in 'our' Mitchell II, FV900 in 'C' Flight, 226 Squadron on an exercise involving air-to-sea firing at patches of aluminum powder in the sea just off the Isle of Wight. I was the navigator/bomb-aimer. On looking back, the mentality of those responsible for sending us off on such an exercise in that area at that time must seriously be called into question. However, possibly even they may have been having second thoughts, for it was just after George Junior' Kozoriz, our Canadian mid-upper gunner, remarked, 'Jeez, look at all them ships out there', that we had a very panicky 'Return to base' message sent to us personally on VHF. We returned.

'On our return we were amazed to find all and sundry being press-ganged into grabbing cans of paint and suitable brushes and painting broad black and white stripes, later to be known as Invasion stripes', on the wings and fuselages of our Mitchells. Being now somewhat experienced, we ourselves, by methods known only to professional aircrew, managed to skive out of this. However, we did not think of invasion but rumour-spreaders had been at work and had accounted for the stripes by saying that we were going to Iceland to protect the Atlantic convoys and the stripes were to help our shipping identify us (partly right, anyway but hadn't they heard of Coastal Command?). Another faction had us going to the Middle East but this did seem a bit unlikely in spite of a claim to have seen 'a hangar full of tropical kit'.

'I had just finished an early supper, unwisely as it proved, washing it down with several cups of strong tea, when my Aussie skipper, Flying Officer Grant Crawford Suttie, a pre-war regular RAAF, appeared on the scene. Old 'Sut' told me with some urgency to report to the Operations Room for briefing, as we were to be 'on' that night. I grabbed my kit, mounted my squadron bike and on the half mile ride to the 'Ops' Room, visualised a course either to Prestwick, Reykjavik or St Eval and ditching in the Bay of Biscay if Gib' didn't come up on ETA. Or were we to bomb Berlin, Berchtesgaden or whatever? No, that's the heavies' job, thank God.

'With such thoughts I entered the Ops Room, having saluted as was de rigueur and was there amazed to see our route already displayed - 'from HARTFORD to POINT OF AIR to POINT OF AYRE, Isle of Man, to TREVOSE HEAD to STURMINSTER NEWTON to BASINGSTOKE' - thence back to base. I asked, as respectfully as I could, 'What the hell?' The Briefing Officer told me that, as far as I was concerned, it was a VHF calibration trip. What it was as far as he was concerned he didn't say, nor did I press the point, being much too relieved by this 'non-op' operational route being presented.

'(Our flight was, in fact, to test specialist communications equipment, although we did not know this at the time. 'C' Flight was code-named the 'Ginger' Mitchell Flight, a very special and secret Flight under the direct operational orders of SHAEF. From early summer, Mitchells were sent out at night over France, ostensibly on 'Nickelling' leaflet dropping sorties - but really as a cover for picking up transmissions from agents. To the normal Mitchell crews were added a number of French radio operators. Later, ours was André Bernheim, who had been a French film producer and was a personal friend of Charles Boyer. Another was Joseph Kassel, the writer. The special operators' task was to receive transmissions on the 'quarter wave' voice system from agents in Occupied France who were equipped with special radio equipment for the purpose. The normal slow Morse transmission was too dangerous because it could easily be picked up and 'homed' on to by Gestapo direction-finding vans. Quarter wave transmissions, on the other hand, were very difficult to detect at ground level but they could easily be picked up by an aircraft at 20,000 feet or above by a special operator using 'Ginger' equipment.)

'I prepared the flight plan with some trepidation, for the met forecast was terrible. Cloud base was 1,000 feet, tops 2,000 or above, Icing Index high. I therefore spent more time than usual on the flight plan. I was to be glad of this. At about 2230 we clambered into dear old FV900, by then fully refuelled but without stripes as I recall. We had not been airborne long before the forecast proved only too accurate. We climbed up through ever-thickening cloud and at one stage, when lumps of ice hurled off the prop were striking the fuselage, I suggested the possibility of a return to base. Young George - he was all of 18 - made the same suggestion but in more forceful terms. 'Sut', however, was the press on' type, so we pressed on. In fact, old 'Sut' really deserved a medal for this trip, for he was on instruments all the way round.

'We saw neither the Point of Air nor of Ayre. We passed our VHF messages but got no reply. All I do recall was a broad North Country voice from time to time saying 'Turret to turret, over'. This meant nothing to us. We were now at 20,000 feet, oxygen full on. The oxygen did make one feel just a little intoxicated, at any rate sufficient to take the rough edges off. The cold was fearful. Cabin heating? Don't make me laugh. I was, in fact, far from laughing, for about half-way between Point of Ayre and Trevose Head my excessive tea-drinking earlier now led to an anti-social accident, the stuff freezing on the floor of the kite and costing me a quid later that day to have the long-suffering ground crew mop up.

'No sign of Trevose Head. We were in and out of solid cotton wool cloud. No 'Gee' - that packed up very early on, so we had to rely solely on the flight plan. We got no messages and no response to our transmissions. We were now heading in the general direction, hopefully, of Basingstoke and I felt that we were at least sufficiently clear of the hills - we were in awe of these - to start our let-down. I informed 'Sut' accordingly, so down we let through the clag. As the altimeter unwound, I recalled the old joke about 'If this altimeter's correct, we're in a ruddy submarine' and as it went off the scale at zero, I prepared for one big bang and oblivion - I had a ring-side seat in the nose of the Mitch. But just then the cloud mercifully broke and there, below, perhaps 200 feet, perhaps more, was a broad, winding river meandering through a built-up area. It couldn't be the Rhine, nor the Seine but. 'OK, Sut, two-six-zero Magnetic - sharpish!' 'I think 'Sut' put our port wing tip into the Thames somewhere east of Putney Bridge. We whipped round in a split-arse turn - to quote the jargon of the day - and headed in the general direction of Hartford. Continuing our previous course might have led to an even greater anti-social accident, costing more than a quid to clear up, for we were headed for Big Ben and the Houses of Parliament!

'Ten minutes or so later, we were thankfully in the good old Hartford circuit, 'Downwind, cleared to finals'. We landed, cleared the runway and finally got back to dispersal. We did our post-flight checks - 'IFF off, Petrol off, Switches off' - and went off to debriefing. In the mess later we were able to obtain our 'operational' eggs and bacon. The kitchen staff believed that we had been on some daring mission over the invasion beaches. We did not disillusion them but ate to a background of 'Mairzy Doats' alternating with 'Lili Marlene'. It was only at about 05.30 on 6 June that we even heard of the invasion.

'Now, if anyone mentions D-Day to me, I cannot help laughing. Privately, I picture myself in a pool of urine trying to avoid a too-close encounter with the Mother of Parliaments. A strange sequel to this was that, on 28 July 1945, a USAAF B-25 Mitchell similar to ours did collide with the Empire State Building in New York. We might have made a similar spectacular impact.'

Flight Sergeant Jack Parker, 'C' Flight, 226 Squadron, 2nd TAF.

Second Tactical Air Force Participation

The part played by the Allied air forces in the build up to the Invasion was crucial. By day the RAF's 2nd TAF, which had been formed in Norfolk on 1 June 1943 under AVM Basil Embry and the US 8th and 9th Air Forces, blasted enemy targets in Northern France and Belgium. On D-Day smoke-laying Bostons of 88 Squadron appeared at 0500 hours to cover the eastern flank and 342 'Lorraine' Squadron the western flank. Each squadron lost a Boston apiece. 18 Squadrons of Hawker Typhoons were available; ten squadrons in 83 Group and eight squadrons in 84 Group. First into action was 143 Canadian Wing, which arrived over the beachhead at 0725 hours. Typhoons dive bombed strong points (Widerstandsnest or 'Resistance nests') at Le Hamel (WN 37) and La Rivière (WN 33) on the eastern end of 'King Red' on 'Gold' and Courseulles-sur-Mer (WN 31) on 'Juno' and Hermanville-la-Brêche (Wiederstandnesten 18-20 on 'Queen White' and 'Queen Red' Beaches) on 'Sword'. Nine squadrons from other wings hit pre-arranged targets, including four gun batteries and two Wehrmacht HQs, at Château Le Parc south-east of Bayeux and La Meauffe near St Lô. During the day attacks were made also on a radar station near Le Havre and armed reconnaissance sorties were flown south of Bayeux, Caen and Lisieux. By dusk on 6 June Typhoons had flown 400 sorties and lost 8 aircraft and seven pilots, four to enemy aircraft and four to ground fire. Three of the Typhoons that were lost with their pilots were from 183 Squadron while positioning to attack a column of tanks south of Bayeux. They were bounced by about twelve aircraft (probably FW 190s of JG 2). Later, Typhoons of 164 Squadron were attacked as they reformed after attacking German vehicles. One Typhoon failed to return having been hit by flak and one FW 190 was seen to hit the ground and explode after being fired on by Squadron Leader Percy Beake.

'We're coming down right low to attack our target; it's a pretty job. We're looking out for the markers now. I don't think I can talk to you while we're doing this job. I'm not a blinking hero! I don't think it's much good doing flash running commentaries when you're doing a dive bombing attack.'

Air Commodore Helmore, one of the RAF's correspondents, as he reported an air strike aboard a Mitchell bomber.

'The German Navy reacted to the massive Allied fleet in the mid-afternoon. Three Seetier-class heavy destroyers from the 8th Zerstorer Flotilla were spotted by Coastal Command reconnaissance off Brest, heading north into the Western Approaches at high speed. Immediately, an air strike was mounted. Fourteen rocket-armed Beaufighters of 404 Squadron, accompanied by anti-flak and escort aircraft, set out in the early evening, arriving in the area of Belle Isle at around 20.30 hours. The escorts dived out of the sun en masse, attacking the flak gunners aboard the vessels with cannon fire. Flight Lieutenant S. S. Shulemson DSO led the 'Buffalo' pilots of 404 in behind them, four releasing rocket salvoes at the leading warship. Nine more Beaufighters assailed the second in line, leaving both destroyers in a badly damaged condition. The last Beaufighter strafed the third ship. Such was the speed and violence of the attack that not a single rocket-Beau was hit. A lone He 111 was spotted near St. Nazaire and promptly cut down by a 248 Squadron Mosquito flown by Flight Sergeant Stoddart.

A second strike took place shortly after midnight, when five more 404 Squadron crews attacked the vessels, causing even more damage. The three ships managed to reach Brest, where hasty repairs were effected. Two nights later they set off again, only to be caught by the Royal Navy. The 10th Destroyer Flotilla sank ZH1 and Z42 and forced the third, the Tartar, ashore near the Ile de Batz. Here it was 'finished off' by twelve rocket-Beaufighters of 404 Squadron the following night. The door from the west was firmly closed.

Beaufighter Strike 1944:The Air War Over Europe June 1st-30th; Over The Beaches **by John Foreman (ARP 1994)**

'When we lived under canvas at Hartford Bridge Stan Adams [the navigator] and I shared a tent. The tent site, which had a large marquee for our messing, was a long walk across many muddy fields from the main camp. It was good fun in a novel but it had its drawbacks. For one thing I ruined one of my best suitcases which had soaked up the moisture through the coconut matting on the grass floor of our tent. However, it wasn't for long and there was a good reason for preparing us in the event of a dire lack of accommodation when we moved across the Channel. As it happened we never saw a tent when moving to France.

'Apart from the three Boston squadrons at Hartford Bridge, we had two Dutch squadrons using the airfield for a short time - 322 with Spitfires and 320 with Mitchells. Their crews were dressed in the uniform of the Royal Netherlands Navy. When we found out how much they were paid, we gasped. Apart from their set pay scale, which was higher than ours, they received extra money for every flying hour. We didn't see a lot of the Dutch chaps for they messed elsewhere, but we often saw in our mess Queen Wilhelmina and Prince Bernhard.'

Mike Henry DFC Boston air gunner, 107 Squadron, 2nd TAF. Eleven squadrons of Bostons, Venturas and Mitchells in 2 Group moved to Hampshire to be nearer the

enemy coast and newer types of aircraft like the de Havilland Mosquito FBVI fighter-bomber and Mustang fighter arrived. Mosquitoes of 140 Wing (21, 487 RNZAF and 464 RAAF Squadrons) specialised in pinpoint bombing of key targets in France in the run up to D-Day. During March-April to simulate the type of tactical targets against which 2 Group would be employed, Boston, Mitchell and Mosquito crews took part in two-week training exercises in full field conditions.

At first light the 344th Bomb Group at Stansted led four groups in the assault by the IX Bomber Command formations upon three coastal batteries at Beau Guillot, La Madeleine and Ste-Martin-de-Varreville at 'Utah' Beach. The Marauders had to be over the targets at precisely 06.09 - 21 minutes before the first landing-craft grounded on the beaches. Most groups mounted a maximum effort of three boxes of 18 aircraft each instead of the normal mission strength of two boxes with one gun emplacement the target of each box of bombers. At Stansted the first aircraft of the 56 that were dispatched took off at 0412 hours. In the lead was Major Jens A. Norgaard flying *Mary Jo*, named in honour of his wife.

'We fly down the sandy coastline, just over the water's edge. The flak is coming thick now, for we are approaching the target. The big red blobs split between us and the wing man and that, my good friends, is too close. I suddenly seize an extra helmet and sit upon it. I wish to God those bombs were gone.

'Somehow I try to pull my head down into the flak suit, knowing full well that it's not much protection, that a fragment of shell goes through as if it were paper. I stare down first right and then left and just then two boats go up in explosions. Apparently they must have hit mines, but they're well beyond our approaching armada.

'German E-boats are firing at us now near shore. Puffs of black shell smoke hang farther back. I do not see it, but one puts an incendiary into a bomber, sets it on fire. Three of the boys bail out into the water. The pilot tries to get his bombs to the target. He struggles with the crippled aeroplane and then in a flesh it blows to pieces. The fire had ignited the bomb-load. That is the only loss our group has. Now inland about half a mile there is a terrible commotion. A patch of hellish smoke and fire bubbles skywards. 'Flak bursts all around, but I pay no attention. Over the phone comes the call: 'Bombs away!' We are approaching that battery of Nazi guns. They look like a series of golf bunkers, neatly ranged like some sandy folly on the beach. I see the racks suddenly empty, the bombs fall down.

'Our wave was over the beaches in about 20 minutes, during which time we bombed every gun installation assigned to us. We flew up the peninsula and circled the island of Guernsey, where we watched destroyers working over the island. They were doing a beautiful job of it.'

Extract from the diary of Jens Norgaard.

John K. Havener was flying as co-pilot in the deputy lead position of the third box:
'The orders were to bomb assigned targets in the clear regardless of how low the cloud cover forced us to descend. Since our normally efficient bombing altitude was 12,000 feet the prospect of going in at a much lower level was terrifying as we would be sitting ducks for light flak, machine gun and even rifle fire! Nevertheless, it was impressed upon us that the entire invasion plan hinged upon our hitting the targets assigned. If we failed, Operation Overlord failed! With the odds of altitude and flak against us and with

no idea of what opposition the Luftwaffe would mount, we figured half of us would not make it back if forced to bomb at a low-level!

'Our groups actually bombed at from 7,250 down to 3,500 feet and finished doing so just three minutes prior to our troops hitting the beaches at 0630 hours. The clouds were in layers varying from 8 to 9/10 coverage and topping out at 13,500 feet. With bases down to 2,500 feet so bombing in the clear was difficult at best from any altitude. All targets along 'Utah' Beach were hit with results ranging from poor to excellent.

'My group formed up in the rain and darkness, as did all the others. As we headed south the clouds broke somewhat and we managed to climb to about 8,000 feet but by the time we left the coast of England they began to thicken and all three boxes had to go down to 6,500, 5,500 and 3,700 feet respectively to bomb. Our target was gun positions on the high ground above 'Utah' Beach at Beau Guillot and each ship carried 16 250lb general purpose bombs. The intent was not to knock out the gun positions but to stun the German gun crews and any infantry in the area, keeping them holed up and to create a network of 'ready-made' foxholes which our troops could use once they'd gained a foothold on the beach. Three other bomb groups carried the same bomb load and bombed specific 'Utah' Beach locations including the beach itself to explode mines, tear up barbed wire barricades and tank traps along with creating foxholes on the beach. The other four B-26 groups carried 1,000 and 2,000lb GP bombs and hit the coastal batteries at Ouistreham, Beneville, Pointe-du-Hoc and Maissy while the three Havoc groups, carrying 500lb demolition, GP and fragmentation bombs, hit a railroad junction near Valognes, German troop concentrations at Argentan and a marshalling yard at Carentan. Their targets were all inland in the areas where our paratroops had landed the night before.

'On the beach the bombing window was so narrow that if we couldn't line up with the target on our first pass, we were to abort the drop and carry the bombs back home. There just wasn't enough time for anyone to make a second pass! Everyone dropped, as all were determined to make the mission a success! Our first troops hit the beach on schedule at exactly 0630 hours and the main phase of the invasion was on!

'As our group approached the IP (Initial Point for starting the bomb run) we came to straight and level and then the German flak started coming up at us. One ship in our first box took a direct hit and did a complete snap roll but recovered and slid back into formation to continue the bomb run! Absolutely amazing since the B-26 was not an aerobatic aircraft! A ship in the low flight of our box also got hit and went down in flames. [On the target approach, flak claimed the B-26B flown by 2nd Lieutenant James B. McKamey, which was hit in the right engine and with a fire in its full bomb bay, the aircraft was pulled out of formation and turned to head back across the Channel, but the B-26 exploded in mid-air. Three parachutes were reported before the Marauder exploded.]

'We dropped our bombs at 06:09 hours and headed west across the peninsula to turn north near the Isle of Guernsey. As we flew northward the entire invasion panorama unfolded before us and we could see the ground fire of tracers and incendiaries squirting up into the groups following us and the first waves of landing craft approaching the beaches. The largest military operation in the history of the world was awesome to behold!

'We returned to our base in time for a second breakfast at 08:30 hours and I can say for sure that this repast was relished much more than the earlier one at 03:30! That one had taken on the form of a last meal before execution!

'Amazingly, only three B-26s were shot down by flak out of 332 that actually bombed from the 424 that originally took off on the mission. Twenty aborted due to mechanical problems, only two were lost in a mid-air collision southeast of London and 67 couldn't bomb because of cloud cover obscuring their targets. Of 135 Havocs launched 132 bombed with three aborting due to mechanical trouble and only one was lost to flak. In spite of these figures, the entire mission was a success as we had done what was expected of us and it was all made possible by two things: 1. The cleverness of Allied Intelligence in convincing most of the German General Staff that the invasion would take place further up the coast in the Calais area where the Channel was only 20 miles wide. We caught them with their pants down! 2. The pre-invasion mission of the 9th to destroy Luftwaffe airfields and aircraft had paid off. Only 20 FW 190 fighters gave the 391st Group any opposition that morning and they shot down one of those! We lost no B-26s or A-20s to fighters!

'Our group flew a second mission that afternoon, as did all the rest and some a third one, but I was not on the loading list so wasn't much concerned. This time they carried four 1,000lb GP bombs each and bombed gun positions in the Cherbourg area. What did concern me, as well as all Maraudermen who saw it, occurred about two weeks later when the first Life magazine printed after D-Day arrived from my wife. To preface this you should know that some of the same USAAF brass that put the 9th on the back-burner had unsuccessfully tried to brush the Martin B-26 Marauder off the stove top completely so as to use the North American B-25 Mitchell as the sole medium bomber of WWII. Life added insult to injury for Maraudermen as there was a full two-page spread in it with an artist's impression of the D-Day landings. It was a beautiful piece of black and white work and showed scores of landing craft heading toward Normandy from balloon-barraged harbours of southern England in the foreground and in the far-off background our Navy shelling shore fortifications above the landing zones while overhead formations of medium bombers were almost at their IPs and higher up the heavies were beginning to appear. It was all pretty much correct except that the medium bombers were all B-25s! The 9th Air Force had no B-25s in its combat inventory!

'To the average layman of the time, a medium bomber was a medium bomber and most were familiar with the B-25 because of the Doolittle Raid on Tokyo while the few who did know what a B-26 was only knew it by the bad reputation earned in early training days that prompted calling it 'The Widowmaker' as one of its many derogatory nicknames. Tragically, the 'Widowmaker' mentality also existed to a great degree in the Air Force itself! Marauder crews in the ETO suspected that the Stateside back-burner manipulators had infiltrated Life's art department and had finally brushed the Marauder off the stove top. The drawing went beyond artistic license and was a slap in the face never to be forgotten!

'At any rate, the D-Day missions flown by the 9th were the first in which they directly supported the ground forces as a true Tactical Air Force should. From then on they continued to do' so and close support became routine. The shadow cast over the 9th's exploits by the 8th's propaganda mill began to shrink but the prejudices and biased actions of the strategic bombing hierarchy continued to defame the IX Bomber Command and the Marauder. Maybe they were afraid the 8th would lose its 'Mighty' moniker since the 9th was actually the largest Air Force in the world with more personnel, more aircraft (gliders included), more commands and more air bases than the 8th! Who knows!'

John K. Havener, co-pilot, B-26 Marauder *Mary Jo*, 344th Bomb Group, Stansted, Essex.

Timeline

0530 6 June Attack by 276 B-26 Marauder and A-20 Havoc aircraft results in all but 67 dropping 4,404 250lb bombs which destroy Wiederstandnesten 5 (WN 5) which covers Exit 2 and all 5 artillery pieces on 'Utah' Beach.

6 June-31 August RAF flies 224,889 sorties and loses 2,036 aircraft (983 of which are from Bomber Command and 224 from Coastal Command). Aircrew KIA/MIA total 1,035 from 2nd TAF and ADGB (Air Defence of Great Britain), 6,761 from Bomber Command and 382 from Coastal Command.

'At 01:00 hours on the 6th I was sleeping soundly, only to be aroused by the GQ at about 01:30 for the morning briefing. I haven't the slightest idea what I had for breakfast. As for clothing, I wore what I usually did to fly a combat sortie - a uniform shirt and trousers over my pyjamas and a flight suit over the uniform, - plus an A-2 jacket. I wore my billed, '50-mission crush' hat because a flak helmet fitted over it. I had on my brown riding boots, which wouldn't come off if we had to bail out - and my fleece-lined flying boots, which fitted better than with the GI boot. In-flight clothing of a sort was added - a Mae West and a parachute harness. I kept my chest pack on the radio operator's table. Over all this went a flak jacket, usually donned when nearing France.

'The mission briefing took place at 02:30 hours. One of the main points I vividly recall was the number of German aircraft that could be brought against us, but not to worry - there would be 7,000 Allied airplanes in the air! The weather was ghastly: low clouds, drizzle and fog. As I recall, we took off about 04:00 hours. The attempt to join up in proper formation was a mess. We missed the main formation and chased the group halfway across the Channel; as the sky brightened we caught up with them and took a position that looked empty. I thought then and still do, that I was in the 13th Marauder to cross the 'Utah' beach-head, regardless of mission logs, group histories and that sort of thing. The 344th had been selected to lead all the other groups, so we were the first.

'Crossing the Channel, it looked to me as if you could walk ship to ship without getting your feet wet. As we neared the coast we could see naval gunfire and some return fire. We were scheduled to be over the beach before the troops came ashore, at about 06:30 hours. 'Because of the low cloud deck, our bombing altitude was low at about 3,500 feet. We flew parallel to the shore line and dropped our 250lb bombs directly on the beach, in the sand. I thought to myself that we were digging foxholes and exploding mines. As far as we were concerned, it was a 'milk run'. The return to Stansted, three hours and fifty minutes later, was uneventful. Thus ended my thirtieth combat sortie.'

Bombardier Charles Middleton in the 496th Bomb Squadron, 344th Bomb Group, Stansted, Essex. Middleton went on to fly 67 sorties and 230 hours of combat time before finishing his tour on 11 September 1944.

'I was a bombardier on the B-26 *Nicks' Chick* in the 495th Squadron, 344th Bomb Group. D-Day was my 22nd mission. We were confined to the post for a week ahead, but I didn't think too much of it because it had happened before. But the night of the 5th we realized from some things that were happening such as the planes down on the flight line being painted with large black and white stripes that this was probably going to be it. All the crews in our squadron got up about 12:30 and we ate breakfast about 01:00.

At 02:00 we went to briefing. When we got into briefing, the colonel told us that this was the invasion and we were to knock out three coastal guns on the east side of Cherbourg. As we understood then, the Americans were landed at Cherbourg and the British on up the beach at Caen. We took off in the dark. We flew No. 2 position in the second flight. We carried a D-8 bomb sight. The D-8 was a simple instrument when compared to the Norden bomb sight, but was accurate at low levels.

'This was to have been my first lead mission if we bombed below 4,000 feet. They told us we were to bomb no matter what. As the weather was bad, if we bombed under 4,000 feet, I was to lead and bomb with the D-8 sight and if we bombed above 4,000 feet, the lead ship was going to use the Norden. As it turned out we could see well enough and he did use the Norden sight.

'When we went across the Channel, the number of ships that we saw were just, well, there's just no way to describe them. As far as you could see there were ships.

'As we got closer to the coast, we could see large warships of some kind shelling the French coast and there were so many of them doing it, it looked like there were fireflies in a big field, just a constant sparkle down there as the big guns went off.

'We were to bomb the coastal battery at twenty minutes before the troops hit so we went across right at the height of the barrage that was hitting the French coast. You could see many invasion landing craft circling to wait until it was the right time to head in.

'As we passed on across, we saw the landing barges start in towards the beach with very close cover by a P-38s. But we saw an awful lot of Allied planes. The skies were full of P-38s and P-51s and it seemed like mostly P-47s.

'We were told the night before that a lot of paratroopers went in and we had heard planes going over constantly all night. Of course, that was not uncommon, but of course this time the volume of them and the length of time we could hear them going over was unusual.

'Anyway, we went in at 5,000 feet. Most of the bombs hit the target. You could see numerous guns on the shore returning the fire from our fleet. The light flak was very intense but we didn't get much heavy flak. After we turned off the target, one ship did explode and go down.

'On the way back across the Channel, we turned the radio to a civilian channel to listen in. No one other than the military knew that this was the invasion. The radio station in England didn't know it. It was sort of strange to be up there with this tremendous thing happening and nobody, none of the civilians knew about it.

'On the way, we crossed over what I was told were the Isles of Guernsey and Jersey and there was some type of warship shelling those islands which had been taken over by the Germans.

'Anyway, we made it back with the loss of just one ship. This was the first time that I had ever been on a mission when we bombed under 11,000 feet.'

Malcolm Edwards, 344th Bomb Group, Stansted, Essex.

'We became aware that the 'big day' was approaching, but when it would be was still a mystery. A feeling of exhilaration consumed us that morning of June 6th for we realized that our efforts, along with all of the others, had made this day possible. The Nazis had taken tremendous punishment from both the strategic and tactical air forces and were reeling. Now it was up to the boys on the ground to finish them off. We knew our task was not finished as we would be required to give air cover and support to the advancing troops.

'On June 5 all officers were instructed to carry their Colt 45 automatic on all future missions. We hit the sack about midnight and after an hours sleep, were awakened and told to prepare for a mission. When we arrived for briefing, the giant map showing our route to and from the target was, for the first time, covered with a sheet. Our Commanding Officer Col. Vance, with a dramatic flourish removed the sheet and announced that the planned invasion of the continent was about to begin. Our targets were the gun emplacements at La Madeleine, Beau Guillot and Ste-Martin-de-Varreville. We, as the lead group, were to start all bombing operations at H-hour minus 20 (06:10 hours) and every two minutes thereafter another wave of bombers would send their regards whistling down to the enemy below.

'As history relates, the weather that morning was horrendous, the worst it had been in over 100 years. We could not reach our normal flight altitude as the cloud cover was anywhere from 4,000 to 6,000 feet, so in essence, we went in at low level.

'As I was flying on my flight leader's left wing I was the 15th plane over 'Utah' on that historic day. Our box of 36 planes led by my squadron commander, Colonel Del Bentley had Ste-Martin-de-Varreville as our assigned target and after dropping our load of destruction at precisely 06:09 hours, we headed west over the Normandy peninsula and then in a northerly direction towards England. As we turned towards home we realized that it was H-hour and the first wave of troops would be hitting the beaches. Our route carried us through an area referred to as 'Shit-Pan Alley', the area between the Alderney Islands and the northwest tip of Normandy. What intelligence briefing did not tell us was that there were anti-aircraft installations at both points and we were caught in a murderous cross-fire of flak. Our lead ship was hit and with one engine knocked out, he dropped out of the formation. The other wing-man and I spread apart to allow the #4 plane to move into position but he just sat there and made no attempt to take over the lead. As a result, I took over the #1 slot and led the formation back to our base.

'Upon landing we noticed that MPs were all over the area. They were making certain that we headed directly to de-briefing. Once there we were subjected to a thorough interrogation and then informed that we could not leave the room which was under armed guard. Obviously high command felt the Germans didn't realize that today was D-Day and they didn't want us calling them long distance to inform them of the day's events.

'As we were still considered on alert status, we couldn't leave the area anyhow so most of us, being slightly exhausted, napped on the benches until later in the morning when a sumptuous lunch of Spam sandwiches was served. We were able to wash this delicious repast down our gullets with our choice of either powdered milk or coffee so strong it was guaranteed to grow hair on the bottom of your feet.

'Sherman was right...'War is hell'.

'Shortly afterwards, mission #2 for the day was called. The French Underground had sent word that a Panzer division was being rushed to reinforce German troops in the invasion area and the estimated time of arrival at the Amiens marshalling yards would be approximately 14:00 hours. We would arrive several minutes later to make certain they would progress no further. As weather conditions were still poor, we had go in at altitude much lower than normal and as a result again received an inordinate amount of anti-aircraft fire. As soon as bombs were away, the formation entered the cloud cover hoping to break through somewhere from 12,000 to 14,000 feet. However the clouds were so dense so dense that it was practically impossible to see the other planes in the formation. I turned 45 degrees to the right and after several minutes reverted to the original heading, climbing steadily until I broke into the clear at a little over 13,000 feet. Ice had started to form on the wings so we desperately searched for an opening in the cloud layer in order to make a safe descent. Within several minutes a small hole was found and I peeled off and dove for the deck. No enemy fighters were visible and we returned safely to our base.'

Harvey Jacobs, B-26 Martin Marauder pilot, 497th Bombardment Squadron, 344th Bomb Group. 'My tour of duty was completed on D-Day plus 1. I flew two missions on D-Day and two additional missions the following day giving me a total of 57. Our Squadron Flight Surgeon, Captain Harry Prudowsky, had observed that my normally smooth landings had become quite bouncy and he had been informed by some of the flight leaders that my formation flying had also become erratic. He ordered a physical examination and discovered a sizable weight loss plus increased tension which had created a sleeping problem. On June 9th the crew was grounded and on June 10th we went to 9th Air Force HQ to meet the Central Medical Establishment. On the 11th I was interviewed by a medical officer and on June 12th, my 22nd birthday, the medical board informed me that we were to be returned to the good old US of A. Almost a month later, July 10th to be exact, our orders came through and we left for Liverpool where we boarded the Mauretania for our trip home.'

'…I gazed with awe at the hundreds of ships and boats off 'Omaha' Beach below. All were headed toward the beach landing site and it appeared from our altitude that one could almost step from one vessel to another and walk between England and France. Our group of about 40 B-17s in close formation began to ease its way into the narrow corridor for the bomb run. At this time the bombardier instructed me to activate the bombs. I climbed out onto the catwalk and after cautiously removing the safety pins from each bomb I notified him that they were now 'live'. For the first time since take-off I now experienced a sense of fear. This was mostly for the unknown because I now began to wonder what the Germans had in store for us in that critical area. As we reached 'Omaha' Beach the lead plane released a smoke bomb, which was a signal for all 40 aircraft to drop their bombs simultaneously. Thus, more than 100 tons of bombs exploded in a matter of a few seconds. This was the only mission over Europe when I actually felt the concussion of our own bombs. The explosions caused our aircraft to bounce and vibrate.

'Obviously, the long-planned invasion had remained a well-guarded secret. We encountered no German aircraft in the target area and enemy gunfire was very light and inaccurate.'

'We were a little apprehensive on our return because of a diminishing fuel supply. We landed at a RAF base in southern England, refuelled and flew on to Horham where we gave an Associated Press reporter our views on the historic mission. Emotions varied. Many of our thoughts, feelings and opinions we kept to ourselves. My pilot, Mathew McEntie, said, 'Thank you men for your fine co-operation as a combat crew. It is doubtful if any of us will ever in our lifetime participate in a historic undertaking of this magnitude.'

'So far nobody has.'

Henry Tarcza, B-17 El's Bells, 95th Bomb Group, 8th Air Force.

Chapter 3

Devils In Baggy Pants

On a farm south-east of the town of Montebourg Friedrich Busch was fed up with soldiering and was in a mood of desperate depression. He had been a schoolmaster in Dresden and wanted nothing more but to go home to his wife and baby. Erwin Müller wholeheartedly agreed with Busch. He too was German but his wife was Danish and he had lived in Denmark for twenty years and thought of himself as a Dane. The Division had been told that American and British paratroopers never took prisoners but there was Jewish blood in his family and he did not care in the least about fighting for the Nazis.

About midnight an air raid alert was sounded by the battalion headquarters in the village of Azeville. That was nothing unusual; there had been one already, earlier in the evening, which had only lasted for half an hour. When the second alert sounded Müller and Busch and the rest of their infantry platoon turned out to man their posts. Busch said to his feldwebel 'I hope I'll see you in battle. I wonder which of us will be the first to get himself killed.'

Events after the American paratroopers began landing moved swiftly towards a dawn which Müller was to remember with horror all his life. Soon after midnight, an order was given to fall in on the road and march to Azeville. On exercises in the past, they had always carried blank ammunition in their rifles and the pouches of their equipment; their live ammunition was stowed in their haversacks. nobody gave them the order to load live rounds, so they set out on their march with blanks still in their rifles, believing the whole thing was another ill-timed exercise but on the outskirts of Azeville they were shot at from the churchyard in the middle of the village and the ammunition was unquestionably live. The whole platoon dropped into ditches beside the road and without waiting for orders they delved in their haversacks and reloaded their pouches and guns. Then, led on by their feldwebels, they crept forward very slowly, from grave to grave. Dark figures dashed out between them and escaped and the firing died away but by the church porch a man was lying dead and Müller, looking down at him, recognized the equipment of an American parachutist and knew the day had come.

It was not very long before the first Americans entered the village. They got into a farmyard opposite the garden gate in a hedge where Müller and his section were waiting and they were sent to clear the Americans out. The feldwebel went first, through an archway into the yard. Friedrich Busch went second and a single shot was fired and killed him instantly.

Müller was shocked by the first death he had ever seen in battle; the more so when he remembered what Busch had said about his wife and baby. It was the first of a series of terrible events of that night which haunted his mind for years afterwards as nightmare memories. By dawn his platoon was cut off and the village seemed to be surrounded. They had no radio and the telephone had gone dead. The feldwebel was ordered by the platoon commander to take a patrol to try to get through to brigade headquarters and ask for orders; and he picked Müller and a couple of younger men. There was an angry argument when the platoon commander told them to go on bicycles. The feldwebel said that was lunacy in daylight. But soon after dawn the four men stole out of the village on foot across the fields. As they crept along beside a hedge out in the no-man's-land of the open countryside, they heard voices and saw two American soldiers in a meadow. Müller and the feldwebel crawled down a ditch. Looking through the thickness of the hedge, Muller was astonished to see that one of the parachutists had a large painting of a pin-up girl on the back of his tunic and the other had the words 'SEE YOU IN PARIS' on the back of his. Müller poked his rifle through the hedge and said 'Hallo.' The Americans wheeled round.

'Hands up,' Muller said and he and the feldwebel broke through the hedge and then saw a third American, lying badly wounded.

'I'm sorry, but we must search you,' Müller said.

'OK, if you say so,' the younger of the two Americans answered; and as Müller began to go through his pockets he added: 'But don't take the picture of my girl.'

'I take nothing but your weapons,' Müller said. In their pockets he found chocolate, silk stockings and elegant lingerie. 'What's this for?' he demanded.

'That's for the little girls in Paris,' the prisoner said. 'And the candy's for me. Have some? Say, how far is it to Paris, fella?'

'I don't know, I've never been there,' Müller said and he accepted the chocolate.

'Don't eat it, it might be poisoned,' one of the young Germans shouted.

'What does he say?' the American asked and Müller told him.

The American laughed. 'It's not poisoned,' he said.

When the second of the prisoners was disarmed, Müller turned his attention to the man who was lying wounded. He was very badly hurt and it was only a minute or two before he died.

'I'm sorry,' Müller said.

The young American knelt down and closed the dead man's eyes and crossed his arms on his chest; and then he began to say the Lord's Prayer. Müller and the other American joined in; and then the feldwebel and the two young German soldiers took up the prayer in German and the six men in their two languages prayed together, grouped round the man who had died.

Erwin Müller was taken prisoner after a week of wandering and years later, returned to his wife. [7]

'About a week before D-Day they moved us from the town of Lamborne, where we had been stationed since arriving in England six months earlier, to Welford airdrome, where we would remain until the start of the invasion. At Welford we were once again hooked up with the 435th Troop Carrier Group, an outfit that we had worked with before, both in England and back in North Carolina in 1943. We were confined in a staging area until the D-Day takeoff. The chow was excellent! Probably about June 3rd our mission was revealed to us. Our battalion would not be jumping with the rest of the 501st. We would enter Normandy with the Division Commander, General Maxwell Taylor and the division HQ group. As it turned out we were more than a reaction force for General

7   Adapted from *Dawn Of D-Day* by David Howarth (The Companion Book Club 1959).

Taylor on D-Day morning - we would be in the very front of his drive to meet the 4th Division coming off of 'Utah' Beach on Causeway #1. On June 4th we were issued live ammunition, grenades and the like and as soon as we were all ready to go they told us it had been postponed. On June 5th we went through the same procedure and this time we marched out to the tarmac to board the planes. Our Regimental Commander, Colonel Howard R. 'Jumpy' Johnson formed us up and made his famous 'knife in the back of the blackest German' speech. Then he did something else that I will never forget. We walked past him and he shook the hand of every man in the battalion! We put on all of our equipment and were helped into the C-47s by Air Corps guys. My platoon had been assigned to the 77th Squadron and one of my friends on the plane, Staff Sergeant Jack Urbank, actually knew the pilot, a Lieutenant Harrison, from previous jumps he had made with the 77th. Like the others, I had a hell of a time getting into the plane as I was loaded down with my two parachutes, four or five grenades, a full cartridge belt of ammo, a SCR536 radio, a M-1 Garand rifle in a Griswold bag, musette bag, canteen, gas mask, first aid pouch, entrenching tool, bayonet and heaven knows what else. They also made us wear, in addition to GI shorts, long underwear and ODs under the impregnated jump suit. Needless to say it was very difficult to move! After we got seated the pilot came out of the cockpit compartment and told us something to the effect that he was going to give us a good flight. As we were taking off it looked like the sun was just going down - and it was 23:30.'

Staff Sergeant Raymond Geddes, Jr., Company 'G', 501st Parachute Infantry Regiment, 101st Airborne.

'At six that evening we dropped everything to make the long drive to Newbury and visit the 101st Airborne. They would be the first troops to land in Normandy behind the enemy lines. Some would be towed over in huge gliders that would settle down quietly in the darkness with their cargoes of young fighting men. Others would parachute down into this heavily fortified area. Ike's last task on the eve of D-Day was to wish these men well... His flag was not flying from the radiator of the car and he had told me to cover the four stars on the red plate. We drove up to each of the airfields and Ike got out and just started walking among the men. When they realized who it was, the word went from group to group like the wind blowing across a meadow and then everyone went crazy. The roar was unbelievable. They cheered and whistled and shouted, 'Good old Ike!' They looked so young and so brave. I stood by the car and watched as the General walked among them with his military aide a few paces behind him. He went from group to group and shook hands with as many men as he could. He spoke a few words to every man as he shook his hand and he looked the man in the eye as he wished him success.'

Kay Summersby, Eisenhower's personal driver, during a visit on the evening of 5 June to visit airfields in the area from which American airborne troops would be taking off. Once the decision to begin the invasion Eisenhower had gone to South Parade Pier in Portsmouth to see the last troops embarking. At lunchtime, Ike and his aide Captain Harry C. Butcher USN returned to Ike's trailer at Southwick Park and played 'Hounds and Fox' and then checkers. Butcher had already arranged for Eisenhower, accompanied by journalists, to go to the airfield at Greenham Common that evening to visit the 101st Airborne Division. From Greenham Common, Eisenhower went to Aldermaston, then to Welford and finally to Membury. Time was

running out, so he did not go on to the fifth airfield, at Ramsbury. Instead, he returned to Greenham Common to watch the take-off.

'Hundreds of paratroopers, with blackened and grotesque faces, packing up for the, big hop and jump. Ike wandered around them, stepping over packs, guns and a variety of equipment such as only paratroop people can devise, chinning with this on and that one: All were put at ease. He was promised a job after the war by a Texan, who said he roped, not dallied, his cows and at least there was enough to eat in the work.'

Captain Harry Butcher, once vice president of CBS. Eisenhower then returned to Portsmouth, telling Kay Summersby during the drive back, 'I hope to God I know what I am doing.' He later told her: 'It's very hard really to look a soldier in the eye when you fear that you are sending him to his death.' Kay's fiancée, Lieutenant Colonel Richard Arnold of the US Army was killed in North Africa in 1943. Ike and Summersby, the former model for the Worth fashion house, who wore uniforms made by Eisenhower's personal tailor, were romantically linked. She first worked for Eisenhower in London in 1942. The two became close friends, sharing stolen moments over lunch at country pubs in between his appointments with generals and politicians. When Eisenhower set up his HQ at Algiers in late 1942, he took Kay with him and there, away from the prying eyes in London, she let herself fall in love. When Eisenhower and Kay flew to Cairo ahead of a conference in Tehran, they sat side by side, daring to hold each other in a crowded but darkened aircraft. 'We were dreamily content,' Kay later wrote.

'Of all his personal worries that day, the worst, he said afterwards, was the thought that his own conscience might find him guilty of the blind sacrifice of these thousands of young Americans. At the airfield, concealing this thought, he strolled round among them talking cheerfully to anyone who caught his eye. They were full of confidence and knew nothing of his fears. One of them, who had a ranch in Texas, offered him a job when the war was over. As darkness fell, they embarked in their aircraft and Eisenhower waited and watched the aircraft take off into the gathering night; a Supreme Commander is always a lonely man. At the same time, others were taking off from airfields all over England and soon the sky overhead was full of the sound of them.

'Probably Eisenhower had hardly noticed the countryside around the airfield, but the parachutists knew it well. When they left their depot at Fort Bragg in Carolina, England had been described to them as a combat zone.

'Many of them, after crossing the Atlantic, had arrived at their camps in Wiltshire in the dark and had had a surprise at what they saw the next morning: gentle green hills, ancient stone pubs and churches, thatched villages with incredible names - Chilton Foliat, Straight Soley and Crooked Soley, Ogbourne St. George and the place which was written Mildenhall and spoken of as Minal. There was no sign of combat, but every symbol of ancient peace and calm. One of the parachutists said he felt as if he had passed out and woken up on a Hollywood movie set.

'It was true that almost nothing could change the peaceful ways of those English villages. Most of their young men and women had gone away. All through the years from Dunkirk, the people who remained had plodded on, working rather harder than they ever had before, urged on by government officials and by their own consciences, to grow more than the land had ever been made to produce and spending what leisure time was left in the Home Guard, the civil defence, the first aid, or the fire watchers. When the Americans came, the people of the villages watched the most extraordinary activities with interest, but without very much surprise. Mass parachute drops on the neighbouring parks and farms became such a common sight that they hardly bothered to go outside to watch.

'But when the Americans suddenly disappeared, the villages seemed very strange without them. On the evening of the fifth, when Eisenhower was at the airfield, the bar of the Stag's Head in Chilton Foliat a couple of miles away was a desolate place. Nobody was in, except the local regulars sitting over their mild and bitter. The bottled ale and the strictly rationed whisky, which had usually all gone by nine o'clock, were left on the shelves that night. The landlord and the regulars, in desultory conversation, wondered where the Americans had gone and agreed that they really rather missed the noise and hustle and reflected how dead the place would have been all winter if they had never been there.

'At closing time, with these thoughts still in his mind, the landlord locked the bar and washed up the few glasses and then went out to shut up his chickens; and it was while he was out there in the meadow behind the pub that the airfield came to life. The aircraft came up over the elms in the park where the American camp stood empty now and silent: in twos, in dozens, in scores, they circled overhead and took up formation and others came over from further north in hundreds. Standing there in awe, he called to his wife to come and listen. 'This is it,' he said.'

Dawn Of D-Day. [8]

'Everyone held their breath at that time when we were watching the plot to see if the E-boats came out from Cherbourg. General Eisenhower, Admiral Ramsay and of course the top brass generally, used to come and pop in for a few minutes, have a look round, look at the plot. They didn't really discuss things in front of us. They tended to come in for a look and then return and obviously had their conferences back in their own headquarters.

'There was certainly some talk. It was not hushed like a church or anything like that. People were behaving completely naturally. After all, we had been exercising in this room for months and so we were quite at home with the situation. The atmosphere was tense, certainly, but everyone was very confident and very friendly. I don't think anyone of us dreamed that things could go badly wrong now.'

Fanny Hughill, a WREN plotter in the Operational Headquarters.

'We returned about 01:15, sat around in the nickel-plated office caravan in courteous silence, each with his own thoughts and trying to borrow by psychological osmosis those of the Supreme Commander, until I became the first to say to hell with it and excused myself - to bed.

'At H-Hour, by coincidence, I was awake, that being 06:40 and was contemplating the underside of the drab tent roof, wondering how come such a quiet night in contrast with other D-nights when this was supposed to be the biggest and most super-duper of all... I tiptoed down the cinder path to Ike's circus wagon to see if he was asleep and saw him silhouetted in bed behind a Western. Ike grinned as he lit a cigarette. I was almost the first with good news, but Admiral Ramsay was just on the phone, telling him things seemed to be going by plan and he had no bad news at all.'

Captain Harry C. Butcher USN, Eisenhower's aide.

8   By David Howarth (The Companion Book Club 1959).

'...There was a moon, that night. The planes mounted and circled, with their wing lights close, and slowly the long sky train straightened out and headed for France. Those who were part of it said it was beautiful: in daylight, the sea, solid with ships, was beautiful too. That giant departure of men for the invasion of Normandy was a terrible and handsome sight.

By 11 o'clock on the night of June 5th all 378 planes, carrying 6,396 paratroopers, had left the fields of England. This was Task Force A, led as before by James Gavin, now a brigadier general. When his men landed in the fields, orchards, marshes and rivers of the Cherbourg peninsula, the long last battle of the war began. As the planes approached the coast of France, fountains of flak spurted up against them. It takes fine and steady pilots to fly the slow vulnerable transports through that stuff. Some planes were hit and crashed in flames, but most of them made it. Bill Walton reports a fragmentary amazing conversation, in his plane, between men shuffling to the open door.

'Please don't shove me, I'll go quickly'...

'Okay, don't shove me either'...

Martha Gellhorn writing in *Collier's Magazine*.

'We were going to be the key that unlocked the door to Hitler's fortress... Our mission was to take and defend the crossing of the Merderet River that led to Chef du Pont and the road that continued to 'Utah' Beach. The main mission of the 82nd was to keep the Germans in the west from mounting a counter-attack on the incoming forces on 'Utah' Beach... that was the set-up and after that we ceased to worry. All we had to do now was to wait for D-Day to come. Meanwhile we ate well, saw a different movie every night, played volleyball and softball and attended briefing meetings that updated us with the latest information.

Jim Kurz of the 82nd Airborne.

'One of the tank crew survived and he came down the side of a hedge after me. I saw him just before he fired. He was wearing very thick glasses. I was hit in the stomach. My pals rolled me into the hedge bottom for safety. I was there for hours before the medics found me. At first they thought that I was dead.'

Ed Wenzel, 508th PIR, 82nd Airborne, who knocked out two tanks at a crossroads near Hill 30 just outside the village of Chef du Pont. Around this village some of the heaviest fighting took place. Two thousand men of the 508th PIR jumped into this area and in the following three days, 336 men died, 600 were wounded and 165 were missing.

'Our takeoff was during the late evening hours of June 5th. We boarded truck with all of our equipment at about 21:00 on June 5th and was driven to our planes. We dismounted from the trucks, put on our parachutes, life preservers, all the other equipment we carried and was issued seasick pills. We boarded our planes about 22:30. It was no easy task getting on the plane with all of our equipment including arms and ammunition. I carried a 30.06 M-1 rifle, a 45 calibre Colt automatic pistol, trench knife and hand grenades. I carried a large bright orange flag which I was to use in signalling any of the Beach landing forces if and when I saw them. We were also issued some French francs. Each of us carried a dime store metal cricket for identification purposes. One squeeze, click-clack to be answered by two click-clacks.'

David 'Buck' Rogers 1st Sergeant, HQ Company, 1st Battalion, 506th PIR, 101st Airborne Division.

'There are eighteen men in the plane, nine facing nine on the chromium bucket seats. The plane is that valuable drayhorse of war, the twin-engined C-47. Scores of other planes, still in formation, fly through the night and the wind, and in all of them sit the quiet men, heavy with equipment, rifle or tommy gun, ammunition, grenades, land mines, first-aid packets, rations and maps, perhaps a radio, a bazooka, or a light machine gun as well - one hundred pounds or more to carry to the ground. This is the long last waiting and their faces and their eyes are blank. What concerns each man now is entirely private and his empty face guards him, where he lives alone. The lucky ones sleep. After all there is nothing to do but wait, everything that can be known is known, the mind only uses itself looking backward or forward; it is good to sleep if you can.

'No man was forced into these planes. Paratroopers are volunteers. There had been months of preparation for this ride, and there was a time, before a man earned and accepted his parachute wings, when he could reconsider and choose some other way to war. In the beginning, at jump school, they were driven through a course of training which was not only intended to harden them and teach them their new trade but was also meant to discourage them if possible. For weeks, from sunup till sundown, they ran until their lungs ached, did push-ups and sit-ups and twirled Indian clubs until their muscles knotted with pain, tumbled from platforms into sawdust pits until they were numb, stumbled and dragged on the ground behind opened chutes, blown by a wind machine, jumped from 35-foot towers and from 250-foot towers and learned to pack their chutes, with the chilling knowledge that they would use these same chutes on their first real jump. Finally, as one of them said, 'preferring certain death to any more training,' they were taken up in C-47s and twice a day they spilled themselves out; having overcome this daylight hazard, they tried it again at night.

'After they got their wings, the training was no less rigorous, but at least there was some praise mixed with the punishment. Nothing that could be taught was left untaught; they were also told that one paratrooper was worth five of any other kind of man. Their confidence in themselves and their units and their division grew to be iron hard, and they were prepared to pay for this pride.

'The time for payment had come. They had been briefed; each man knew what was expected of him and knew the plan that directed them all. They also knew what can go wrong. They knew that a chute can fail to open, a 'streamer' they call it. They knew a man can land and break his legs, his back, his neck for that matter. They knew a man can be shot as he floats to earth, or hang in a tree as a helpless target. They knew there is no guarantee that they will be dropped where they expect. They knew for certain that wherever they dropped the enemy will be all around them, waiting, and they can only hope that darkness and surprise will give them that edge of time they need. The moment for thinking and knowing is past; the red warning light has flashed and the jumpmaster gives the command that belongs to them alone: Stand Up and Hook UP! Seventeen men rise and fasten their static lines to the main cable.

'Check your Equipment!'
'Sound off for equipment - check!'
'Number ten okay!... Number nine okay!... The voices count off, above the motor and the noise of the wind.
'Are you ready?'
'There is a full, roaring shout.
'Then the final words: 'Let's go!'

'The officer disappears into the wide loud night; men shuffle fast down the length of the plane; hurry, hurry, the faster you get out the nearer you will be to your buddies when you land; the plane is empty. In seconds which cannot be measured in time, men have descended into battle.'

Stand Up and Hook Up! by Martha Gellhorn writing in *Collier's Magazine*.[9]

'It was a grave-faced group that boarded the planes the night before D-Day. Gone was the habitual wise cracking and blonde talk. In its place was a sense of responsibility and a tense anticipation. After countless months of training, learning how to get the other fellow first, our men were ready.

'The plane ride lasted nearly two hours - two hours of physical as well as mental discomfort, for the cumbersome equipment, the flak, the chute opening and where and what you'll land in and on, can occupy even the calmest individual's mind in such circumstances. The wind was high, and the plane bounced about plenty, but no one got sick. Finally, the crew chief yelled that we were 20 minutes out from the drop zone. 'OK guys, let's stand up and hook up,' came the quiet voice of the jumpmaster. Everybody shuffled into line. Now was the time when all Paratroopers get the old 'Butterflies' - the time spent between hooking up and waiting for the jump order. We must have checked our straps and equipment a hundred times. Then, suddenly, the jumpmaster's command: 'Let's go!'

'The nervousness had lifted, just as it always does when the crucial moment comes. We all pushed towards the door - come what may. We were ready and wanted to get it over with. Out I went. Then with a jolting jerk that temporarily leaves you breathless, the old silkworm has blossomed again. Looking toward the ground, I am suddenly very clear headed and alert. Tracer bullets are coming up all around us. It seems almost as if you are walking down a fiery stairway. Coming to your senses, you see the ground right below you and get ready to land. With a dull thud, you hit the ground. Then, in a nervous jumble that seems like years, your thumby hands, clumsy with tension, unfasten your straps, and you are free-for action. First, we must reorganize. At night, this is a real problem. Picking up men here and there from the widely scattered parachutes, you assemble as many as possible and then, when the flare goes up, you proceed to the Battalion assembly area.'

Joe Stanger, 505th PIR, 82nd Airborne.

'Late in the afternoon we began loading our equipment on the planes. It did not get absolutely dark until about midnight so it was light when we finally took off. We flew south and west. It was dark and the formations had tiny blue lights around the wing edges and down the fuselages, arranged to be seen only by the other aircraft. We homed on a sub somewhere, turned south for a spell then east and hit the west coast of Normandy on an azimuth of 113 degrees. We supposedly had a few minutes to go to drop zone and the red ready light went on. All men stood up, hooked up and moved in position to jump. Flak at night is magnified; similar to flying over the fairgrounds into the fireworks. The plane began jumping from the concussion but I don't think we took any hits. We flew and flew and flew. We knew something was wrong. I could no longer see the formation light of other planes. The guys were getting edgy and that line was

9   An abbreviated version of *'Stand Up and Hook UP'* appeared in the *Saturday Evening Post* entitled *82nd: Master of the Hot Spots.*

surging and pushing. And there was some profanity. Then the crew chief came up to me and said: 'Lieutenant, we can't find the drop zone. We are lost. Do you want to go back to England? Gawd almighty! Go back to England? Those guys would have thrown me out and jumped anyway or killed me when we got back to England. I said, 'Are we over France?' He said, 'Yes.' I said, 'Give us the green light, we're going.'

Lieutenant Robert Clinton Moss, Jr., Company 'H', 508th Parachute Infantry Regiment.

'Evening chow was a very quiet time as I recall, with all of us thinking about what lay ahead. We knew the risks. We had been told way back through jump school at Fort Benning that very few of us would survive in combat, or if we did, it would be in an incapacitated status. Our chances of returning were dim, but no one believed that applied to him. We had heard all these stories many times in training, but it was that very training that gave us the proper mental and physical state of readiness. We were at a high pitch. Our physical fitness couldn't have been better. We were in essence, ready! In fact we had spent just enough time at the airfield to be in the right frame of mind to take on anybody. Let's get out of here and get on with it!

'Well, we did get on with it! After supper we donned our equipment that was to be loaded on our persons. I had already put on my jump suit, which had been impregnated against gas attacks and I began to place my K-Rations in my left side pants pocket and the balance in my musette bag. I put on my shoulder harness with ammo belt and filled all the pouches with 30 calibre rifle ammo for my M-1 Garand that would be carried in three pieces in a separate pouch behind my main chute. My first aid pack was on my helmet, so I placed atabrine tablets for water purification in a small bag with other toilet articles in the musette bag. I slung two bandoliers of 30 calibre rifle ammo across my chest in opposite directions, like a Mexican bandit. I placed the gammon grenade in my right pants pocket. I was quite doubtful about this piece of explosive and I treated it with due respect and hoped not to land on that side.

'I stowed an orange smoke grenade in my musette bag and some other equipment that I would not need immediately. When the signal came at 21:00 hours to assemble I grabbed my chutes and put them on but left the straps open. I would complete the connection at the planes. The sergeants and platoon lieutenants with the squad leaders checked each mans equipment and then we trudged toward the planes. My helmet felt quite heavy with its liner and wool cap plus the camouflage netting. I was glad that I had not placed anything heavier on my helmet than the first aid kit, otherwise I would be lopsided. I was a loaded ammunition dump. Row after row of planes met us as we looked for the one assigned to our group. There must have been hundreds of them all lined up almost touching each other.

'We reached our craft and unloaded our chutes for the final adjustment of all our gear. We all had trouble getting our chutes tightened over everything else and the Mae West that we were required to wear got in the way of all the other stuff. I wondered how the hell I was going to get out of my chute and assemble my rifle and other equipment before I was shot by the enemy. Even the heavy duty suspenders seemed to sag under the load. Being right handed I had earlier strapped my trench knife around my right ankle and before I could secure my chutes I had to place the 9" Hawkins mine into my bag which would ride under my emergency chute across. The cardboard between the detonator and outer ring really concerned me. I would be glad to place that on our roadblocks as soon as possible.

'I tightened my ammo belt and adjusted my canteen and entrenching tool then secured my gas mask in place. I tied the end of the shovel around my left leg to keep it from flapping in the breeze and started to put on my main chute when Jack Blankenship called me to assist him into his chute and buckle the waist band. Jack was about the tallest trooper in Company 'H' standing about 6' 8" tall and trying to buckle his chute was a real job. He had to bend over slightly so I would have room to work. I finally got it in place and pulled it tight and after I finished his he helped me strap mine tight. I had all my stuff on now with the exception of my helmet which I had laid on the ground nearby. I could not bend over to pick it up. My M-1 rifle container under my emergency chute made that manoeuvre impossible. Several C-47 crew members were assisting us get our equipment on and one sergeant lifted my helmet and placed it on my head saying, 'You'll need this trooper.'

'Thanks' I said. 'I can hardly move with all this stuff strapped to me.'

'I believe them when they gave the estimate of weight of a paratrooper when fully loaded for combat to be about 100 pounds additional. Heavy Man! Some of the troopers were walking around trying to shake the equipment into a more comfortable position. The order to board the planes came as their engines began to rev up. The sound was deafening with all of them humming into one great crescendo. I was concerned about the two grenades attached to my harness lapels. They seemed to be in a vulnerable spot. Perhaps that is why I carried my New Testament in my left pocket over my heart. We would certainly need the power of God with us this night and the days to follow. Whoever invented those narrow steps to board the planes heard the wrath of thousands of paratroopers that night. What a struggle! As each boarded and took his bucket seat along the fuselage. Battalion Commander Colonel Krause and his aide would lead off our stick of Company 'H' paratroopers. Most of the troopers on my plane were first platoon Company 'H' men. I was in the ninth position. Sergeant Buck Knauff, Norman Vance, Francis Gawan, Corporal Robert Coddington, Glen Carpenter, Richard Vargas and Larry Kilroy were in front of me along with Colonel Krause and his aide and after me in line were, Marshall Ellis, Hans Frey, Leon Vassar, Jack Blankenship and others. We had about 21 troopers on board plus the C-47 crew. I do recall being number nine in the stick of paratroopers and how someone had given me a shove from behind to assist my boarding the aircraft.'

Pfc Leslie Palmer Cruise, Jr, Company 'H', 505th Parachute Infantry Regiment, 82nd Airborne.

'I had a large, sharp, GI knife in a boot holster with a lanyard to my belt, a carbine (.30 calibre) and a .45 pistol which was cocked and ready in a shoulder holster. Thus I departed the good old C-47. I knew there was something bad on the ground but it didn't worry me particularly. I was happy to get out of that plane. This feeling is shared by all troopers. My chute opened as usual. I checked the swing somewhat. A strong breeze was blowing and I knew I was moving fairly fast in some direction. I was not going straight down. What looked large pasture below me was really a flooded section of the Merderet River. I removed my reserve chute and dropped it to have no interference when removing the back pack on the ground. I knew we had jumped about 700 to 800 feet which is not bad. Then I realized I was moving backwards. I could have turned my body to come in forward but said to hell with it, I'll go in as the Good Lord permits. The 'pasture' was gone now and I could see houses below. I realized I was coming in fast, mostly horizontal. More so than vertical. Then WHAMMMM'. I had trained for this with that thatched roof. I was swinging in the corner of a room. Bang-right wall, bang-left wall. Then I knew - nobody told me - I had come through the roof of a stone barn. I saw the joists, about two feet apart and up to a peak like any house roof. I pulled the knife from my boot and slashed through the nylon suspension lines that go from the shoulder to the parachute. I was now swinging by my left shoulder and still banging the wall. Left right, left right.'

Lieutenant Robert Clinton Moss, Jr., Company 'H', 508th Parachute Infantry Regiment.

'We daubed on our war paint - big white stripes on our ships so our own ground troops wouldn't shoot them down. Grim-faced, high-ranking officers gathered for secret councils. Enlisted men sat around aircraft reading letters from home, wondering when they would get back. Planes sat waiting on the ground. The MPs stopped soldiers at the gate. The radio operator sat reading a comic book in the sudden hushed silence of his shack. We dug our fox holes and waited...

'At first it was just a fuzzy spot of light, a dim glow, hovering like a cloud-obscured star on the northern horizon. The briefing room clock said 11:20, the S-2 calendar said June 5, 1944. It was quiet. The dim blob of light didn't move - it just grew. It grew too big to be a star. And then it just hung there, taking on colour. First there were little pin-pricks of amber, then red, then green. Still nothing happened. There wasn't a sound. Still it grew. Larger and larger. Then hung there like a little toy Christmas tree in the clouds... red, amber and green.

'Here and there a grease-stained mechanic glanced carelessly across the low, dark valley to the north, then started, paused, stood transfixed on the dew-wet wing of his airplane and stared like a pilgrim beholding a vision...

'For Chrissake Joe! What's that?'

'Joe took his hands from the cold, oily womb of an engine and squinted intently at the still night sky. 'What's what?'

'There - right there!'

'Then Joe saw it too...' 'Oh-h', I'll be', I'll be a son-of-a-bitch!'

'Slowly men arose from their work and turned tired faces to the wonder in the northern sky. Still it was quiet. Still it grew. Bigger. Brighter. It didn't appear to move, just grew. Grew until it looked like a great big Christmas tree floating in the clouds. Still there wasn't a sound. It grew until it looked like a huge, magic city floating in the sky. Then you could see it move - slowly, majestically. Then you could hear it move. Or maybe felt it first. The whole sky, the soft night air, alive with a tremendous throb - the low, deep throb of countless churning engines. Then you could see them - planes! Dozens of planes! Great big lumbering C-47s. Troop transports. Scores of them. This is IT! D-Day! Invasion!

'They came right over the field at 500 feet; ours was their last airfield this side of France. We knew they couldn't hear us, but we shouted anyway - 'Go get 'em Yank!' We waved, we shouted, we even prayed. For three solid hours they came. Wave after wave. After the Yanks came the British, towing big Horsa gliders behind them.

'A thousand planes that were going to flyover the coast of France at 500 feet - with their lights on. God, what a target! Oh, what a sight!'

HQ History, 474th Fighter Group, 9th Air Force at Warmwell, Dorset.

'...the sky over our house began to fill with the sound of aircraft, which swelled until it overflowed the darkness from edge to edge. Its first tremors had taken my parents into the garden and as the roar grew I followed and stood between them to gaze awestruck at the constellation of red, green and yellow lights, which rode across the heavens and streamed southward towards the sea. It seemed as if every aircraft in the world was in flight, as wave followed wave without intermission, dimly discernible as darker corpuscles on the black plasma of the clouds, which the moon had not yet risen to illuminate. The element of noise in which they swam became solid, blocking our ears, entering our lungs and beating the ground beneath our feet with the relentless surge of an ocean swell. Long after the last had passed from view and the thunder of their passage had died into the silence of the night, restoring to our consciousness the familiar and timeless elements of our surroundings, elms, hedges, rooftops, clouds and stars, we remained transfixed and wordless on the spot where we stood, gripped by a wild surmise of what the power, majesty and menace of the great migratory flight could portend.'

Sir John Keegan, at that time a ten-year-old schoolboy living on the outskirts of Taunton in the West Country, *Six Armies In Normandy.*

'My ears were very sharp and I would hear a faraway drone, like myriad bees flocking, away over to the north-east, but not from any particular point of the sky. Then quite suddenly the sky above the horizon was filled with dots, like a huge widespread flock of homeward-bound crows on a summer's evening. It was a while before they came close enough to make out silhouettes - most of us were pretty skilled at aircraft recognition, when life might pivot on the knowing of a Messerschmitt 109 fighter from a Hurricane or a Spitfire. From the vantage point of the Woolwich Common we watched the hundreds of aeroplanes, some singly, some towing the Hamilcar troop- and equipment-transporting gliders. The aircraft were mainly American-built Douglas DC-3 Dakota transport planes, the air-workhorse of the war. The width of the flock was at least ten miles wide and it took at least a quarter of an hour to fly overhead. Even if the separation was 100 yards between aircraft there must have been close to two hundred aircraft abreast. Then they were somewhere above central London, with St Paul's Cathedral's dome and towers shining, as if so proud that England was at last striking back at the grey-clad, half-million-strong German VII Army. A thrill of excitement ran through me as I stood alone, for a little while, watching approaching aircraft that surely and steadily carried the airborne troops that were to drop behind the Normandy beaches and have such a crucial bearing on the successes of that day: Tuesday 6th June 1944.

'One thousand bomber raids had become common by the Allies over Occupied Europe - but thirty thousand? No, it could not have been, although it certainly looked like it.'

Alex Savidge, a boy living in London.

US Airborne Forces	
82nd Airborne Division	
Major General Matthew B. Ridgway	
505th Parachute Infantry	508th Parachute Infantry
507th Parachute Infantry	325th Glider Infantry
101st Airborne Division	
Major General Maxwell D. Taylor	
501st Parachute Infantry	506th Parachute Infantry
502nd Parachute Infantry	327th Glider Infantry

An A-20 Havoc of the US 9th Air Force sporting D-Day invasion stripes with an 8th Air Force B-17 in the 381st Bomb Group in the 1st Bomb Division below. (USAF)

Painting D-Day invasion stripes on the wing of a 9th Air Force B-25 medium bomber. (USAF)

General Eisenhower speaks to Lieutenant Wallace 'Wally' C. Strobel the jumpmaster (for plane number 23) of Company 'E' of the 502nd Parachute Regiment, 101st Airborne Division at Greenham Common on 5 June. Strobel, whose 22nd birthday it was on 5 June, wanted to see Kay Summersby, Ike's attractive driver but when he went down company street near the 502nd's 'Tent City' he met Ike coming up so he never got to see her! Strobel has said that Ike asked him where he was from and when he replied 'Saginaw, Michigan', Ike said: 'I've been there and liked it. Good fishing there!' Eisenhower, his round of visits to the paratroopers completed, shook hands with General or and wished him good luck before walking to his waiting staff limousine to return to invasion headquarters at Portsmouth. His aide, Captain Harry C. Butcher USN noticed that there was a tear in Ike's eye. ((Lieutenant Lee Moore)

Kay Summersby, General Eisenhower's attractive driver attaches a pennant to Ike's staff car.

A group of Pathfinders before they boarded their C-47s to be the first to land in Normandy during the first few minutes of D-Day. On the left, back row, is Tony DeMayo; standing on the far right is Robert Bales; fourth from the right, back row is Larry James; far right in the middle row is James J. Smith. In Normandy, when two men either side of Mayo were killed by an exploding artillery shell, DeMayo felt a blow on his chest and when he looked at the bible he carried in his breast pocket, he found a piece of shrapnel embedded in it. If it had not been for the bible he would have been killed. DeMayo returned to Loughborough Parish Church in 1945 to marry his girl Ethel and take her to New York. He had met her while playing darts in the Loughborough Hotel in Baxter Gate, with her father. (US Army via Deryk Wills)

Tense and anxious, a platoon from the Third Battalion, 82nd Airborne barely managing a smile just before they boarded their C-47 for D-Day. One aircraft carried a stowaway, 20-year old American Oglala Sioux Indian Herbert Buffalo Boy Canoe in Company 'D'; a veteran of the Sicily and Salerno jumps, who had been ordered not to go on the D-Day drop but there was no way that the 505th PIR were going to jump without him. Canoe ended the war with the Silver Star, a Bronze Star and two Purple Hearts. (US Army via Deryk Wills)

Soldiers of the Royal
Electrical and Mechanical
Engineers (REME) reading
their French guide books
for the benefit of the
camera.

One of Colonel Wilson Wood's 323rd Bomb Group B-26 Marauders bombing Utah Beach before the landings.

Lieutenant Joe Hamil's crew in the 94th Bomb Group at Bury St. Edmunds (Rougham) Lieutenant Abe Dolim, the navigator, is far left. (Dolim)

General Sir Bernard Montgomery addressing troops of the Royal Ulster Rifles in the run up to D-Day.

Right: Feldmarschall Erwin Rommel with baton during his inspection of the Merville Battery. Rommel seldom spent daylight hours at his HQ at Château de la Roche-Guyon, choosing instead to inspect his troops on the Atlantic Wall in his Horch staff car accompanied by no more than two officers.

Below: Feldmarschall Erwin Rommel and Feldmarschall Gerd von Rundstedt, Commander-in-Chief West. Rommel commanded Heeresgruppe (Army Group) B which comprised the Wehrmacht armies in northern France, Belgium and the Netherlands with 7th Army west of the River Orne and 15th Army east of the river.

General der Artillerie Erich Marcks commanding LXXXIV Corps.

8th Air Force Fighter Command Mission Board on D-Day. (USAF)

Opposite Page: B-17 Flying Fortresses stockpiled on the runways at a Base Sub-Depot in the build up to D-Day.

Exeter, during the evening of June 5th - platoons of the 506th Parachute Infantry regiment move towards C-47s of the 440th Troop Carrying Group.

ANNA CATHARINA

British paratroops boarding their suitably inscribed Horsa glider.

3150

Captain Stanley E. Morgan the surgeon of the 3rd Battalion of the 506th PIR has his equipment inspected by Colonel Robert L. Wolverton.

Left: Mohican cropped Clarence Ware and Chuck Plauda, two of the 506th Regimental Demolition men who were assigned for a special mission on the Douve River bridges apply war paint using the same black and white paint that was used to make 'Invasion stripes' on the wings and fuselages of the C-47s at Exeter airfield.

Right: Major Frederick C. A. Kellam, First Battalion Commander (left) and Colonel William E. Ekman, CO, 505th Regiment, 82nd Airborne at Cottesmore waiting for D-Day. Kellam, whose nickname was the 'Jack of Diamonds' (note the Diamond insignia on their helmets) was KIA by an exploding mortar shell. (US Army via Deryk Wills)

Below: Hurry up and wait!

P-47 Thunderbolt 42-25871 Nigger II flown by Captain Richard M. Holly CO, 84th Fighter Squadron, 78th Fighter Group. The Thunderbolt was named after Holly's always-suntanned wife. (via Andy Height)

Colonel Hubert 'Hub' Zemke, CO, 56th Fighter Group, one of the great US fighter leaders of WWII, admiring his wing guns for the benefit of the camera. (USAF)

Ninth Air Force C-47 *Forty Niners* in the 49th TCS, 313th Troop Carrier Group at Grantham (St. Vincents). (Rose via D. Benfield)

British paras boarding a Halifax for the trip to Normandy.

Major David E. Daniel, CO of the 87th TCS, 438th Troop Carrier Group in the Ninth Air Force with his aircraft, C-47 42-100738 *Belle of Birmingham.*

Opposite page: Rows of Horsa gliders and their C-47 glider tugs ready for flying to Normandy.

American paratroopers in the 101st 'Screaming Eagles' emplaned for Normandy. (Lt Colonel Daniel via D. Benfield)

Major John Howard who commanded the coup de main party of 150 men - 4 platoons of 'D' Company and two attached platoons from 'B' Company, 2nd Battalion, Oxfordshire and Buckinghamshire Light Infantry and 30 men of 249 Field Company (Airborne) Royal Engineers. After the capture of the parallel bridges over the Canal de Caen at Bénouville and the River Orne at Ranville their task was to hold the bridges until relieved.

Captain John Sim MC 12th Battalion, the Parachute Brigade.

The danger was that the assault from the sea could be contained either at the coast or within the narrow-necked pocket formed by the wider flooding of the river valleys. Montgomery therefore had insisted (in spite of AVM Trafford Leigh-Mallory's objections) that airborne troops must be used to secure the beach exits and river crossings and he determined to turn the German inundations to his own advantage. 'Monty' planned to drop the two American airborne divisions in depth across the neck of the peninsula in the hope of sealing it off at one blow and isolating Cherbourg by establishing a defensive line along the northern edge of the flood-waters. Two weeks before D-Day an 'Enigma' decrypt revealed that Rommel had moved a fresh division into the very area of the 82nd Division's dropping-zones around Ste-Sauveur-le-Vicomte. This fortunate knowledge prevented almost certain disaster, for Bradley was able to modify the original ambitious design.

Two parachute regiments of the 101st Division were to drop just west of the coastal lagoon, silence a heavy battery and seize the western exits of the causeways leading from 'Utah' beach and head off an eastern German advance. One parachute regiment were to drop north of Carentan, destroy the rail and road bridges over the Douve and hold the line of that river and the Carentan Canal so as to protect the southern flank of the Corps. The 82nd Division, landing farther inland, were to drop astride the Merderet River south and west of Ste-Mère-Église, block the Carentan-Cherbourg road and extend the flank protection westward by destroying two more bridges over the Douve and secure the Merderet crossings, thus forestalling any attempt to contain the invasion forces behind the inundations and opening the way for an early drive to the west coast of the peninsula.

This modification avoided the dangerous dispersion of the earlier plan and brought the zones of both divisions within easy reach of the seaborne forces, but Leigh-Mallory's fears were not allayed. A week before D-Day he expressed them again in a letter to Eisenhower, warning him that loss of aircraft and gliders might run as high as 80 per cent. He pointed out that the troop-carriers and tugs would have to fly a steady course at 1,000 feet in moonlight over an area thick with flak-guns and searchlights, that the ground was heavily garrisoned and was unsuitable for large-scale landings from the air because of the flooding or obstruction of the only open areas and because of the close nature of the remaining country. Serious as these objections were, Eisenhower felt compelled to overrule them and the airborne assault went in as planned.

'On May 30 he [Leigh-Mallory] came to me to protest once more against what he termed the futile slaughter of two fine divisions. He believed that the combination of unsuitable landing grounds and anticipated resistance was too great a hazard to overcome. This dangerous combination was not present in the area on the left where the British airborne division would be dropped... To protect him in case his advice was disregarded, I instructed the air commander to put his recommendation in a letter... I telephoned him that the attack would go ahead as planned and that I would confirm this at once in writing. When, later, the attack was successful he was the first to call me to voice his delight and to express his regret that he found it necessary to add to my personal burdens during the final tense days before D- Day.'
Dwight D. Eisenhower, *Crusade In Europe.*

At 15 minutes after midnight on 5/6 June Captain Frank Lillyman's team of 101st pathfinders parachuted into occupied France. Behind the team came 6,000 paratroopers of the 101st 'Screaming Eagles' Airborne Division in C-47s of the IX Troop Carrier Command. On the western flank of the invasion beaches it was planned to drop 13,000 paratroopers from the US 82nd and 101st Airborne Divisions using 882 aircraft on six drop zones - all within a few miles of Ste-Mère-Église. Running into heavy German flak as they approached the drop zones, many of the troop transports took evasive action and scattered the parachutists over an area 25 miles long by 15 miles wide and by nightfall, only 2,500 men could assemble in their units. Many men, much equipment and almost all their glider-borne artillery, were lost in the flooded areas of the Merderet and Douve Rivers.

'I have just witnessed the take-off of first serials of the 438th Troop Carrier Group carrying paratroopers of the 101st Airborne Division, spearheading the invasion of Europe. It was a model of precision flying and air discipline. The C-47s, zebra-striped for identification, took off at 11-second intervals. General Eisenhower told the grease-painted paratroopers and the air crews: 'The eyes of the world are on you tonight.' Before take-off I talked to Colonel John M. Donaldson, pilot of *Birmingham Belle* leading the first element and most of the other flight leaders. The were grim but calm. *Birmingham Belle* was airborne at 2248 hours and the invasion of Europe was on.'

Major General Lewis H. Brereton, Commanding General of the 9th Air Force, who was on hand at Greenham Common to watch the first serials of troop carriers take off. First dispatched were six pathfinder serials (a serial being a number of planes specifically assigned to drop on one zone or area) with three planes to each serial, except one with four planes. Their mission was to drop at least one of three airborne pathfinder teams on each of the six drop zones assigned. The teams were to mark the zone with lighted tees and radar beacons 30 minutes before the arrival of the main body. The pathfinders were also to drop two teams to mark a special glider landing zone. All drops were accomplished. While the pathfinders were operating, 821 C-47 and C-53 transports plus 104 towing as many Waco CG-4A gliders were ready to be dispatched in 28 serials from fourteen airfields from Lincolnshire to Devon.

The flak grew more intense as the serials behind the leaders reached the French mainland at 'Muleshoe' the IP (Initial Point). From 'Muleshoe', the transports nosed down toward 700 feet and reduced speed to 125 mph. As Birmingham Belle reached the drop zone her radio man, Staff Sergeant Woodrow Wilson was slightly wounded by flying shrapnel. Then the Belle slowed to the 110 mph speed necessary for the paratroop drop, the dropping point was identified and at 0016 hours of 6 June the first paratroopers of the invasion dropped toward Normandy, With their cargoes delivered the first planes headed north for the coast at 'Paducah' from which point they continued north to 'Spokane' before turning west to 'Gallup' where they returned to the original corridor which took them back to England.

'The horseman guiding his steed sideways to get him squared away for his jump over a high bar and broad pit, then turning, loosens the reins and feels the surge of power ripple through his spirited mount, knows something of how I felt on the night of June 5th/6th as I turned our formation of 81 troop carrier C-47s at the last check point in the English Channel, leading in the first group of the 50th Troop Carrier Wing and started on the final straight run-in to the German-held Normandy. Not that I'm kidding myself about the lumbering old C-47 Skytrains being powerful or spirited, but the potent fighting cargo we carried, the eager tough young paratroopers of Colonel Sink of the

101st Airborne Division, gave us that sense of power and spirit.

'Crossing the coast at 1500 feet, I saw a cloud bank too late to get under, so started over and the Group was on instruments temporarily, until I found a hole and went down to 700 feet. We were fired on by machine guns and flak to within a few seconds of the DZ, located three miles short of the opposite coast. My No. 2 element was badly shot up and one ship toward the rear was shot down, piloted by Sargent Capeluto and Muir were shot down in flames, but got their paratroopers out safely we think; they were in the 2nd section of 36 led by Major Harry N. Tower.

'Returned to base at 0230 with only three planes unaccounted for. We brought back only two paratroopers, one of whom had been shot through the leg twice, but who was going to jump anyway. The other had been knocked silly on the side of the door as he started out. Colonel Sink and I bet £5 that I couldn't put him within 300 yards of his DZ point, 'T' or no 'T'. The Pathfinders had left no 'T' lit but had a radar in operation. I believe I put him within 200 yards.'

Colonel Charles H. Young, commander of the 439th Troop Carrier Group, who led the 50th Troop Carrier Wing in, flying his radar C-47, D8-Z. Three weeks later one of the officers of the 506th Parachute Infantry came back and told Young that Sink was all right. He also paid him £10 for Sink as he had put the paratroop commander within 200 yards of his DZ point. [10]

'We were restricted to base and briefed on the pending missions. There was no outgoing mail. On the afternoon of the 4th after the briefing, all flight personnel were segregated from the non-flying personnel. Black and white paint was used to paint the invasion strips on the aircraft to aid naval forces in identifying allied aircraft. On the evening of the 4th, the mission was postponed. For several days the airborne troops had been moved onto our base and slept on cots in the hangars. They were sweating out the mission also under severe restrictions. On June 5th we proceeded on schedule on double daylight time. All crews and airborne reported to their aircraft at 2200 hours. This provided about 40 minutes to help load the paratroopers and check out the aircraft. We had to help load the heavily burdened paratroopers. All had leg packs tethered to their waists. These packs would be lowered after the jump so the sacks weighing 40 to 80 pounds would hit the ground first. We had worked with the airborne before and they were cocky, unruly characters but this time they were very serious. A couple of them had us lace the strap from their backpacks so they would have to cut the strap to get out of the chute.

'We started the engines at 2240 and taxied into take-off position so we could get the planes up and in a V of Vs formation very quickly. Take-off was at 2300. We had a very precise route to follow over the Channel and across Normandy. The return route brought us back over the out-bound route. Although we experienced many night formations with paratroopers in the States and in England, the plan for getting the troops to the Drop Zones in Normandy was the most complex and ambitious mission we had ever faced.

'There were several changes in altitude and direction over the course. There were no check points from the IP to the DZ to aid in maintaining the desired course. The pathfinders who were supposed to be on the DZ did not reach the area and no signals were emitted.

10 *The Ninth Air Force in World War II* by Ken Rust (Aero Publishers Inc. 1967).

'Our serial of six waves of nine planes each was led by Lieutenant Colonel Kreyssler of the 79th Troop Carrier Squadron followed by the 80th TCS and 85th TCS. Len Hayes and I were in the left flight lead position of the first wave. Len was in the pilot's seat and I was in the co-pilot's seat (right side). Everything was working fine as scheduled until we got to the last light boat at which time we were to turn off the amber down light and reduce the formation lights to half power. The formation lights (shielded blue lights on top of the fuselage and wings) were controlled by a rheostat - there was no half-power position.

'The pilot flying on Kreyssler's left wing turned off the formation lights so low they were not visible. At that time Hays could see nothing of Kreyssler's wing man from the left seat, so I flew from the right seat since I could see the exhaust stack glow and the phantom outline of the plane. We maintained our position flying as tight a formation as possible. When entering an unexpected cloud bank we continued on without any appreciable difference in visibility. We maintained the course and when coming out of the cloud bank we could see tracers coming up from many angles. The lines of tracers arched over us as we flew under them. There was a tremendous racket such as experienced when flying through hail. I had very few glimpses of the ground since I had to keep the outline of the plane in sight. It was standard procedure for the serial leader to show red or green lights from the astrodome so that all pilots would signal the jumpmasters. It was done this way so that all the troopers would jump in unison.

'Shortly after getting the 4-minute red warning light (stand up and hook up) I got a glimpse of a steeple of a church about a half mile ahead and off to the right about a quarter of a mile. Assuming this to be Ste Mère-Église, I felt we were on course and that DZ 'A' lay straight ahead. There seemed to be a delay in slowing down to the jump speed of 110 mph. When Kreyssler did slow down it was too fast. Wingmen had to cut power and hold the nose up to keep from over-running the lead planes, which in turn was followed by a blast of power to keep the plane from stalling out. The net result was that when we got the green light, we were flying about 105 mph and pulling a lot of power. The paratroopers went out in a terrific prop blast, which was the last thing we wanted to happen. We dropped our troopers at 0102 on June 6th. As soon as the paratroopers were out, Kreyssler dove to get down to 100 feet. Before I could follow in the dive, the lead flight was out of sight.

'We had another ticklish problem also. As the troopers jumped we had a strong stench of gasoline in the cockpit and cabin. When I lost sight of the lead flight, Len Hayes took control, descended and turned to the new heading. I checked the gas tanks and found the main tank we were using for the right engine indicated empty. I switched to the auxiliary tank even though the engine was still running.

'Being busy, I did not see the beach after we left the DZs. Norbert Milczewski, navigator, told Hayes when three minutes were up to turn again. We checked frequently to see if our wingmen were still in position. Wank and Butz were on our right wing and Camp and Shurman on the left. They stayed with us all the way to Membury.

'The trip home was uneventful even though no one dared smoke in this potentially dangerous situation. Coming back across the Channel at 3,000 feet, planes and gliders at 500 feet lit up a continuous column going into Normandy. I didn't envy those glider pilots having to fly and land in the dark. When we landed at Membury, Hayes turned off into the first available hardstand and very cautiously shut down the engines.

'When Hayes and I alighted, Norb Milczewski, Hoytt Rose and Tom Anderson were already standing about 100 feet away in the grass. Gasoline was running out of the tail and the moisture drain holes along the trailing edge of the wing. Later it was found that a 30 calibre slug had punctured the tank and lodged in the float. The hole in the tank was the only hit we had.

'I have always assumed the steeple I saw was at Ste-Mère-Église. Lately I learned there are at least seven steeples in the eastern part of Normandy. I cannot be sure which one I saw. I have never heard of any of our crews that saw a steeple. For our missions over enemy lines we used every conceivable means to assure safety for the crew.

'Typically we wore flight suits or fatigues. Everyone wore a Mae West. The pilots wore chest pack harness over their Mae Wests. It was too cramped in the cockpit to wear seat pack parachutes. We used chest pack parachutes that were stored behind the cockpit. If necessary the chest packs were clipped onto the harness while en-route to the door to exit the aircraft. Other crew members wore regular seat pack parachutes. We were issued British flak suits which consisted of two pieces, front and back, which were fastened at the shoulders and sides. Most used a third piece to sit on. Pilots wore goggles and a steel helmet in case the windshield was damaged or blown out. Basically the C-47 was unarmed, lacked armour and self-sealing fuel tanks - sometimes referred to as a 'sitting duck'.'

Second Lieutenant Roger Airgood, born Indiana 1 March 1921, C-47 pilot, 436th Troop Carrier Group at Membury in Berkshire.

'D-Day arrived for glider pilots in England. Breakfast was at 04:00 featuring honest-to-goodness fried eggs and a huge piece of chocolate cake. I suspected that the cook believed that he was cooking a last meal for us and that the food glider pilots liked most was fried eggs and cake. Where he got the fresh eggs, I'll never know. We hadn't had any in the previous four months we'd been in England. 'The condemned ate the hearty meal,' chirped one wag. When I arrived at our glider the other pilot and I carried our parachutes onto the glider between two rows of airborne infantrymen who were already seated on either side of the glider. We put our parachutes in the seats, actually, because the seats were built low on purpose to accommodate a seat pack and still allow tall pilots room for their head. About that time, a burly airborne paratrooper lieutenant stuck his head in between us two pilots and said, 'There's no use in you two fastening those 'chutes. We'd never let you use them anyway.' I thought that was putting it plainly, so I didn't even bother to drape the straps over my shoulders. You didn't argue with an airborne infantry officer. One C-47 pilot in our squadron was quite a comic. It happened he was a co-pilot on a goonie-bird that pulled me into France on D-Day. All we had for communication between the airplane and the glider was a telephone wire stretched along the tow rope. As we flew along the east side of the Normandy peninsula, waiting the right hand turn into the 'Utah' Beach landing area, I noticed numerous splashes in the water below us. 'Anderson', I asked on my phone, 'what's making all those splashes?'

'Those are P-51s dropping their tip tanks.'

'Anderson,' I replied, 'you're a damn liar. There aren't that many tip tanks in the whole Army Air Force.' The splashes must have been German shells falling in the water. 'Two good glider pilot buddies in my squadron were Johnny Bennett and Charlie Balfour. Those two were as close as friends could be, but they were forever arguing about one thing or another. One bone of contention concerned whether or not glider pilots would ever be committed to combat in Europe. Charlie said yes and Johnny said no, right up until D-Day. They asked to make the Normandy invasion together and flipped a coin to see which would fly as pilot and which as co-pilot. Bennett won the toss and along with a string of hundreds of gliders, they crossed the English Channel, flew inland over 'Utah' Beach and then Bennett released his glider from the tow and started his descent from 900 feet. They glided silently for a few seconds and then Balfour broke the silence with these words: 'Johnny, they'll never fly gliders in combat.' For several seconds, there was hilarious laughter between the pair, despite the hail of bullets that started coming up from the Germans below. The airborne troops sitting at the rear must have thought the two were slightly nutty. Luckily, all of them got on the ground unscathed.

'When the other pilot and I cut ourselves free from the tow planes for the Normandy landing, we caught a burst of machine gun fire from the ground which missed my head by about a foot and then stitched the right wing from end to end. The first bullet - I was flying co-pilot - just missed my head as we turned our plane to the left and that why it didn't get us. If we'd gone another half second farther it would have gotten us both right in the face and we'd have probably all gone down. Germans had flooded our proposed landing area so we landed in 3 feet of water. I went out the side of the pilot section by tearing off the canvas and tumbling in the water after first removing my flak vest. One guy didn't have the presence of mind to take off his jacket and fell into a hole where the water was over his head. Luckily for him, the other glider pilot rescued him after a series of frantic dives. It was pretty funny, though, to watch this big tall pilot as he dived down, came up, shook the water out of his eyes, looked around and then dived again. He must have dived down about three times before he found his little co-pilot.
'Our general instructions were to get back to the coast as best we could and get on a ship for the return to England. We landed about a mile and a half from Ste-Mère-Église. I spent some time with some artillery guys manning a 105mm cannon and with a communications outfit of the Army. I saw a burning C-47 aircraft on the edge of the field where I landed. I could still make out the number on the tail and I knew it had been flown by a good buddy of mine. All aboard were killed, I heard later. I guess I was just lucky to get off so easy. A lot of other guys weren't so lucky.'

Flight (Warrant) Officer 'Chuck' Skidmore Jr., combat glider pilot, 91st Troop Carrier Squadron, 439th Troop Carrier Group.

'This is the story of the first phase of the invasion as I saw it from the air in the early hours of D-Day. At 1:40 am we were over Carentan, in the Cherbourg Peninsula, in an American Ninth Troop-Carrier Command 'lead ship' - some 20 paratroops, the flying crew and me. A moment later the plane was empty. The paratroops were making one of the initial descents of the Second Front and the enemy from the ground was firing the first shots of this most momentous of all campaigns. All around the plane, rocketing less than 100 feet from the ground, a 'Brock's Benefit' of flak rainbowed us for something like eight minutes on end by my watch, though I could have sworn it was at least half an hour. It was dusk as our air fleet, advance guard of the invasion, left an airport in England - left twinkling lights for dark hazards. So closely had the secret of D-Day been preserved that not all the flying crews themselves knew the signal had been given till they took off. The paratroops had been in barbed-wire enclosures for some days. No one had any chance to talk.

'The previous day I had flown into London and back on urgent business. Immediately on my return I was summoned to a squadron headquarters to sleep. But they didn't show me my room. Instead they lead me right out to the airfield, to the first of a line of waiting planes. 'This is It!' they remarked. It had come at last - just like that...'

'As I climbed aboard, paratroops, steel-helmeted, black-faced, festooned from head to foot, were in their planes in the bucket-seats lining each side of the fuselage. The co-pilot, Major Cannon, was reading a historic message from General Eisenhower. It spoke of the 'Great Crusade' and ended: 'Let us beseech the blessing of Almighty God on this noble undertaking.' As the door slanged to on us, sitting there in the dusk, we realized that we had suddenly passed from one world to another. Perhaps that was partly the effect of the all-red lights on the plane. They made our faces look slightly blue. They turned white the red tips of our cigarettes. I think that perhaps all of us had rather a sinking feeling in the pit of the stomach. But that didn't last long. Somehow we seemed to leave it behind on the ground.

'Almost before we realized it we were off. Here and there lights, friendly lights, winked at us. Other planes, their red and green wing lights twinkling cheerfully, fell into close formation behind to left and right. As everyone adjusted parachute harness, flak suits and Mae Wests, our mood brightened to a spate of banter. 'Say,' someone sang out suddenly, 'what's the date? I'll feel kinda dumb down there if some guy asks me and I get it wrong.' We laughed uproariously at things like that - the littlest things, the silliest things. We exchanged cigarettes and we talked on - but somehow never about things that mattered.

'Among the paratroops were a doctor and two medical orderlies. They were going to drop with the rest to set up first-aid posts wherever opportunity offered. There was a chaplain, too. They all wrote their names and addresses and some messages in my notebook.

'Down below a beacon flashed out a code letter. We made a sharp turn over to the coast. Then our roof lights, our wing lights and the lights of all the fleet behind abruptly flicked out. We were heading out to sea. We fell silent, just sat and watched the darkened ghosts sailing along behind us in the twilight. I noticed a red sign on the jump door, just one word: 'Think.' I tried to remember what the jump master had told me: 'If you have to bale out, don't forget to pull this tag to strip off the flak suit'; 'when you jump remember to count to two before you pull the rip cord'; 'if you hit the sea you MUST unbuckle this 'chute clip here before you pull the tassel to inflate the Mae West, or it'll choke you.' 'While I was reflecting that I was certain to forget something, shore lights flashed in the distance. We could just make out land on the horizon under a glimmer of moon. The coast of France....

'This was it - the Great Adventure everyone had lived for and worked for so long and so hard. I hated to see it; and yet it thrilled me. Hitler's Europe.

'Those lights went out. A flare went up. Had they seen us? Had they heard us? The moon silvered the fleet behind.

'A pity' someone said. 'We were going in here,' one of the paratroopers remarked suddenly. We knew what he meant. He was talking of that extraordinary report that reached America some hours before that the Allies were already landing in France. Well, as it turned out, it was right. We WERE going into Northern France. Up here, now that lives were at stake, someone's idiocy didn't seem amusing.

'We took a sharp turn towards the land. And here I must pay tribute to the planning. So cunning was our routing, so many our twists and turns, that at no time till we reached our objective could the enemy have gained an inkling as to just where we were bound.

'The land slid by, silent and grey. And still nothing happened. Some of the paratroopers chorused 'Put that pistol down, Momma,' and 'For Me and My Girl.' Someone called out: 'Ten minutes to go.' The paratroop battalion commander talked quietly to his men. A final briefing. I shall never forget the scene up there in those last fateful minutes, those long lines of motionless, grim-faced young men burdened like pack-horses so that they could hardly stand unaided. Just waiting....

'So young they looked, on the edge of the unknown. And somehow, so sad. Most sat with eyes closed as the seconds ticked by. They seemed to be asleep, but I could see lips moving wordlessly. I wasn't consciously thinking of anything in particular, but suddenly I found the phrase 'Thy rod and Thy staff' moving through my mind again and again. Just that and no more. It was all very odd.

'Then things began to happen. Below we saw fires on all sides. Our bombers had done their work well.

'Corporal Jack Harrison of Phoenix, Arizona leaned over and thrust a packet of cigarettes in my hand. 'You might need them on the way back,' he said.

'I said, 'What about you?' He just shrugged. Then he lined up with the others.

'The jump door opened, letting in a dull red glare from the fires below. The time had come. We were over the drop zone.

'I wish I could play up that moment, but there was nothing to indicate that this was the supreme climax. Just a whistling that lasted for a few seconds - and those men, so young, so brave, had gone to their destiny. I'd expected them to whoop battle-cries, to raise the roof in that last fateful moment. But not one of them did. They just stepped silently out into the red night, leaving behind only the echo of the songs they had been singing.

'Then we got it. The flak and tracer came up, from all sides. Through the still-open door in the side of the plane I could see it forming a blazing arch over us - an arch that lasted for minutes on end, so close it seemed that we could not escape.

'It felt very lonely up there then in that empty C-47. I think I sat on the floor. About the only thing I can be sure of is that I was bathed in perspiration.

'I knew we were a sitting pigeon. We didn't have a gun or any armour-plate. Our only safeguard was our racing engines and the cool-headedness and skill of the pilot, Colonel Krebs, as he twisted and dived.

'I thought their fighters would be after us. But, fortunately, not a single one showed up from start to finish.

'Well, we came back. Three of Colonel Krebs' fleet didn't. 'We had luck,' said the colonel as we streaked for home.

'Standing behind him in the cockpit, you could see fleets of planes passing in each direction, guided by beacons on the water in a perfectly organized system of traffic control. The sea seemed full of ships. Soon the first seaborne forces would be going in....

'We came back. Our paratroopers hadn't - yet. At the moment, they're too busy to tell their story.

'Just in case Corporal Harrison happens to read this, I'd like him to know that I'm keeping his cigarettes for him. Perhaps he might like a smoke on the way home. But if he can spare them I'd like to keep them always.

'Back at the base, as we ate, two young officers walked in to breakfast and flipped over the morning papers. 'So the Allies have taken Rome,' they remarked. 'Well, it shouldn't be long now before the invasion starts.'

'They didn't know, yet....'

'I Saw Them Jump To Destiny' by Ward Smith, BBC *'News of the World'* Special War Correspondent who flew with the 440th Troop Carrier Group at Bottesford into Northern France with the first wave of Paratroops. Lieutenant Colonel Frank X. Krebs was the CO. The 440th TCG dropped troops of the 101st Airborne Division on D-Day, losing three aircraft. Vital supplies were carried to the same area the next day and a Distinguished Unit Citation was awarded to the Group for its efforts.

'The flight over to France was uneventful. It was dark and it took about two hours. I looked out the window once and saw a red light down there somewhere. Then someone said, 'We are over land!' I looked out the door. It was sort of moonlit haze. Shortly thereafter the red light came on and the drill started - 'Stand up! Hook up!' etc. Then the plane started to bounce around in a manner which I had never experienced before. We also began to hear explosions and what sounded like hail hitting the plane. We heard a loud explosion at the same time as a large flash of light. One of the planes in our group had gone up in a giant explosion. Someone called out, 'Look, those guys are on fire!' I leaned over and looked out the left windows and could see bits of flaming wreckage as the plane next to us also began to go down. I saw tracers from anti-aircraft fire all over the sky and I realized that the 'hail' hitting the plane was flak. Along with others I began to yell to our jump master, 'Let's get the hell out of here!' or words to that effect. Then our plane went into a dive and we tried to keep from falling down. The plane levelled out just above the ground. I learned later from Sergeant Don Castona that the pilot had passed on the message for our jumpmaster, Lieutenant Barker to come up to the front of the plane. During the time Barker was in the cockpit Castona noticed that the plane had changed course. We began climbing and suddenly the green light came on.

§'Immediately the line started out the door and we jumped. We were going fast and the opening shock was terrific! I remember seeing a farmhouse below and then I was on the ground. My harness was so tight I couldn't get myself free. Cows were all around me as I reached for the knife attached to my boot. It was gone, pulled loose when the chute opened. I finally got hold of my jump knife, which I had stored in a pocket in my jacket and destroyed government property by cutting myself out of the harness. I stood up and checked my radio operator's watch, which I noticed had stopped, from the opening shock, at exactly 01:25.

'I was very glad to see that I had not lost my M-1 rifle, stored in its Griswold bag. I assembled the rifle and moved off, trying to find someone. There was noise coming from every direction, planes overhead and shooting on the ground, but I was totally alone. Finally, in the moonlight, I saw some helmets. I gave one click on the 101st recognition signal (a toy cricket) and waited for the reply of two clicks. There was no reply. I tried again. Still no answer. I was reaching for a grenade when, thank God, I saw the shape of the helmets. I called out and found that the soldiers were men from my company. They told me they never heard the cricket. I found out later that we had landed in the centre of Drop Zone 'C', exactly where we were supposed to be (near Hiesville), one of the few units in the whole US Airborne to make that statement. [11]

11 'Fifty five years later I learned that Lieutenant Harrison had saved our lives by diving away from the anti-aircraft fire that shot down the other two planes in our flight. He flew past the DZ and then, after talking to Lieutenant Barker, he turned 180 degrees and dropped us in the middle of the DZ going the wrong way. He deserved a medal and he got it, but it took 60 years.'

'I have only a few memories of events between the time I joined up with Company 'G' and sunrise. I remember how beautiful the German tracers looked as they flew into the sky looking for targets. I watched a plane explode. I also remember that I fell into a ditch and found it was full of dead soldiers - I still don't know if they were Germans or Americans. One thing I do remember is that at dawn, when I could see, I took my trusty jump knife and dropped my trousers so I could cut off those damn hot GI long johns.

'While we were in the assembly area my company commander, Captain Kraeger, told me to contact the other platoons with my radio, but no one answered. Today I know that the reason that I couldn't contact anyone, all the radio operators were dead. Finally we moved out, towards Exit 1 from 'Utah' beach. I was on the left side of the road and Captain Kraeger was opposite me on the right. I remember seeing General Taylor and another General, who I now believe was Anthony McAuliffe, who became famous at Bastogne. There were also a lot of high ranking staff officers wandering around.

'We put out some scouts and began moving down toward the beach, which was some distance away. As we came around a turn in the road we ran into a German patrol and a brief fire fight took place. All of the Germans were killed. We kept moving and came to an intersection and more shooting started, this time from a sniper. A major by the name of Legere, who had been walking with us, was hit and fell in the centre of the road as the rest of us jumped into the ditch. A medic from out Company named Eddie Hohl went to the major's assistance and the sniper shot him too. Hohl never made a sound. He just slumped over on the major. I called out to him to see if he was OK, but he never answered. [12]

'We started down the road one more time and arrived in the town of Pouppeville, where there was a fight with the German garrison. We lost some more men, including one of the platoon leaders, Lieutenant Marks, who was leading the attack. Captain Kreager was wounded, but stayed with the Company. At one point during this fight I was again in a ditch and had several rounds clip the top of the ditch only inches from my head - I quickly moved.

'The Germans gave up after we had pushed them all into the house they were using as a headquarters and I was put to work placing German prisoners in a barn next to the German HQ building. Many of the 'Germans' weren't Germans at all. We figured out that they were Polish soldiers who had been drafted into the German army. Several of our Company 'G' guys could speak Polish and we learned a lot about local defences from the prisoners. We left the German bodies where they fell. I was assigned to collect the German weapons that seemed to be lying around everywhere. I was just a kid and I loved guns, so I decided to fire one of them at some ornamental balls on the roof of the HQ building. As soon as I squeezed the trigger I was in trouble. Everyone thought the single shot was from a sniper! I had a very difficult time for the next few minutes with all sorts of people yelling at me, especially our First Sergeant.

'After a time in Pouppeville we saw American soldiers coming up the road. Of all the American units in Normandy, it was Company 'G' of the 501st PIR that was the first airborne unit to meet up with the 4th Infantry Division coming off of the beach and I was there. That is my single claim to history.

12 To this day that incident makes me angry. Hohl was wearing a helmet with red crosses on it and had another red cross on his sleeve. I have spent the last 65 years hoping that the bastard that shot Hohl was one of the Germans who we later killed. I believe that a group of our guys went after the sniper, but I don't know if they got him. I visited Normandy in 1996, and stood at the location where Hohl was killed.'

'Later that afternoon we moved off with the rest of the 3rd Battalion to provide security for division HQ at Hiesville. I remember during the walk seeing a paratrooper lying face down next to the road with a bullet wound in the back of his head. He was wearing brand new jump boots. It's funny what you remember, because the rest of D-Day for me is pretty much forgotten.'

Staff Sergeant Raymond Geddes, Jr., Company 'G', 501st Parachute Infantry Regiment. 'June 7th was not a lot of fighting for us. We were held in division reserve. We felt the concussion of bombs and artillery. At one point some German prisoners from the 6th Parachute Regiment were brought in and we all wanted to see what our opposites looked like. Captain Kraeger, who had been wounded in the left hand, who was on his way to the aid station told us to take care of ourselves. I never saw him again as he was killed in Holland. He was a good officer. Late in the afternoon, as we were preparing more defensive positions, a Horsa glider crashed near our position. Unlike the CG-4A, which was made of aluminium and fabric, the big Horsa was made of plywood, which goes everywhere when it crashes. Everyone in the glider was seriously injured. I pulled a Thompson submachine gun out of the wreckage but threw it away when I could not figure out how it worked. June 8th turned out to be my last day in combat and my last day with G/501. Our battalion was now part of an attack towards Ste-Côme-du-Mont. Later in the morning I received my first wound of the day, in the leg, from an artillery shell. I also picked up a replacement watch from a dead German soldier. We kept advancing towards a major road intersection that today is called 'Dead Man's Corner'.

The battalion commander's radio operator had been wounded and I was sent to operate Lieutenant Colonel Julian Ewell's SCR300 radio in the back yard of a house that we had captured. (At the time the house was being used as a German aid-station - today it is a museum.) Colonel Ewell had me calling in artillery fire on German positions when a round landed in the yard and I was struck in the left eye by a piece of shrapnel. It felt like I had been slapped. There were no American medics around and the Germans had a big red cross on the roof, so I went inside to see if I could get some help. A German medic sat me down and looked at my eye. After a few seconds he said 'nicht kaput'. He put some powder on the wound and left. Then to my amazement, someone started talking to me in English. It was a German doctor from their 6th Parachute Regiment. I commented on his excellent English and he said, 'I should, I got my medical degree in England'. As he moved on to help his wounded German soldiers I noticed that he had left his hat next to me. I believe his name to be Karl-Heinz Roos. I was put into a jeep with other wounded for evacuation to England on a landing craft. We were told that no weapons or ammunition were allowed on the ships. I had hidden a $10 bill behind the butt plate of my rifle before we jumped on D-Day so I put the ten dollars in my wallet. In England the surgeon who operated on my eye said he could send me back to duty or send me home. 'You decide.' I asked him if I could return to Company 'G' and he said, 'Probably not'. I thought they would put me somewhere I did not want to be and told him I might as well go home. Several weeks later I arrived at Mitchel Field on Long Island and I used that $10 bill to buy a train ticket to Baltimore and be with my family.'

'We were dropped exactly on target... I dropped in an orchard which was a short distance from Amfreville and from a German garrison post... The lieutenant who jumped ahead of me broke both of his feet and he was captured. The second in command, Lieutenant Ames, took over the group and seven of us assembled at the point where we were to set up our ground-to-air-communications, our radar equipment... We were being attacked by small-arms fire. Much of the drop zone was flooded with water two to four feet deep... I could hear the men that had dropped into the water, their cries of anguish; cries for help. They were weighted down with equipment so that they had to struggle in the water to get out. In the deeper water some of them were drowned. It was really quite a harrowing experience, not only for them but for me, knowing that the signal we were sending out was dropping them into inundated areas.'

Pathfinder, Rolland Duff, 507th Regiment, 82nd Airborne Division.

'The C-47 was really vibrating as its motor turned over chugging and coughing as the pilot was endeavouring to get it running smoothly. The crescendo increased as the planes began moving into line for the takeoff. I wondered if they would get off the ground with their heavy loaded cargoes. Trying to talk was useless over the increasing noise. This was the time in the jump process that I became the most nervous, just before the takeoff. I believe that the uncertain sound of the motors contributed to my intensity. Tremendous excitement filled the air and much more on the way. I was chewing gum with a passion unknown before. The planes were all lined up and stopped at the runway waiting their turn to lift off as the crews checked their instruments. One by one the planes filed onto the runway revving their motors in anticipation of the impending acceleration for takeoff. We could hear the louder roar as each plane following the leader accelerated down the runway and lifted into the air. Our turn came and the quivering craft gathered momentum along the path right behind the plane in front. Stubbornly it clung to the ground as if uncertain of its role, but finally it reached the proper speed. Rising slowly over Cottesmore it gently lifted its load as those before it had done. We kissed old England goodbye. We knew we were in for real trouble now and parting wasn't easy. All the little chickens had assembled into formation at the assigned altitudes and we were on course for Normandy and all those other names we had learned in the past week.

'We knew from our indoctrination that we would be approaching the Cotentin Peninsula from the west side, which meant that the planes would be heading back towards the English Channel and England as they disgorged their loads, That's us! The Colonel who was nearest the door was nudging the one beside him and pointing downward as we flew over the channel. We all turned as best we could to look out the small windows to see what he was so excited about. In the partial darkness below we could make out silhouetted shapes of ships and there must have been thousands of them all sizes and kinds. If we had any doubts before about the certainty of the invasion, they were dispelled now by what was revealed in the dim light below our flight path. I could not hear what was being said near the doorway, which was open, due to the motor sounds and it was necessary to shout to get the attention of those across the aisle to look at the armada on the channel. The invasion of Normandy would begin and we the airborne troopers would spearhead the armies. God help me to commit myself to the task ahead and help me to be a good soldier and save me from all harm.

'I was constantly checking my equipment and mentally running through the sequences and procedures that I was to follow as soon as I hit the ground. Other troopers smoked incessantly since the smoking lamp was lit, while others like me were chewing gum with a similar intensity. Some feigned sleep. Most, if not all of us, were hoping to get out of the plane before we were hit by flak and hopefully there would be no malfunctions of our parachutes. Any talking had to be done by shouting to be heard over the roar of the droning engines of the plane.'

Pfc Leslie Palmer Cruise, Jr, Company 'H', 505th Parachute Infantry Regiment, 82nd Airborne.

'Stand up and hook up.' The silence was broken and we jumped up and snapped our hooks onto the wire. Then the sergeant called, 'Keep your hand on the D-ring when you leave the plane.' 'Sound off for equipment check.' I shouted, '17 OK.' The next man shouted '16 OK.' The countdown continued until, '1 OK.' 'Stand in the door.' My heart was pounding and I said a prayer to myself. I shouted, 'What time is it?' It was 02:30, although I don't know who answered. I don't know why I asked for the time, but I suppose it relieved the tension. I felt I was all alone and continued praying. The first man held his position in the doorway and we all shuffled up tightly and kept the pressure on him until we heard, 'Are you ready?' All together we yelled, 'Yeah!''Let's go!' With the roar of the engines in my ears, I was out the door and into the silence of the night. I realized I had made the 'JUMP INTO DARKNESS.'As the chute popped open, my head snapped forward and my feet came up; my helmet was pushed slightly over my face. The jolt of the opening chute soon made everything a reality. I looked up at my chute to make sure it was OK, then looked down and couldn't see anything but blackness. I unfastened the main belt, unsnapped my reserve and let it drop to the ground. I opened the chest strap. Now all I had to do on the ground was remove the leg straps and I would be free of the parachute. For a few seconds on the way down I looked around and saw red and green flares. The brightness of tracers flying into the sky and the sound of machine guns firing seemed to be all around me. I thought, '... just like the Fourth of July.' Looking up at the chute and then down at my feet, I had the shock of my life. I plunged into water. My heart was pounding and my thoughts were running a mile a minute. 'How deep is the water? Can I get free of my chute? Am I too heavy? Will the weight keep me on the bottom?'I hit the water in a standing position and when my feet touched the bottom I was leaning slightly forward. I straightened and kicked up for air. The water was not as deep as I had expected, so I held my breath and tried to stand. The water was almost above my nose! Quickly I stood on my toes and gasped for another breath of air. My heart was beating so rapidly that I thought it would burst. I pleaded, 'Oh God, please, don't let me drown.' Below the water I went and tried to remove the leg straps. They were too tight and wouldn't unsnap. Needing more air, I jumped up and as soon as my head was above water, I began splashing around. I started to pray, standing on my toes with my head barely above water, my heart beating faster. After a few seconds I calmed down and decided to cut the straps. 'God, 'my only chance is the knife. Please let it be there. 'Going down into the water again, I felt for my right boot. 'Yes, yes, it's still here.' I slipped my hand through the loop and tightly gripped the handle. With a fast upward motion, I removed the knife from the sheath. Quickly I jumped up for more air and stood still for a while thinking, 'Now I have a chance.' Holding the knife tighter as I went below the water, I slipped it between my leg and the strap, working back and forth in an upward motion. Nothing happened! In a panic, I came up for another breath of air and thought my heart would burst from fright. I wanted to scream for help but knew that could make matters worse. I told myself I must think. 'Think... Why can't I cut the strap? My knife is razor sharp!' As I was gasping for air I kept saying Hail Mary's. It seemed an eternity before I realized I had the blade upside down. 'That's it! I'm using the back of the blade!' I touched the sharpened edge and made sure it was in the upright position. Taking another gulp of air, I went down again to cut the leg straps. With a few pulls of the knife on each strap I was finally free of the chute. Getting rid of the chute calmed me a little, but the weight of the musette bag and land mine was still holding me down. With a few rapid strokes of the knife, I cut loose the land mine. Then I unfastened the straps of the musette bag and let it fall. I adjusted the rifle and bandoleers of ammo into a more comfortable position. Then I cut away the gas mask and removed the hand grenades from my leg pockets and put them into the lower jacket pockets. Reaching up, I unfastened the chin strap of the helmet and let it fall into the water. After taking another deep breath I bent down to retrieve the musette bag. Except for the wool cap, the entire contents were disposed of and the bag was then thrown over my head to hang behind me. I became conscious of the rifle and machine gun fire in the distance and I was gripped by fear. All the training I had received had not prepared me for a landing like this - in water!! The equipment I still carried was heavy and I was terrified I would drown because of it. I hesitated to move for fear of walking into deeper water. I needed to find a spot where the water was a little lower though, so I could get off my toes and rest. Moving slowly, inch by inch, the water became shallower. When it was chest height, I stopped and rested, trying to decide which way to go. My eyes strained to see a landmark, but I could see nothing in the darkness. I was cold and began to shiver. We had been told at the briefing to go in the direction of the next plane coming in if we were separated from the squad. 'Suppose there are no more planes... then what should I do?' The water seemed to be getting colder now. My shivering got worse and my teeth were chattering. 'I must keep moving; then I won't feel the cold so much.' The water was now at waist level and I believed I was walking toward high ground. I kept moving, but the water then became deeper. I turned and returned to the waist-high water. In the distance to my left I could hear the sound of airplane engines coming in my direction and getting louder. All Hell broke loose as rifles and machine guns began firing and I watched the tracers flying into the air. Suddenly there was a huge burst of orange flames coming from both engines. As the plane came down it sounded like the scream of a human being about to die. I could not believe what was happening. I just stood still... seeing, hearing. Suddenly I realized the plane was heading straight for me in a ball of flames and screeching for help. As fast as I could, I moved to the right, trying to get out of its path. 'Oh my God, it's banking towards me!' In a panic, I tried to run the other way. The flames lit up the darkness and with screaming engines, the plane crashed. It was dark again and became very quiet. As I stood shaking in the cold water, I wondered if the troopers had bailed out before the crash. 'I'll head in that direction and maybe I'll join with some of them. I have to get out of this water before daylight -- if I'm spotted by the Germans, they'll use me for target practice.' I was still shoulder high in the water and was pushing my way through some weeds. 'No, it couldn't be. Did I hear a voice?' Pushing the weeds away as I walked, I heard the password, 'FLASH.' I recognized the voice to be Dale Cable's. Pushing the weeds from side to side, my right arm hit against a hard object and I heard the click of a trigger. Cable hollered 'FLASH' again, while he cocked the bolt of his weapon and put a round in the chamber. Immediately I replied, 'THUNDER.' He recognized my voice and proceeded to give me Hell for not answering the first time. His rifle was a few inches from my face. Meeting Tommy Horne made us feel better and the three of us proceeded toward the plane. While walking through the tall weeds, we again heard the password and replied. This time we found Tom Lott and asked him if he thought there was anyone else in the water. He said he hadn't heard any other movement except ours. Time was running out. Hoping to join up with other troopers, we moved as fast as we could. We knew it was imperative that we leave the water before daylight. We were moving along in single file, but with some space between us. I heard splashing. Tom Lott was making noise as though he were going under. Horne and I rushed over and pulled him above water. We couldn't understand what had happened until Tom told us he could not swim. We decided to keep a tight single file and we put Tom Lott between Dale Cable and me. Tom Horne led. Cable told Lott to hold onto his rifle barrel and to stay as close to him as possible. Daylight was coming upon us fast and we could now see the outline of trees. We all knew what would happen if we failed to reach land before daylight. In our haste to reach high ground, Tommy Lott let go of Cable's rifle and went slightly to our right, falling below the water. This time I thought we had lost him for sure. Rushing over, I grabbed him and kept his head above water. He was coughing loudly, so we rested for a few seconds. We all told him again and again to stay close! Now we could see land clearly and Horne was moving us faster. Just as we reached the bank he went under, but managed to struggle to his feet again. Lott was afraid to move so I pulled him by the hand while Cable pushed from behind. We finally got him onto high ground. The four of us collapsed on the bank, completely exhausted. It was almost daylight when we took cover in the hedgerows. The hours spent in the cold water left us shivering. Water was dripping from our uniforms and sloshed in our boots. I made a clearing in the brush and removed my combat belt and bandoliers of ammo. I shook the water from my M1 and removed the clip of ammo, then looked down the barrel to see if it was clogged. It appeared to be clean so I replaced the ammo and then sat down. While removing my boots and socks, I noticed that my pistol and holster were gone. After squeezing the water from my socks, I put them back on and laced up my boots. I took off my combat jacket and wool undershirt. Wringing the water from these was difficult but I did the best I could with both. After putting on the damp undershirt, it gave me the shivers and my teeth began to chatter. Reaching for my musette bag, I took out the wool cap, gave it a few squeezes to remove the water and put it on my head. My knife was still hanging over my wrist. Before putting it into the sheath, I gave it a little kiss. If it weren't for that knife, I'd still be in the swamp, struggling.... Or drowned.

'Zipping up my combat jacket, I slung the ammo over my shoulder and sat down beside a tree. Resting my back against the trunk, I reached into my pocket for a chocolate bar, had a few bites and then put it back into my pocket. My teeth were chattering and I was shivering from the cold. I prayed that God would be good to us and make the sun shine. My prayers were answered. In the bright sunlight, we slept for a little while. Tom Home suggested that we move out and try to contact some of the other men from our regiment. Lott and Cable agreed, so we ran across the field to a hedgerow, spotting a road. Looking to the left, we saw a few troopers walking down the road towards us. We jumped over the hedgerow with our guns levelled at them. They gave us Hell for keeping them covered, but after speaking to them for a few minutes, we were convinced they were Americans. They told us we took a Hell of a beating on the initial jump, losing many men in the high water of the swamps along with most of our gliders. The situation looked very discouraging at the time. We asked about the 508 men and if they had met any down the road. They told us the men they had met were from different regiments. These troopers were from the 507th and were trying to find their own regiment. Wishing each other good luck, we went our separate ways. We continued down the road, running short distances at a time and taking cover in ditches. Further down the road we heard more voices and stopped, took cover in the ditch and listened. We recognized the American voices and came out with our rifles in a hip firing position, while advancing toward the troopers. We were standing outside a small building and after identifying each other, we asked what was going on. They told us there were many wounded inside, so we entered and spoke to some of them. None of the GIs being taken care of by the medics were from our company. After leaving the building we went further down the road and came upon a glider that had crashed. Immediately we went to see if there were any wounded inside. To our surprise there was a medic attending the wounded in there. Except for one, all the glidermen had died in the crash. His leg was crushed and the medic was about to remove it. The glidermen didn't have much of a chance. I hadn't seen a glider that wasn't badly damaged or which hadn't crashed. Paratroopers have a great admiration and respect for the glidermen. They had it a lot tougher than us. Horne, Cable, Lott and I were still together at this point. There was some shooting down the road and we could hear more voices. Cautiously we ran down the road and met a few more troopers. They had some Germans pinned down and Jack Schlegel was trying to talk them into giving up. Jack was doing a lot of shouting in German and then waiting for a reply. When he received no answer, he gave a burst from his machine gun. After that a few Germans gave up to him. Right after they surrendered we received mortar and rifle fire and scattered from the hedgerows to take cover. That was the last time I was to see Tom Horne, Dale Cable or Tom Lott.'

Private Thomas W. Porcella, Company 'H', 508th Parachute Infantry Regiment, 82nd Airborne.

'June 6th was the biggest day of my life. It was D-Day for me and all of the Airborne. I was quite scared but not as much as I had thought I would be. Finally the time came. The jumpmaster said 'Let's go.' Well, everybody started to go when we were hit by ack-ack. Half the stick got out easily but the ninth man was hit as he reached the door. We were all knocked down. We got up except for the wounded man who couldn't move. When the last man had left, the wounded trooper got to the door somehow and followed him out... The night was beautiful. I didn't like to see our boys being shot in their chutes, while still in the air... I stayed in a ditch for a while until some troopers came along. We continued to move until daylight when we were boxed in by enemy fire. The Germans spotted us and began firing on the ditch where I was hiding. One of the boys carried a prayer book. He asked us to say a prayer but I told him I didn't know a prayer. All I could say was: 'God, if you could ever do anything for me, please do it now as I need it.'... We started out of there and kept moving until we met up with our General. We joined others who were ordered to take a town. We took the town and held out there until the troops reached us from the beach. We had lost some men but the Germans lost three to our one... I hope every general is as much of a man as General Gavin proved he was in combat when he led us in such a victory.'

Private M. G. Thomas, 82nd Airborne.

'He was only eighteen. The men in his company used to call Private Tony Vickery the 'Milk Bar Commando' - milk shakes being his strongest and favorite drink. As for women, he didn't have any. His mom, back in Georgia, was his only and best girl... The jump was uneventful except for flak and a few ambitious Jerries on the ground. Out of the entire planeload, he came across one man and together they started off in the direction of the Drop Zone. On the way they picked up eighteen more troopers and that night they chalked up three machine gun nests and about twenty-five or thirty Jerries. Daylight made it necessary for them to take cover and dig in but Tony stayed on the alert. His vigil was not wasted for not more than six hundred yards away a skirmish line of German grenadiers broke out of a wooded area and advanced on the trooper's positions. He waited until the Jerries were about fifteen feet away before he squeezed the trigger of his Tommy gun. The fight lasted about twenty-five minutes and when the smoke cleared away he lay in a heap at the bottom of the ditch. Four slugs from a machine gun pistol got him in the throat. It was a rotten way to die, but if you looked on the other side of the hedgerow you would have seen the bodies of at least thirty - three dead Germans and the kid got everyone of them.'

Corporal Jules Stollock, 82nd Airborne.

'Our parachute troops were to land on three drop-zones and the gliders on one, located three to four miles behind the beach. Parachute pathfinder teams carrying lights and radar beacons for guiding in the planes were to drop shortly ahead of the main body and mark the landing areas. Theirs was the unenviable task of dropping in darkness into enemy-infested territory and announcing their own presence to the Germans by turning on their lights and beacon signals. These pathfinders were among the real heroes of D-Day.

'With the invasion set for 5 June I began on 28 May to make the rounds of the 17 marshalling areas scattered over Wales and southern England where my troops were sealed up and receiving their final instructions. Standing on the top of a Jeep, I addressed every unit in the division, trying to communicate to the men my feeling of the historic significance of the drama in which we were to be key actors and the pride we would feel someday in telling our children and grandchildren that we had been in Normandy on D-Day. Henry V had said it much better on St. Crispin's Day, but I was encouraged by the bright-eyed attention of the men and their visible eagerness to get on with the hazardous business which seemed to hold no terrors for them.

'...Promptly at 11 pm, our plane placed itself at the head of the squadron departing from the field. Lieutenant Colonel Frank McNees, CO of the 435th Troop Carrier Group, one of the most experienced pilots of the Troop Carrier Command, gunned the engines, we hurtled down the runway and we were off on what was to be, for most of us, our greatest adventure. To me, it was a moment of relief to be off after so many months of laborious preparation. I was content in the feeling that I could think of nothing which we had left undone to assure success. Now it only remained to go into action in the spirit of the verse of Montrose which Montgomery had quoted to the Allied commanders at their last conference:

He either fears his fate too much
Or his deserts are small,
That dares not put it to the touch
To gain or lose it all.

'Our parachute planes circled in the dusk over England for more than an hour as the successive squadrons rose from the airfields to join the airborne caravan which now included not only the planes of the 101st but also those of the 82nd arriving from their fields in central England. In all, there were over 800 transport planes in the formation as it turned toward France, carrying about 13,000 parachutists of the two divisions.

'By the time my plane reached the Channel, it was dark with a faint moon showing. We were flying very low in a tight V of Vs formation to keep below the vision of the German radars on the French coast. As I stood in the open door of the plane, I felt that I could touch the sparkling waves of the Channel so close below. The men were strangely quiet, some seeming to doze on their hard metal seats in spite of' the load of their equipment. They, too, seemed to have left their cares behind.

'Our route was across the Channel from Portsmouth to an air corridor between the islands of Guernsey and Jersey on the west and the Cherbourg peninsula on the east which then turned eastward across the base of the peninsula to our drop-zones. As we came abreast of the Channel Islands, from my post in the door I could see a great grey wall to the south-east where the Cherbourg peninsula should be. It was unexpected fog, the enemy of the airman, which was to be the first disrupting factor in our well-laid plans.

'The air column, still flying in orderly formation-at low altitude, made its final turn eastward and headed into the fog bank. It was very thick at first, so thick that I could not see the planes flying on our wing-tips. Almost immediately, the formation began to break up as the flank planes, fearing collision, veered to the right and left and some increased their altitudes. But there was little time for worry about the fog in our plane. The hook-up signal came on quickly and Larry Legere, four years out of West Point, had us in the aisle attaching the static lines of our parachutes to the overhead wire which would trip the opening device on our chutes as we jumped. We checked our equipment and stood in file, each crowding against the man in front to ensure a rapid exit when the time came. I was almost riding on the back of Legere who was to lead the stick out the door.

'Soon, the fog became broken and we could see patches of ground from time to time as we flashed over the Merderet River; by the time we entered the landing area, it was almost completely clear of fog. It was a thrilling sight to see: the sky ablaze with rockets, burning aircraft on the ground and anti-aircraft fire rising on all sides. The green light flashed - the signal to jump - and out we went shouting 'Bill Lee!' in honour of our former division commander instead of 'Geronimo!' the traditional war-cry of the American parachutists.

'As the plane roared away, I was left floating to earth in a comparative quiet, broken only by occasional burst of small-arms fire on the ground. Since we had jumped at about 500 feet, to shorten the time during which we would be floating ducks for enemy marksmen, there was little time to try to select a point of landing. At the last moment, a gust of air caused me to drift away from my comrades of the stick and only by a mighty tug on the shroud lines did I manage to escape becoming entangled in the top of a tall tree. Then I came down with a bang in a small Norman field enclosed by one of the famous hedgerows which compartmented the countryside. In most places, these hedges consisted of rows of trees planted on earthen banks which, in combination with the trees, presented formidable obstacles to military operations of all sorts. Many a parachutist that morning found himself suspended from one of those tall trees, from which he could only hope to lower himself by a rope before a German rifleman found him.

'At last on the soil of Normandy, I began to struggle out of my parachute, expecting that some of my men would appear to help me. But looking around I saw not a single soldier, only a circle of curious Norman cows who eyed me, disapprovingly I thought, as if resenting this intrusion into their pasture. I was still attempting to extricate myself from my 'chute when a German machine pistol opened up in the next field with the tell-tale sound of a ripping seat of pants which energised me to frantic struggles to free myself. In the wet morning grass it was a terrible job to unbuckle the many snaps and I finally gave up and used my parachute knife to cut my way out. Then, reluctantly abandoning my leg bag and its contents, I started out, pistol in one hand and identification cricket in the other, to find my troops - a lonely division commander who had lost or at least mislaid his division.

'Moving in the shadow of the hedgerow, I became aware of the smell of freshly-turned earth and soon came upon some newly-dug trenches, a warning that the Germans were probably nearby and to proceed with caution. This I did, creeping in the shadows along the hedgerow to the end of the field. There, I heard someone just around the corner of the hedge and veered toward the sound ready to shoot. But then there was the welcome sound of a cricket to which I quickly responded in kind and jumped around the corner. There in the dim moonlight was the first American soldier to greet me, a sight of martial beauty as he stood bare-headed, rifle in hand, bayonet fixed and apparently ready for anything. We embraced in silence and took off together to round up others of our comrades who were beginning to appear.'

Major General Maxwell Taylor, commanding the 101st Airborne Division.

'My plane took off at 23:15. It was not quite dark at this time. There was some flying time used to get this huge number of planes in the proper formation for the flight to Normandy. We eventually headed south toward our destination and found ourselves flying at about 500 feet elevation over the English Channel. There was not a lot of talking during the flight across the Channel. I think most of the men were contemplating what was about to happen. As we neared Guernsey the planes began to turn eastward toward the Normandy coast. When we were over the coast, the planes entered a cloud or fog bank. It was at this time that some of the planes lost formation. The pilots had been told to hold formation at all cost; most did but some did not. As a result of this, some of the paratroopers were dropped miles from their drop zone. The pilot of my plane stayed the course and we flew directly over our drop zone C. A mortar cart that was to be pushed out the plane door before we jumped was slow in getting out delayed us a bit.

'When my parachute opened I was directly above the church steeple of the church in Ste-Marie-du-Mont. The moon was full and there were scattered clouds which made everything on the ground easy to see. When I looked down, I saw the picture of Ste-Marie-du-Mont. It looked just like the picture I had studied so intensely at Upottery. I knew without a doubt that I was over the church steeple in that small French village. I drifted to the edge of the village and landed with my parachute caught in a small tree in a fence row. I was probably 75 feet from some buildings. I got out of my parachute and was looking around the area when I saw a shadowy figure about 150 feet along the fence row moving toward me. I clicked my cricket and received two clicks in return. We moved toward each other and I met Isaac Cole, my Battalion Sergeant-Major. We were extremely happy to see each other.

'At this time, troop carrier planes were still flying over and gunfire sounds were coming from every direction. It wasn't long before Sergeant Cole and myself had gathered together six or seven other paratroopers, none of whom I knew. We didn't bother to ask their names or what unit they belonged to. We were just glad to have this small group together in one place. After some consultation, we decided to move toward the church and the centre of the village. As we moved along the street, we decided to knock on a door and try to get some information about the enemy. An elderly Frenchman answered our knock. One of the men in our group could speak some French and he asked him where the Germans were. Waving his hand over his head, he said, 'everywhere.'

'We proceeded on to the church and decided that we would enter and have half of our group stay on the ground floor and the others would go up into the steeple. Sergeant Cole, me and three of the other men would go up the steeple. After going to the upper reaches of the steeple, we found that we had could fire in every direction and had a good view in most every direction. We would do our best to prevent any German troops from moving through the village.

'Daylight was not long in coming and when it did I looked toward 'Utah' Beach and saw the most awe inspiring sight I had ever seen. There were hundreds and hundreds of ships of various kinds lying off the beach. I could see some of the ships firing on the beach. Later there were planes dropping bombs. After some time had passed, we saw the boats caring the landing forces moving toward the beach. We now new the sea landing forces were on their way.

'We later saw a lone paratrooper moving along the sidewalk hugging the buildings as he moved. He was passing the corner of a building where another street entered the church square when he collapsed to the sidewalk. We heard the shot and we knew he had been hit. He didn't move after he fell so we knew that he was probably dead. This was a sobering event. At that moment, we realized that we were in a deadly game of kill or be killed. After a few minutes, a German soldier came from around the corner of the building where the dead paratrooper lay and begin to go through the trooper's pockets. We began to fire our weapons at the German and he dropped across the paratrooper's body.

'Later that morning two German soldiers came riding into the village driving a small vehicle. When they came into view below us we opened fire. One of them, I remember he had red hair, jumped of the vehicle started running along the sidewalk below us. He was looking left and right trying to determine where the gunfire was coming from. He didn't go far before he dropped to the sidewalk dead. The driver of the vehicle had placed it in reverse and it was moving backward. It backed into a building and stopped. The driver was slumped over dead by the time the vehicle stopped.

'In the early afternoon I saw an American tank about 175 yards distance with its gun pointed toward the steeple. I unfolded the flag and waved it at the tank. That wave did not save us from some shell fire. It was not the tank that was firing at us. An artillery shell came screaming by the church steeple. From the sound, we knew the shell was coming from a different direction than the tank. A moment or two later we heard another artillery shell screaming toward us. This one hit the steeple above us with a very loud explosion. Debris began to fall from the explosion and a big hole was opened in the steeple. It was a miracle that none of us were hurt.

'Some beach forces and other paratroopers arrived in the village soon after the artillery shell hit the steeple and we came down from the steeple. Cole and I went and pulled my parachute from the tree. I cut two panels out of it which I folded and placed in my back pack. I still have this piece of my parachute that lowered me to the ground in Normandy. We moved out of Ste-Marie-du-Mont late that afternoon and went to Holdy where we had learned that my company commander, Captain Patch and other members of my company were located. When we arrived at Holdy we were told that they had captured four artillery guns and that Sergeant William King had bore sited one of the guns and fired it at the church steeple they could see in the distance. They thought that the steeple was being used by the Germans to direct artillery fire.

'The area around the four guns was littered by dead Germans and a few paratroopers. The dead paratroopers were from our company mortar squad. They had landed in and around the area of the guns and were immediately killed before getting out of their parachutes. By this time it was getting dark and we learned we would be heading toward Carentan the next morning, June 7.'

David 'Buck' Rogers 1st Sergeant, HQ Company, 1st Battalion, 506th PIR, 101st Airborne Division.

'At Saltby airfield, 50 miles north of London, at 23:00, June 5, a Monday night, the C-47 troop carrier planes were lined up on the flight line loaded with paratroopers and engines were idling as pilots awaited the order for take-off. When the order came, planes began their take off and circled as they formed up in an 850-plane formation. Air crewmen were wearing their flak suits and, where possible, steel helmets. Take off for 50th Squadron planes was 23:38. The skies began to clear as the planes flew south. In the bright moonlight as the formation made its way across the English Channel, a vast armada of naval vessels could be seen below. The flotilla stretched for miles and miles. Every type of vessel one could imagine, large and small, was lined up in a convoy several ships wide. To observe such a scene while flying overhead made an indelible impression upon the mind. It revealed the determination and commitment of Allied forces to place the men and materials into battle to obtain the victory. At an altitude of 500 to 700 feet, the 314th Troop Carrier Group made its paratroop drop at about 02:10 on June 6. Following the dropping of the paratroopers, the flight formation continued crossing the Cotentin Peninsula on its way out to the English Channel. All 18 planes of the 50th Squadron returned to base. However, Lieutenant Sidney W. Dunagan, piloting one of the planes, was killed in action while making a second pass over the drop zone. Two paratroopers had fouled their rip cords as the plane passed over the drop zone and other troopers had jumped. These two were not able to exit the plane at that time. The problems quickly resolved, Dunagan circled to make a second pass over the drop zone to allow the two to jump. While making the circle, he was hit with a bullet in the left side of his chest, killing him instantly. Lieutenant Walter D. Nims, co-pilot, flew the aircraft on the return flight to home base. On this mission, the 50th Squadron delivered 319 paratroopers, 1,868 pounds of ammunition and 13,935lbs of combat equipment into the drop zone.'

Robert E. Callahan, radio operator in 1st Lieutenant M. R. Perreault's C-47, 50th Troop Carrier Squadron, 314th Troop Carrier Group.

'We formed into a very tight formation. Through broken clouds and a bright moon we headed for the coast. Over the Channel you could see hundreds of boats starting towards the Continent. I had the feeling we were part of a big chunk of history. Looking out of the window in every direction were planes. About 1 am one of the guys yelled 'There she is boys.' We all knew what it was - the coast of France. At 9 minutes to drop zone, flak and machine-gun tracers could be seen to the right and left. It looked just like the Fourth of July. About that moment a plane on our right blew up; hit the ground in a large ball of fire, 18 to 20 men wiped out. This was no Fourth of July celebration. Welcome to the real war.

'The red light in the door came on. We stood up and hooked up. Then the green light and we were out of the door. Quite a struggle because of all our equipment. Someone fell down and had to be helped up and out the door. When I jumped it looked like every tracer in the sky was zeroing in on me. I'm sure the rest of the guys felt the same way. I don't know how high our plane was, but I'm sure it was very low because I remember swinging about twice and then hitting in the middle of a road. I could see a man and a woman standing in the front yard of a house just beneath me. I hit the road, took about two steps and went head first through a wicket fence, knocking out two teeth and cutting my lip. I rolled over, tried to get my carbine out, couldn't, sat up and the man and woman were gone. I finally got out of my harness, pulled my folding stock carbine out and could hear some soldiers coming down the road. I started up a hedgerow but it felt like someone was holding me by the belt. I stopped, tried to move again, same thing. I slowly turned around and found the shroud lines from my parachute were tangled up in the fence. I could hear the boots getting closer and closer. I finally got the shroud lines unhooked, climbed to the top of the hedgerow, fell over on the other side and in about a minute 35 or 40 Germans came marching past where I had just been. I could have reached out and touched them. After they passed by I moved in the direction I thought our plane had come in. Being alone behind enemy lines is a unique, indescribable feeling. You just feel so helpless, so alone.'

George M. Rasil, 101st Airborne Division.

'Struggling to carry out the mission of the 101st to clear and secure the exits from 'Utah' Beach for the arrival of the 4th Infantry Division, small groups of soldiers valiantly did their best under the difficult conditions. Major General Maxwell Taylor could only assemble about ninety men in the meadows before he set out the two miles to secure the southernmost causeway leading to 'Utah' Beach. Among them were one other general, General Tony McAuliffe, his artillery commander and at least four colonels. The rest were staff officers, artillerymen without artillery, clerks, military police and Robert Reuben a war correspondent from Reuters. Not one of the officers or men belonged to either of the two battalions which should have been there and should have attacked the causeway but one of the colonels, Lieutenant Colonel Julian J. Ewell was commander of the 3rd Battalion of the 501st Parachute Infantry and about half the men were his. Ewell was a professional soldier, a graduate of West Point and young at 28 to be a colonel. This was his first combat. Taylor put Ewell in charge of the ill-sorted force and told him to do what he could at the southern causeway. Referring to his brass-heavy group, General Taylor said to Ewell, 'Never were so few led by so many.' [13]

'It was just twilight and the sound of all those men marching in single file to their

---

13 They made their first contact with the enemy on the outskirts of Pouppeville where the column halted while Ewell organised his attack. The resistance was light but it was a time-consuming task to clear out each house and eliminate the snipers and the attackers mopped up the village by about noon. They captured 40 prisoners and suffered about 20 casualties. One of these was Larry Legere who received a severe hip wound which resulted in his evacuation for long hospitalisation in the US. Ewell and his men held the village until the leading troops of the 8th Infantry, 4th Division could pass over the causeway. Utilising the communications of the 4th Division, Taylor conveyed the welcome news of the historic linkup between the airborne forces and the landing forces to General Bradley.

planes was like a drumbeat. Nobody was talking. The roar of engines was everywhere. I looked out of the door of the plane and saw all those English people, cooks and bakers watching us. It was like a silent prayer, or salute. As young as we were, we all knew it was the biggest thing in our lives.

Private First Class (later sergeant) William 'Bill' Tucker of Cambridge, Massachusetts, Company 'I', 82nd Airborne. During the four or five days spent at Cottesmore getting things ready Tucker had had time to get started on a book, *A Tree Grows In Brooklyn*. His father, who taught him pride and to reach for intellect, would read the morning story that US airborne troops, had landed in Western France. On his long subway trip to work he stopped at an old church in Central Square, Cambridge. [14]

'Outside the engines of the tow planes were warming up and the noise was such that any verbal communications had to be shouted. At last this was it, this was what we had been training for and we were ready to go.

'Sitting there, there was a feeling of anticipation. How would the flight go, the landing and after? There wasn't any external or internal signs of fear - this was a great adventure and, after all, what could happen to a twenty-two year old. It could happen to the guy across the way, or the one next to you - but never you.

'Soon the roar of the lead C-47 was heard as it inched forward slowly on the runway at Membury airfield. The tow line began to uncurl like a serpent from its preset configuration and the lead plane was off at 20.37 hours.

'Then it was our turn, the tow-rope unravelled, tightened and with a slight jerk our Horsa glider began to roll forward. We gathered speed and soon the rumble of the wheels on the runway was silenced and we were airborne. The glider lifted off first and the taut tow-rope lifted the tail of the tow plane. We were veering off and climbing to the preset altitude for assembly.

'Our serial was completely airborne with 418 airborne troops, thirty-one jeeps, twelve 75mm pack howitzers, twenty-six tons of ammunition and twenty-five tons of other equipment.

'The troop carriers were unaware the 82nd Division was diverting our flight to landing zone 'O' because of the supposedly better landing conditions and that landing zone 'W' was dominated by German weapons. The glider pilots had been briefed to turn 180 degrees to the right after releasing instead of the previously directed left turn because of the German strength in the area of 'W'. This turned out to be a mistake because at 'O' the German strength was to the right.

'The two serials joined up and in a column of fours headed across Southern England in a ten-mile wide corridor, out over the English Channel heading for France. For the 200 mile flight we were accompanied to the French coast by groups of Allied fighter planes. Whereas the parachute drops approached Normandy from the west of the Cherbourg Peninsula, the gliders came in directly over the 'Utah' Beach area, roughly from the north.

'I peered out of one of the port-holes lining the length of the Horsa and I could see the lines of tow planes and gliders droning on over the increasingly darkening water below. We passed over the armada of fighting ships; the larger ones, parallel to the shore, belching great balls of yellow and orange flames towards the shore.

14 *Put On Your Boots and Parachutes!: The United States 82nd Airborne Division* written and edited by Deryk Wills (self published, March 1992).

'As we approached 'Utah' Beach the rushing noise of the wind passing over the wings and the side of the glider increased. The gliders were usually towed at about 100 mph, but as we approached the shore the C-47 pilots increased their speed to what felt to be about 125 mph so that they could get in and out as fast as possible.

'The sun had set a few minutes before we crossed the coast and as we headed inland the ground began to get darker and it was more difficult to make out objects below, even at 500 feet. I could see what appeared to be a group of fireflies milling about on the ground in the darkness and then ascending in single file, increasing in velocity as they approached in streams until, with a swish, whizzed by the window. Realising they were tracer bullets, I felt that I had nothing to worry about because they could be seen. It was the other four or more bullets between each tracer that you had to look out for. The intensity of the ground fire increased and more and more fireflies went streaming by. The glider pilot finally cut loose, the noise of the rushing wind became silent and starting a 180 degree right bank we began to descend into the darkness. I continued to peer out of the porthole, searching for any recognizable land feature. That was the last thing I remember. [15]

'The next thing I recall was total darkness and the continual sound, of what seemed to me, of crunching and splintering caused by someone jumping off a roof of a house into a large pile of wooden match boxes. I realised it was someone tearing away the plywood from on top of me. Then some dim shadows with arms extended to assist in extricating me from the wreckage.

'There were two other men, one sitting each side of me; so that I was sandwiched between them and they must have absorbed some of the impact. I recall seeing a Fourth Division insignia on one of the rescuers. While laying on my side, I spotted, about ten to fifteen feet away, the jeep tipped over on its side with a complete oval-shaped section of the glider floor still attached to it by the tie-down ropes. I felt relief that it had not landed on me.

'Blood was running down my face and my entire body was sore and aching. I had a swelling and a gash about an inch above the outside corner of my left eye and a number of slashes across the top of my head in an ear-to-ear direction. Someone bandaged me up with two compression bandages; one across the top of my head and tied under my chin; the other over my left forehead and tied at the back.

'Amid the usual din of war I made my way, in the darkness, to a nearby stone wall. I pulled up about me an abandoned parachute and leaned back, hardly moving to prevent antagonising the soreness I felt all over. There I sat to see what the six hours of summertime darkness might hold in store.

'When daylight came, I made my way to an Aid Station that had been set up at a nearby crossroads. The tent, marked with a Red Cross, had wounded lying on stretchers around it, tagged and waiting to be evacuated. I was cleaned up a bit and tagged. Orders were that anyone with a head wound was to be evacuated immediately. Waiting outside the tent I

---

15 'The first glider release in our serial occurred at 2255 hours, five minutes ahead of schedule. A large portion of the gliders were released over a mile short of Landing Zone 'O', while six gliders were released at least five miles to the east. The change in the landing zones took the tow planes and gliders over the German defences and into heavy ground fire. Small fields, some only a hundred yards long, hedgerows, tall trees, darkness, enemy fire and some glider pilots disregarding orders to land at a slow speed, all played havoc with the landings. Including some damage done by enemy fire after landing, of the 84 Horsas, only 13 were undamaged. Fifty-six were totally destroyed. Eight of the fourteen CG-4A's gliders were destroyed. The eight surviving were damaged. Ten of the 196 glider pilots were killed, at least 29 wounded or injured, and seven reported missing. Of the troopers, 28 were killed and 106 wounded or injured.'

noticed a P-47 fighter plane that had seemed to have been hit by enemy fire and was obviously in trouble. I recall subconsciously asking myself why the pilot didn't bale out. I was relieved when I saw a human form falling from the plane. I waited for the chute to open, but the figure continued to plummet earthwards and disappeared into the trees down the road.

'When we reached the beach a DUKW took us out to an LST waiting off-shore. Back in England I remember being in a cot in a large circus-like tent and being checked over by a nurse. They shaved my head around my wounds. I was then sent to the 62nd General Hospital further inland from where I was later released to return to Market Harborough to await the return of my unit from Normandy.

'Both the men on either side of me in the crash suffered broken vertebrae in their necks. The gilder pilot had a bullet in his leg. The Lieutenant who had acted as co-pilot sustained a broken back and was unlucky enough, while waiting on the beach to be evacuated, to be strafed and killed.'

Pfc Joseph G. Clowry, 319th Glider Field Artillery. [16]

'We took off from Cottesmore airfield where we had been isolated under strict security for several days. I was the jumpmaster on our C-47 which carried 18 paratroopers. Our machine guns and mortars were in bundles slung beneath the airplane and could be released and dropped by parachute when we jumped. [17] I had a beautiful view of the English Channel as we crossed. The door of the plane had been removed and as I sat by the open door I watched the moonlight shine on the waves. It was a peaceful prelude to the violent invasion. I can't recall all my thoughts as we flew in. I do recall one personal concern. We had removed six Fulminate of Mercury blasting caps from our demolition kit because of the danger of leaving them packed with the high explosives in the bundle under the plane. I had taped them in a wooden block to my left foot. They were very sensitive and I was afraid they might blow up when I hit the ground.

'Shortly after we crossed the western coast of the Cherbourg Peninsula the anti-aircraft fire filled the sky. This continued at intervals in the distance until we reached Ste-Mère-Église. My primary concern was that the pilot would locate our proper Drop Zone and that we would be able to assemble all our men and equipment. The red warning light finally came on and I gave the order to 'Stand up and hook up'. This order was relayed from man to man over the roar of the engines and each man checked the parachute of the man in front of him. Beginning with the last man '18-OK', the count was relayed from man to man until the man behind me shouted 'Two - OK' then I knew we were ready.

'The plane's engines slowed down and I knew we would receive the green light to go soon, but I still could not see the lights which were to be set up by the Pathfinders who had jumped earlier to mark the D-Z. Suddenly we made a sharp left turn and I picked out the blue lights in a 'T' formation directly in front of us. Just at that moment the green light beside

---

16 *Put On Your Boots and Parachutes!: The United States 82nd Airborne Division* written and edited by Deryk Wills (self published, March 1992).

17 At Spanhoe just before take-off a Gammon grenade carried by one of the men of the First Battalion HQ Company exploded. Four were killed in the C-47 of Flight Officer Harper of 43 Squadron, USAAF; 15 were wounded, one being the aircraft's radio operator. The only man unharmed was Corporal Melvin Fryer, who, not wanting to be left behind elbowed his way on to another plane. He was killed twelve days later in Normandy. *Put On Your Boots and Parachutes!: The United States 82nd Airborne Division* written and edited by Deryk Wills (self published, March 1992).

the door flashed on and giving the order 'GO', I jumped. I had no trouble on landing despite all the equipment we carried. As soon as I got out of my parachute harness and stood up I saw the green light which was our Battalion's assembly signal, a short distance away.

'The first man I encountered was our Battalion Commander, Lieutenant Colonel Benjamin Vandervoort. He asked if I had found my medical aid man but I told him I was alone. At the time he did not mention that he was injured, but he had broken his leg on the jump (and fought for weeks with his leg in a cast). [18] He ordered me to continue to locate my men. This I did for the next hour and we were able to assemble the First Platoon and Company Headquarters of Company 'E'. The Second and Third Platoons were dropped away from the drop zone. After we had located as many men and weapons as we could, we moved towards Neuville-au-Plain, which was our original objective. However, before we reached our objective we were ordered to turn south to Ste-Mère-Église.

'We entered the town just at dawn. One man came out of a house and spoke to me. He was the only person I had the opportunity to talk to during my brief stay in Normandy. He spoke little or no English and I spoke only a little French, but I understood him well enough to sense his concern. He wanted to know if this was a raid or if it was the invasion. Our orders were not to disclose any information on the invasion, so I could not tell him that this was the day he had waited four years for. I did reassure him of one thing: 'Nous restons ici.' As for us, we were not leaving Ste-Mère-Église.

'Our Company was assigned an area in the town along the sea road, east of the church. We were not called on for action until about noon when my platoon was ordered to go north to Neuville-au-Plain to provide the rear guard for a Platoon from Company 'D'. This was commanded by Lieutenant Turner Turnbull (he was part American Indian blood and we called him 'Chief')[19.] They held the Germans north of the town but were outnumbered and we were to give them orders to return to Ste-Mère-Église and cover their withdrawal.

---

18   Lieutenant Colonel Benjamin H. 'Vandy' Vandervoort broke his left tibia about one inch above the ankle on the jump into Sainte-Mère-Église but carried on with his jump boot tightly laced and a rifle as a crutch. He later 'persuaded' two 101st Airborne sergeants to pull him rickshaw fashion on a collapsible ammunition cart until he transferred to a glider-borne jeep and managed to borrow crutches from a crippled French housewife in Sainte-Mère-Église! After the battle for Sainte-Mère-Église Jim Gavin, surveying the scene a day or two later with Vandervoort said in jest: 'Van don't kill them all; save a few for interrogation.' Vandervoort was awarded the Distinguished Service Cross for his actions in Normandy. His ambition was to remain in the Army after the war but he was later wounded, losing the sight of one eye. He retired from the Army in 1946, spending 26 years with the CIA. He died in 1990 aged 75. In the film *The Longest Day,* the role of Ben Vandervoort was portrayed by John Wayne.
19   Turner Turnbull was half Cherokee. At about 1300 hours as Colonel Vandervoort was taking up the defensive positions for Ste-Mère-Église, talking to Turnbull whose platoon had set up a road block; a Frenchman rode up on a bicycle and announced in English that some American paratroopers were bringing a column of German prisoners down N-13 from the north. When they looked, there appeared to be paratroopers on each side of the column waving orange flags but Vandervoort noticed that two tracked vehicles were following in the rear. He ordered Turnbull to have his machine-gunner fire a short burst just to the right of the approaching column, which was now about 800 yards away. When the machine-gun fired, the flag wavers and the marchers dived into the ditches and opened fire. Turnbull's men returned the fire and pinned down the infantry. The two self-propelled guns continued to move forward and at 500 yards they opened up. Their first shots knocked out the bazooka team at the road block but a 57mm gun with some fast and accurate shooting knocked out both vehicles. Meanwhile the Frenchman had wisely disappeared. The next day Turnbull was killed by an artillery round and is buried in the Cemetery at Ste-Laurent. He was recommended for a Distinguished Service Cross, but ultimately was awarded the Silver Star. It was Turnbull's defence of Ste-Mère-Église in the early stages that enabled the 82nd Division to stabilise its position. John Keegan in his book, Six Armies In Normandy, commenting on Turnbull, stated: 'He belongs with those who saved the invasion.' Put On Your Boots and Parachutes!: The United States 82nd Airborne Division written and edited by Deryk Wills (self published, March 1992).

'We arrived at the southern edge of Neuville-au-Plain just as the German troops were cutting east along a road which would have cut Turnbull off completely. We engaged the enemy and prevented him from going any further in his plan of encirclement. We were able to hold them even though we were outnumbered. In the meantime Turnbull got his surviving men out of Neuville-au-Plain and on the way to Ste-Mère-Église. My platoon then moved back to our position in the town. We did not lose a man in this action, but we inflicted many casualties on the enemy, principally by very accurate mortar fire provided by our mortar Sergeant, Otis Sampson.

'Shortly after returning to Ste-Mère-Église, gliders began to land in the area. I was standing in a ditch along the sea road when a glider suddenly came crashing through some trees. I had not seen it coming and of course it made no sound until it hit the trees. I just had time to drop face down in the shallow ditch when the glider hit the road, crashed across it and came to rest with the wing over me. I was not injured, but had to crawl on my stomach the length of the wing to get out from under the glider. The trees had split open the fuselage and many men were injured inside. We helped carry them out, but the best we could do for them was to inject them with morphine from our first aid kits and put them in trenches wrapped in parachutes. The men who survived left to remove their artillery piece from a glider nearby.

'Enemy artillery had begun to hit about us as we were removing the injured from the glider and it continued to fall heavily on our position during the night. We were well dug in however and only one of our men, Private Benoit, was wounded.

'The next day I received an order from our Company Commander, Captain Clyde Russell, to go to the beach by Jeep with two men from Company 'D' and try to make contact with the Fourth Division. We were in desperate need for one of their artillery observers to give us fire support. I was able to reach a unit of the Fourth Division as they were moving off the beach, but they had only one observer left alive and could not release him to aid us. I noticed a tank unit along the road and explained our needs to the lieutenant colonel in command, but he could not release any tanks to me without orders from his command. It was frustrating to see all those tanks not engaged while we were fighting so hard a few miles away. But there was nothing a Lieutenant could do, so I returned to Ste-Mère-Église with one bit of helpful information: the tank commander was in radio contact with tanks which were assigned to us. He told me they were on their way to Ste-Mère-Église on a round-about route through Chef-du-Pont.

'As soon as I reported back to Battalion Headquarters we were given an order to move into a position north of Ste-Mère-Église to prepare to attack the enemy who were closing in on the town. The Platoon took up positions along a road which runs west from the main highway. It is the road which has the last house on the north edge of the town. We were told that the 8th Infantry Regiment of the Fourth Division would arrive on our left flank, but by the time of our assigned attack no contact had been made.

'While we were waiting for the preset time to attack, a tank unit came up from the sea road, but in the confusion of war they drove up the highway north to Neuville-au-Plain, apparently never knowing that they had passed both us and the enemy. I am not certain, but I think these tanks were the same ones that I had seen on the beach. If so, it was the second opportunity to help us that was missed. They went so far north that they did not contribute any aid in the battle that was about to begin. However, two tanks which had been assigned to us had arrived and they would cover our open flank as we attacked.

'There was heavy machine-gun fire coming across the field from our front. My original order was to take my Platoon across this field, but in the interval before our jump off time, 17.15 hours, I got permission to take them north up a dirt road on the left of the field which provided better cover and concealment. We advanced up this road with the tanks following and when we reached the intersection of another dirt road running east to the highway we found the enemy behind the hedgerow. Luckily we had come up on his flank and by pure chance he had left it unprotected. We poured fire up the ditch from our positions. One of the tanks joined in with its heavy machine-gun and after about fifteen minutes a white flag appeared in the ditch. I called for a cease fire and it was with some difficulty in all the noise of battle that I was able to get our firing stopped.

'Lieutenant Frank Woosley, our Company Executive Officer and I went up the road to accept the surrender, but before we got very far two hand grenades came over the hedgerow. He dived into the ditch on one side of the road and I went in the other. We thought at the time that we had walked into a trap.[20] We returned to our position and resumed fire. This time we did not cease firing until the enemy ran out of the ditch into a large field next to it with their hands raised. When I saw that there were over a hundred of the enemy running into the field I went through the hedgerow with the intention of stopping them and rounding them up. But as soon as I got through the hedgerow into the ditch on the other side I was hit by machine pistol fire. The Germans had not yet quit. One of my men followed me through the hedgerow and fired an abandoned German machine-gun up the ditch ending any further resistance from the enemy.

'In this battle Company 'E' with two platoons, (the other commanded by Lieutenant Theodore Peterson) captured 160 prisoners. We again received accurate supporting fire from Sergeant Sampson's mortar from a position which can be located today about 50 foot south of the 82nd Airborne Division sign at the intersection of the main highway at the north end of Ste-Mère-Église. I do not know the number of enemy dead left in that ditch. Lieutenant Peterson's platoon, which was on my right flank, captured the German Battalion Commander. Corporal Sam Appleby shot one German captain as he tried to escape the trap. A platoon of Company 'D' commanded by Lieutenant Thomas McClean captured a great number who tried to escape across the main highway and ran into his position.

'I was given first aid after the prisoners were collected and rode back on a tank to the Battalion Aid Station in the old school in Ste-Mère-Église. The next day I left the town in an ambulance to return to England and hospital. The ambulance took me from the 505 Aid Station in Ste-Mère-Église, drove for about an hour and then unloaded its wounded on stretchers in a large field. The men who needed immediate attention and surgery were taken into nearby hospital tents. I had been shot through both buttocks this time, the bullet being somewhere just below my left hip. Naturally, the Medics could not spend any time on me. They took one look at the holes in my rear-end, slapped the bandages back and gave me a shot of morphine.

'I didn't know where I was in Normandy, but I did learn that I was in the 82nd Airborne's 307th Evacuation Hospital and that I would not be operated on until I got back to England. Just before dark on D plus 2, I was loaded into an ambulance with five other wounded and headed for the beach. By coincidence, I recognised the glider pilot

20 'I learned from M. Alexandre Renaud's book [Sainte-Mère-Église: Première Tête de Pont Americaine en France] 25 years later that these troops were Georgian. They were probably the ones who wanted to surrender, but the German officers and NCOs were fighting on.'

that I pulled out of the crashed glider in Ste-Mère-Église on D-Day. We didn't do much talking, however, because both of us were half out of it from the morphine and were not making much sense anyway.

'The ambulance was bouncing over the rough roads and one of the wounded moaned constantly. I realised that his wounded leg had bounced off the stretcher and when I was able to replace it and secure it with a blanket, his moaning ceased. We finally arrived at another field hospital on the beach and spent the night there. It was impossible to sleep however, because of our artillery firing nearby.

'The next day I was loaded into the hold of a Landing Ship Tank (LST) with hundreds of other wounded men and we sailed for England. I spotted another Company 'E' man, Private Eads, on a stretcher near me and was able to determine that he was not seriously wounded and eventually would recover. We landed at Plymouth and travelled by ambulance to the 55th General Hospital in Quonset huts at Malvern Wells, Worcestershire. After the bullet was removed and I could get around, I went looking for Company 'E' men in the hospital but I didn't find any. However there were several officers that I knew from the 505 in my ward.'

Second Lieutenant James J. Coyle, a platoon Leader in Company 'E', 505th Parachute Infantry Regiment, 82nd Airborne Division. After about three weeks he was discharged from the hospital. The regiment returned from France about a week later. Coyle learnt that Lieutenant Roper Peddicord had been killed and that Lieutenant 'Pete' Peterson was in hospital with a leg wound. He and 'Pete' received battlefield promotions to First Lieutenants. [21]

'We passed the northern portion of the peninsula and made our final turn to the assigned flight path toward our drop zone when we heard the distinct sound of ack-ack. Anti aircraft shells were bursting all around the planes and the reality of our situation bore in on us for all we could do was to wait for the green light before we could get out. I hoped that the pilot would keep us on course and that the German gunners would be nervous and blind to our location. All before this was practice. The roar of the C-47 almost drowned out the sound of the guns below, but as we peered through the small windows and the open doorway we could see that it looked like the Fourth of July outside the plane. I cringed trying to make a smaller target, as I sat in the bucket seat weighted down with all my equipment. The rations, rifle in case, ammunition, grenades, loaded musette bag and the ever present parachutes tightly strapped front and back. Each time a flak shell burst nearby, I cringed again and again. With all that stuff coming up, some is bound to be effective and the plane rocked and shook with each blast. We were very tightly packed in the plane seats and the weight of our equipment helped us stay in our positions. This plane must be full of holes, I thought, as the pilots fought to control its flight path. Along with the flak, tracers rose by the millions to greet us.

'Suddenly the red light flashed and the command 'Stand up and hook up!' was shouted by Colonel Krause who was in the number one position. Almost as one the troopers arose and hooked up to the static line in the centre of the plane ceiling. 'Check equipment!' came the next command. Over the noise inside and outside the craft we could barely distinguish the replies of '21 OK, 20 OK, 19 OK, 18 OK' and up to me. 'Nine

21 *Put On Your Boots and Parachutes!: The United States 82nd Airborne Division* written and edited by Deryk Wills (self published, March 1992).

OK' I yelled and belted Taylor in the rear in case he didn't hear me. The last trooper yelled 'OK'! and the command to close it up and stand in the door came as we neared the drop zone. The green light flashed. 'Let's go', yelled the Colonel as he leaped into the dark Norman night. Quickly we followed and number nine wheeled out the door leaping in perfect jump school form into the flak ridden sky. The day of the Normandy Invasion was now official! No turning back, no siree! The past is indeed prologue, the present, the reality. The chute tightened in my crotch, as the planes droned overhead and I knew that my chute had opened though I could hardly look up to see it. I had suddenly slowed as the chute fully opened and I floated in space, as I began my more leisurely descent. Leisure is not the best word as tracers whistled by and I began to hear again as I never heard before. Alert to every sound as I floated earthward I wondered whether I would be killed, wounded, or what? How, when and where would I land? Were the Germans below with me in their gun sights? Would I see my buddies from the stick of 21 chutists? Can I get my rifle unpacked quickly and assembled fast enough? I could see a fire in the distance and silhouettes of parachutes passing through the glare of the fire and I realized that some were nearby. The staccato sound of machine gun fire broke my trance. It was to the left. No, it was to my right as I kept turning in my chute I couldn't tell where it was coming from. Rushing past a twenty foot high hedgerow, I landed with a thud as I tumbled backward hitting the ground and striking my head on the Normandy turf. I had jammed my helmet over my eyes which blinded me momentarily. I couldn't see. I had to remedy that situation in a hurry.' Come on, for crying out loud', I muttered. I could hardly move.' Get the chute off!' I said under my breath. Struggling with my chute, I unbuckled the strap and yanked out my rifle case quickly unzipping the side, I eagerly pulled out the three pieces of the M-1 rifle and quickly assembled them loading the chamber with one eight round clip.

'I rolled over and came to a kneeling position forcing my musette bag, which had hung below my emergency chute in front, up and over my head to my back and snapped it tight under my arms to my shoulder straps. I loosened the balance of the chute off my gear and I was now ready as I listened for any sound of other troopers with their cricket, the signal of friendly troops. What seemed like an eternity only took several minutes, if that.

'From my kneeling position, I was ready for the enemy as I peered skyward the planes kept droning above in the flak ridden sky. Occasionally one large flash appeared and I would see a plane silhouetting earthward. 'Oh my God', I thought, 'There goes a whole plane load of guys'. I was rudely brought back to the happenings around me as one by one troopers came down crashing into hedgerows or banging into the ground unceremoniously, cursing as they floated in. As far as I could discern in the darkness, I was situated in what appeared to be a three acre field. To my right was the twenty foot hedgerow I had so recently missed. To my rear was some kind of road which was some six foot below the field. I could see the shadows of several men as they emerged from the hedgerows about the field heading towards me and then I recalled that I was in the middle of the stick of parachutists and they would gravitate in my direction. This was standard procedure to gather on the middle man. I gave the cricket snap and heard the reply in two clicks. One gave the sign 'Flash' and I replied 'Thunder' - sign and counter sign given as the troops assembled in my area by ones, twos and larger groups. Within a short time our platoon was intact along with many from other third battalion companies. Many troopers arrived with the much needed equipment from the bundles dropped from each of the aircraft. These supplies were distributed to all to help get them to our objectives where they would be give us the additional firepower that we required. I carried two containers of machine gun ammo in addition to my already heavy load. Along the road below I could see a group of officers talking to a Frenchman who had arrived on the scene and he was pointing out some directions, at least he was waving his arms in several directions. Perhaps no one spoke French.

'Captain DeLong gathered Company 'H' platoon officers together to pass along the orders given by Colonel Krause. The battalion numbering over several hundred men plus some troopers who had missed their drop zone would move on Ste-Mère-Église where the glow in the sky was showing and take the town and defend it. We could hear sounds of machine gun and rifle fire all around, but nothing was from our immediate location. We had secured our area and were waiting orders to move which came after the confrontation with the civilian who had been convinced to join our group by a group of troopers. With the assistance of our new found friend we moved out towards Ste-Mère-Église with Company 'G' in the lead followed by Company 'H' and 'I' groups. Some groups were missing by the plane load and we had no idea where they were, but we could not wait for them because time was very important to the success of the mission.

'It was quite difficult to see where we were going in the dark surroundings as we stumbled down the embankment to the roadway and moved down the road in single file. We had trouble staying in line and following the men in front. I assumed we were heading for Ste-Mère-Église and I hoped that the colonel knew our route. The trees and hedges screened the silhouettes of the men to my front and I was taken by surprise when he suddenly seemed to vanish when I realized that he had turned right off the road into what appeared to be a cattle trail through the hedgerow and about three feet below the surface of the road. I damn near fell flat as I stumbled onto the trail fresh with cow manure. 'Where the hell are we going?' I murmured to myself. This path was almost like a tunnel through the brush which was hanging low over our heads as we meandered along, staggering in the soft turf. I heard low muttering from others, but loud noises would give us away to the enemy, who must know we are in the vicinity. Just as suddenly as we had entered this path, we now began to exit onto what looked like a main road where we paused momentarily to reconnoitre and check locations.

'Company 'H' men were ordered to set up road blocks on this road and several others as each platoon was assigned an area to cover while the other two companies moved into town to gain control and form a perimeter defence of the town. The platoon CP was set up somewhere near the inter-section of two roads and my squad held a road block that faced toward a town called Chef du Pont where we deployed our land mines, glad to unload them from our mussette bags, where we had stashed them in England about three hours ago. Three rows of mines were placed in front of our defence line and we hoped they would stop any German tanks that might try to dislodge us. We were assigned positions to the right and left of the road as well as on either side of it in the ditches and some troopers were given the areas in the fields to cover our flanks.

'Some troopers were assigned to dig in on each side of the roadblock about 50 feet behind the mines we had deployed across the road. Vance, Ellis, Gawan and several others from the first squad of the first platoon were located there and some troopers were assigned to the left flank along the hedgerows facing away from Ste-Mère-Église. Jones, Coddington, Carpenter, Beckwith and Gamelcy were among these. Cruise, Vargas and Larry Kilroy were on the right flank above an embankment at the roadside and about 50 feet from the road. Slightly off to their left were men of the second squad commanded by Sergeant Edward White with Nielsen, Cusmano, Horn, Zalenski and Davis plus others spread out towards the next roadway where they linked with other Company 'H' squads.

'In the pre-dawn darkness Vargas, Kilroy and Cruise started their foxhole with one of us watching while two dug and then we exchanged diggers until completed. We were located in front of a three foot high hedgerow that ran perpendicular to the road and we positioned ourselves so that we could cover effectively the field to our front. The hedgerow would provide some cover when we communicated with those on the road. In scanning the area I realized that we were very close to the hidden trail we had taken to arrive in our present spot. I had gotten used to the darkness and though it was cloudy we could see shapes and outlines of things near us, but the high bank near the road obscured the men there.

'We were certainly surprised and not quite prepared for what was about to occur in our area in the predawn darkness. After the planes that had dropped the paratroopers had cleared the sky lanes for several hours, the second wave of C-47s arrived overhead towing glider borne troops with artillery pieces. We would really need those artillery units for our defence of the newly liberated Ste-Mère-Église. The first town liberated by Allied forces on D-Day we would learn later. About an hour after we had secured our position off the road block, we heard the unmistakeable drone of the planes. These C-47s would be try to release their loads near our objective assuming we had control over the drop zones. Once again as if on cue, the anti-aircraft guns began to chatter as the planes came directly over our area. We knew that gliders were being released and would be descending nearby. The sounds of the planes receded and we could hear the crashing sounds gliders slamming into trees and other obstacles such as farm buildings, which could not be seen clearly by their pilots.

'One of those gliders had landed about 300 yards from our roadblock. We could hear the noise as they were getting out and removing equipment. Over their shouting we heard the noise of a jeep motor starting and several troopers left the confines of our position to help. Before they reached the landing spot a jeep rushed down the road passing them even as they shouted a warning about our mines ahead. The occupants of the jeep were in a big hurry as we at the roadblock heard their running motor coming in our direction. Above all the noise, the distinct yells at the block of 'hit the ground' were heard clearly and we all buried ourselves in the dirt of our foxholes. The driver must have thought our men were Germans and was not about to stop. Down the road they rode on full throttle. KAPOW! BLOOEY! BANG! BOOM! A deafening crescendo of explosives sounds as a number of our mines blew the jeep and its troopers into the air. All Hell broke loose flashing lights with pieces of jeep and mine fragments raining down around us. Directly across the middle of our mine field they drove and immediately their direction became vertical and in an arching skyward path they landed in the hedgerow beyond. We could hear the thump and bangs of falling parts all around us. The men had left the jeep on first impact and they had become the first casualties in our area, but they would not be the last. We had lost about half of our mines, which we had so carefully delivered and they would be sorely needed in case the krauts should attack. Those GI's sure wrecked the hell out of our defences. The troopers at the road surveyed the damage when all the raining of pieces had ceased and they ventured forth from their protective positions. They had to be careful lest another mine explode amid the smouldering scene. We would have to locate some more mines to fill in the voids and reinforce our tank defences. Those of us nearby also came over to see the damage and the smoking remains of the jeep were lying in the ditch at roadside. My first experience with sudden death as the men were extracted from their perch and quickly moved by several medics to the rear areas.

'All around our sector we could hear the chatter of machine guns and rifle fire in the darkness, but after our mine field disaster things became rather quiet through the early morning hours. The infantry forces were due to hit the beaches at 0630 hours and we could be expected to hear the barrage that would precede their landings at 'Utah' Beach. The rumbling began around 0600 and it sounded like distant thunder which vibrated the ground even in our area some 6 or 7 miles inland. The cannonading was softening up the shore defences and the landing crafts would be starting towards the shoreline. We inland were holding off the Germans from getting to those forces, that is, those of us who had reached our objectives and were defending them. I wondered if all those ships we saw during the night flight were firing because the sound was continuous as they pounded the land forces. We didn't know from our positions how other paratrooper units were faring in their battles nor could we account for all our company men. Whole plane loads had not yet assembled in their assigned area we had learned, but we figured when daylight came we would see many of them. We began to receive some artillery fire in our area and we concluded that some of the large calibre shells landing in our area were from the invasion fleet miscalculation of the shore location.

'Several hours later when the firing had ceased, a French farmer approached our road block from the direction of Chef du Pont and tried to communicate to us that a German soldier was holed up in his house and wanted to surrender. He had been hiding there since he had become separated from his unit during the night. This information was gathered by one of our troopers who was of French descent and spoke the language. He had been called from his position to interpret. Private Kilroy and Les Cruise, two Philly lads were ordered to go with the Frenchman, check out his story and bring back the kraut with his 'hans en haut', or something that sounded like that. The Sergeant didn't want anyone shooting him prematurely or us by accident.

'We cautiously started up the road with the Frenchman in the lead while we trailed behind on opposite sides of the road, keeping a respectful distance from the native and watching all sides to avoid an ambush. About a kilometre or two from our roadblock at Ste-Mère-Église we arrived at his farm cottage which was set back from the road way several hundred feet. Warily we checked the road ahead and surveyed the land around the house. We had some protection from the house direction because the road had an embankment about five feet high which bordered his field on that side. His home was white with a dark thatched roof. He was standing in the middle of the road as though no one else was about and we had flattened ourselves against his bank keeping a low profile. We motioned for him to move to his house and tell the kraut to come out to American Paratroopers over by the road. We were very uncertain of this situation and quite suspicious, constantly looking around for any of the enemy. At our bidding, he apparently understood and proceeded towards his house and entered the doorway. We waited impatiently for something to happen, but several minutes passed without any indication from within. We discussed the situation and decided to approach the house one at a time while the other covered from the road. We were all set to make our move when the Frenchman stood in his doorway and motioned for us to come to the house. Apparently the German soldier wasn't anymore sure of his predicament than we were of ours. I told Kilroy to cover me and watch also his rear area and I would go up to the house and rout out the enemy soldier. I wished I had eyes all around to be sure of my safety, but I proceeded anyway reasoning that I was covered by Kilroy. I arrived quickly ay the door of the house meeting the owner there. He was jabbering too fast for me to understand with my limited high school French, but I stepped around him into the room of the home with its masonry floor and walls and wood beams and there standing without weapons was a young German soldier in the green uniform of the Wehrmacht. The dreaded enemy! I confronted him with my rifle and attached bayonet and motioned for him to move out the door in front of me. As he passed by me I thought that he must be about my age. He certainly didn't appear to be more than twenty. I followed out the door, thanking the French people at the home for their help with 'Merci! Merci!' but not taking my eyes off the enemy, who had stopped in front of the house uncertain of my intent. In front of him now, I motioned to him to move towards Kilroy and said in my best German, 'Komen sie here mit hans en haut', or at least that is what I thought it was supposed to sound like. He wasn't moving fast enough, so I prodded him against his butt with my bayonet and loudly ordered him to move more quickly.

'Impatiently I moved him forward with my rifle hips high, bayonet gleaming in the morning light and urging him onward towards Kilroy at the road, all the while with the 'Hans en haut and komens sie here'. I prodded him with my bayonet, gently of course. He got the point! I had checked him at the house for any weapons, so I wasn't afraid, just wary. I continued to point the way with the bayonet. At the road we joined with Kilroy, waved to the Frenchman and started down to Ste-Mère-Église from whence we had come. We motioned to our prisoner the direction to go as Kilroy followed watching sides and rear for any of the enemy. We neared the roadblock and Larry moved ahead to warn our troopers not to shoot Cruise or the German prisoner. That thought might have occurred to some.

'The men at the roadblock cheered and jeered as I moved the German through the mine field we had re-established earlier. 'Hey, where did you find that Kraut; why didn't you shoot him?' I knew some of their diatribe was directed at the new man in the outfit, or at least since March when I had arrived in Camp I was new to them. 'Bunch of smart jerks with all those comments' I thought. 'Gotta keep proving yourself all the time' I mused. Kilroy remained at the defensive position while I was directed by the Sergeant to take the man to our compound near the town hall in Ste-Mère-Église. I continued on my way back into town where I hadn't been before. Past the Company first aid station and along the main road into town I cautiously moved my souvenir as I passed other troopers going about their assignments. Those in town, curious as I passed. I came to the stone walled compound and turned my trophy over to those in charge of captives with their thanks for another helper. They had put some other prisoners to work caring for our wounded and theirs. I had my first look at the devastation in the town from our troopers who had battled there several hours earlier and thought that it might get worse when the krauts recover from their initial surprise. Shortly I arrived back at the roadblock and returned to my position with Kilroy and Vargas and opened a K-Ration box for my lunch.

'The Germans had regrouped from their earlier surprise in the predawn darkness with all the confusion and chaos that our arrival had precipitated and they now began to probe our defence perimeter that was enabling us to control Ste-Mère-Église. We had roadblocks set up on all the roads leading out of Ste-Mère-Église and in the adjacent fields troopers from the third battalion were covering their flanks from foxholes dug during the night and early morning. We were receiving artillery blasts of mortars and eighty eights and it was very difficult to determine where the stuff was coming from. We hugged the bottom of our foxholes and wished they had been deeper. The different sides of our perimeter were being attacked by squads of krauts, but our particular road was only under artillery fire. On one road block Atchley and another trooper had manned a 57mm piece and blasted a German attack hitting two armoured vehicles and scattering the occupants and troops following.

'Vargas, Kilroy and I were busy watching our front between ducking for cover and popping up again when the sounds of artillery abated and suddenly a runner appeared ordering us to move to the left flank, because several of our men had been wounded and killed during that barrage and the gap left needed to be filled. We were selected to fill it. We would have to cross an open area between us and the roadblock some fifty yards long. The messenger had crawled over this area and probably was not seen by the enemy. Anyone standing would be visible in that open space. Except for the small hedgerow, we would have no cover until we reached the road. We gathered our equipment that was within reach beside our hole and strapped it all on replacing my hand grenades back on my lapels and re-strapping my musette bag on my back. Vargas and I were ready about the same time, so we grabbed our rifles and started to traverse the open space quickly. Kilroy had to gather his BAR ammo and took longer to get going. Vargas and I reached the road safely and climbed over a barbed wire cattle fence at the top of the embankment and slid down about eight feet to the road gutter. We had held the barbed wire for each other to pass through, but Larry had no one to assist him and got himself tangled in the wire. While he struggled with the wire, we started to cross the road when Kilroy yelled even as we heard the artillery shells coming in. 'Hit the dirt', he yelled and with no further urging we dove for the wooden open gate in the hedgerow on the other side of the road as the shells exploded all around us and buried ourselves into the Norman soil.

'Kilroy had freed himself from the barbed wire even as he yelled and had dropped to the gutter and flattened himself. Vargas and I had flung ourselves to the ground belly first, rifle and arms out front. We landed on the dirt as the shells hit all around us. The din was almost unbearable as winced with each detonation. We were being covered with dirt and debris as the air was filled with flying fragments. We hugged the ground body to body when through the racket I heard the distinct sound of whimpering next to me. Vargas had been hit by an exploding shell! He was crying and in great pain! Amid the noise I rose on elbows and peered at his body to see where he had been struck. Right pant leg already red with blood. Had to move him to cover, I knew instinctively. 'Can you move', I shouted. He could only shake his head, no. I was quickly on my knees, then up on my feet as I grabbed his shoulders and dragged him behind the hedgerow for protection, I turned him on his back, face up. A mortar shell had exploded right next to him and his whole right side from thigh to ankle was covered with blood. His jump pants were shredded in the same area with dust mingling with blood. I quickly knelt over him and loosened his belt to use as a tourniquet. I grabbed my trench knife from my left ankle and sliced his trousers down his leg and almost fainted at the sight of multiple punctures all along his leg. I suppressed a gasp at the sight and muttered to myself, 'Tourniquet! Tourniquet!', 'I've got to get one on!' Quickly I applied his belt around his upper thigh and tightened it. As I was struggling with the tourniquet, Kilroy crawled around the gate opening. Seeing him I hollered above the explosives sounds for him to get a medic right away! Roddy, or anybody else. I would stay with Vargas and try to hold him together until he returned with help. In a crouching run, Larry headed through an adjacent hedgerow toward Ste-Mère-Église and I continued to comfort Vargas where I could, wincing with each shell blast still falling, but farther away.

'While I waited, I gave Vargas a shot of morphine in his arm from his first aid kit and later would use mine. He was moaning and crying because even the morphine was insufficient for the pain from his shattered limb and I had my doubts about the effectiveness of the antidote. I was fearful, that if Roddy or some other medic did not arrive soon, Vargas would be lost. How inadequate to the need I was! Why wasn't I a doctor? I tried to cover his wounds with some of the bandages from the aid kits after I applied some sulpha powder along the cuts. I exhausted both kits. I kept checking the tourniquet for tightness. He must have realized the hopelessness of his situation and he appeared to be lapsing into shock as he grabbed my arm and softly said, 'Pray for me'. I was shaking with my own trauma of striving with an unfamiliar task and the Lord's Prayer did not come easily to my lips. I almost choked over the words, as I repeated them to him. I recalled his nightly rosary sessions beside his cot in out tent at Quorn and I knew that as a Catholic of Mexican descent, he believed in God. His visual expression confirmed it. I kept reassuring him that help was on the way and he would be okay and finally Kilroy arrived with a medic. I outlined to him what I had done and he took over the care of Vargas.

'Larry said to me that we were ordered by the lieutenant to move to our new location right away. Reluctantly, I departed with Kilroy realizing that the medic was more proficient than I and he appeared to know what he was doing. I begged the medic to see that he got to the aid station.

'Somehow the remainder of that day seemed uneventful and I was operating in a mechanical fashion not really aware of what was happening. I took off my musette bag to get some K-Rations to chew on as I sat in my new hole and much to my surprise, I saw that the bag was full of little holes. It was mute testimony to the nearness of danger to my own body that I had escaped and as I checked it over and cleaned it out, I recovered a number of small pieces of jagged metal from its contents. I was thankful that I had not been wounded in that deluge of shells. When I completed my chow time, I thought that I should get to the aid station and check out Vargas. I informed my squad sergeant that I wanted to see how he was and since things had quieted down somewhat, he concurred. I headed back into Ste-Mère-Église rifle and ammo belts in place, to locate the aid station and found it after some direction from another trooper nearby. At the station I enquired about the condition of Vargas and was quietly informed that Vargas died before he reached the aid station. He had lost too much blood and the shock was too great for his body to sustain life. I was in a state of angry shock myself after hearing that news. I had really tried my best to save him. I felt that if we had gotten the medic fast enough he would be saved. I could not find out what happened after we had departed to our new positions. No one could clearly answer my inquiries. I knew that they had their hands full with many others. I turned and left the aid station and proceeded to cross the street where I sat down against a stone wall and cried. There was nothing else I could do for Vargas. My efforts had been in vain. His shattered body could not cope with the trauma he endured. A short time ago my friend was alive, breathing, talking and eating with me and then mortally wounded, now dead. A lifetime gone in a few moments! I would remember this day for the remainder of my life and these hours of June 7 would not fade or pass from my memory. A short time later I was back at the roadblock, but how I got there I do not recall.

'The road to Chef du Pont was protected by our roadblock and though we did not see any krauts we could feel the sting of their attacks. Their artillery was aiming at our position and bouncing 88 shells off the road at our spot. We could hear the guns fire, ricocheting off the road and land with explosive force in the fields beyond us at almost the same time. The rifle velocity of the 88s created a deafening tumult of sounds. We could hardly hear, much less think. It was like some great continuous earthquake, with debris flying in all directions and the earth vibrating with each crashing explosion. I had been moved to the roadblock position to help defend that area in case the Germans would attack there as they were in other areas of our perimeter defence around Ste-Mère-Église. I had dug a long narrow foxhole in the gutter at roadside about 30 inches deep, which was as deep as I could go because of rocks in the gutter which caused my entrenching tool to rebound with each ringing stroke I made. I was burrowing myself as deep as I could hugging the bottom as the shells zinged across the hole and landing beyond yards away. I never heard anything like this before, Fort Benning infiltration course and manoeuvres notwithstanding. I was literally petrified by the noise and danger. No false bravado, I was scared. Who wants to be blown apart by one of these shells? I remembered Vargas and I had no desire to be incapacitated. This dangerous crescendo carried an ominous sign of the possibility that the beach force may not arrive, or break through as planned. I was unnerved by that thought and my earlier experiences with human pain.

'We were continually pounded by German artillery and frontal assaults all around our Ste-Mère-Église perimeter during June 6th and June 7th and late in the afternoon of the 7th one of our troopers at the road block was wounded by shell fragments and I was ordered to get a medic, because the man was not able to be moved. I headed down the road towards the town centre and was passing a six foot high stone wall bordering a roadside property when a terrific explosion rocked the opposite side of the wall sending me sprawling amid the debris from the blast at the wall. I had heard the whine of the shell and was on my way down as it hit the side of the wall. I beat the stones to the ground by a half second. I lay there stunned by the impact of sound and debris on my body. Who could see me from enemy positions? I thought that I was pretty well concealed from easy view. Why are they trying to kill me with all that artillery? Do they have a spotter somewhere? They have been here for years so they do know the terrain very well, certainly far better than we did. I rallied my senses when I saw a soldier about a hundred yards down the road near the aid station and I shouted to him to get a medic, but he headed for me thinking I was hit, I waved him off as I arose dusting myself off and shouted that I was OK, but we needed help for another trooper. I continued to move towards him and the station to be sure someone would come. Once there I relayed the information and a medic and I hurried back to the roadblock to do what needed to be done. Satisfied that my job was done, I returned to my side of the block and sat on the ground with my legs dangling in my foxhole ready to jump in if necessary. My buddies then informed me of Glen Carpenter's fate. During the recent barrage that I thought was all for me, a mortar shell had landed directly in his foxhole. I was again anguished by that news and was glad that I was not a witness to such destruction.

'Kilroy, Ellis and several others at the roadblock were conversing across the macadam road from their respective foxholes about the day's events when a second squad trooper appeared from the hedgerow and announced that Sergeant Ed White had been killed and was laying beside the small stream on the others side of the hedgerow from us. It had happened during the same barrage that got Carpenter and sent me flying. Several of us wended our way through the hedges to where the Sergeant lay. There in the thick growth beside a small brook, not far from the stone wall that had protected me, lay Sergeant James Edward White, eyes wide open starring at the sky from whence he had come, killed by concussion from the shell burst that covered me with debris. I stood still for a few moments and looked at the ashen face as light as his blond hair. Not a mark of wound or blood on him, yet there was no life in the body. Another good soldier gone!

'The original plan which had allowed 12 hours until the beach forces reached us it now expanded into almost 48 hours as June 8th dawned. What had happened on the beaches? Where were the relief troops that were due late Tuesday? Rumours on late Wednesday indicated that some troopers had contacted patrols of one of the regiments of the 4th Division and they would be joining us soon. It could not be too soon for us because we were running low in ammunition and many had been killed or wounded and our ranks were thinned. We were all suffering exhaustion from lack of rest and we needed a morale boost. The early morning Thursday was rather quiet compared the two days earlier and we began to wonder what happened to the krauts.

'Sometime after 11 am we were surprised by the rumbling sounds of tanks to the front of our roadblock and several troopers ventured up the road to take a look from cover and to our ecstatic surprise, these were from our own 4th Division spearheads at last joining up with our unit from the beaches. We broke out with cheers. Some of the troopers climbed up on the tanks to shake their crew's hands and for a ride into town. Our relief had arrived. We recovered from our initial joy and began to give them hell for taking so long. 'What took you guys so long?' we queried. 'Where have you been?'Did you stop somewhere for gas?' It was all good natured and a release of tension for us. We were really more than glad to see them. It provided a few moments of respite from all the prior pressure of the past several days. It was a time to rejoice in our mutual success.

'Several of us troopers cleared the land mines from the roadway so the armour vehicles could make their way into town. The link up was now official and we knew that the beach landings had been successful though not without trials. The Normandy Peninsula of Cotentin was being liberated bit by bit and supplies and reinforcements would be pouring in for the continuation of the battle. Our reunion did not last very long for about two hours later, Sergeant Blubaugh appointed four selected Company 'H' volunteers to join up with like members of Company 'G' with one Lieutenant to be a reconnoitring patrol to scout out our front and bring in stragglers and other lost troopers. Corporal Jones along with Privates Cruise, Wands, DePalma and Vance stepped forward as ordered. The Sergeant indicated that we were to report back to him as soon as the mission was completed. He said, 'I don't know where we will be, but find us.' I believe that the Lieutenant in command of the patrol was Lieutenant Gensemer.

'We moved out from Ste-Mère-Église with the Lieutenant in charge and patrolled to the northwest and westward directions from the town covering a great deal of territory. We encountered small groups of troopers from the 507 and 508 Parachute Infantry Regiments holding a bridge, or crossroad. Many spent parachutes in the area and dead cattle and several parachutes hanging from trees with their harness dangling empty the occupant long gone, where we did not know. Crashed gliders with much equipment scattered about them unable to be used by the occupants, who were either killed, or in too much of a hurry to gather everything. The countryside was covered with the debris of war. I could not bear to see the everything covered with dirt and blood. Our hearts and minds burned with hatred at these encounters. Though death was all around, I was not willing to concede to it. We were beginning to accumulate much dirt ourselves from climbing, crawling and trudging through the hedgerow country looking for either friend or foe.

'We assured those that we met, that the landings on the beaches had been successful and that support was on the way. We could see why the Germans were having so much trouble massing their forces. With so much diversion, they had their hands full with airborne troops all over the area. I do not recall whether we met any of our own regiment's stragglers, or lost men, but we met others from attached regiments.

'Our patrol was not without a bit of humour. It was necessary to ford several streams along our route through hedgerow country and keeping dry was paramount. In one particular area we reached a stream that was just a little too wide and turbulent to jump across even for our best athletes and the lieutenant had two men get a nearby tree limb of sufficient girth that we could use to walk across the barrier. They returned with the news that there was a limb across downstream a short distance away, so off we trudged to that location. The log appeared to be about 6'to 8' in diameter which would seem OK to travel across the water. No sweat! Our intrepid lieutenant led the crossing with one long step on the log and cleanly leaping to dry ground beyond showing us how it could be done. I was bringing up the rear and watched as each trooper one by one cleared the stream. 'Duck Soup', I thought as my turn came. Someone must have greased the wooden pole, because my first step sent me reeling off the log and into the water to my waist. Rifle dirtied, ammo wet, soaked uniform and wounded pride; but the first laugh that we had since early am on June 6. They all helped me out of the water laughing as they hustled me up to the bank. We made a brief pause for me to quickly clean my rifle, which had gotten wet and muddy in the flip. I would have to dry off as we travelled. Fortunately my jump suit had been impregnated before leaving England's Camp Quorn causing the water to run off quickly. I was hoping that we would not run into any krauts, thinking that my rifle might get jammed from the exposure in the water.

'When the patrol leader was satisfied that we had reconnoitred the area that was assigned and that further coverage was unnecessary, we headed back towards our own lines. Where ever they were. I am certainly glad that our leader knew where he was headed because we seemed to have been marching in a series of arcs. We reached the outpost and sign and countersign given, we passed through as the lieutenant enquired about Regimental Headquarters location. The troopers on the line pointed the way and we located the HQ after passing a line of hedges with about twenty dead German soldiers strewn along it in a grotesque fashion, lying as they had been killed. The headquarters was just beyond under a stretched camouflaged spent parachute tied between several trees in a hedgerow. There we met General Ridgeway and Colonel Gavin who heard the Lieutenants report and also questioned some of the other patrol members. All comforts of home in a French farm yard. We got some hot coffee from the HQ group and ate some of our rations. We were instructed to remain for the night and return to our Companies in the morning. I cleaned my rifle for the second time that day. This wasn't my last patrol, but it was the most humorous. That ended the first three days in Normandy for me.'

Pfc Leslie Palmer Cruise, Jr, Company 'H', 505th Parachute Infantry Regiment, 82nd Airborne.

'I heard voices and I recognized the tongue. They were not French. A Schmeisser machine pistol started firing through the door and through the window of the barn but I was swinging behind the window and not close to the door and they missed me. I could make out two persons outside the barn and they were coming close. I pulled my .45 out of the shoulder holster - it had a hair trigger and it went off as I pulled it out. Remarkable I didn't shoot my arm off - and I kept firing, nervous reaction and just as I reach the door with my rapid fire this German came in still firing and the .45 slug caught him somewhere and knocked him up in the corner. A .45 is a rough damn gun. I did not see this man move again. I grabbed the lanyard on my knife and pulled it up and slashed the suspensions lines on the left side and dropped a foot or so to the floor. I went down flat and crawled to the door. I saw the other one standing about five or six feet away and shot him. He spun around, went backwards, fell and lay there. Still on my hands and knees I crawled through the doorway (there was no door) around the side of the barn into a driveway to a road behind the barn. There was gunfire but not right there. I dashed across the road into what was an orchard and stopped to survey the situation in the dark. I could not see more than thirty yards, if that.

'Reconnaissance - that is a military positive and it comes up front - reconnoitre - patrol - and that's what I did. There were 17 or 19 men on my plane and we would have come down in a generally straight line. I did not know about the river then. I was in the village of Chef du Pont but did not know where I was.

'I spent about one hour going from end to end of that place which was spread out with several fields and many open places along a main drag. No lights, no sign of habitation. The natives were lying low. I found none of my boys. How much time went by I can't recall and I was ready to leave the village and make toward some firing that had started up I don't know just how far away. I could tell from the sound that our rifles were firing.

'Actually, I was heading cover behind fences, posts, bushes - just like a good soldier doing it by the book. That was the easy part. I was back at the orchard and I heard someone moving. The weeds were about knee high. A normal pace through could make noise and I was tuned for a pin drop. I went down in a prone position, brought my carbine up on this figure I could make out as he came toward me and - why I didn't take that perfect shot, only God knows. Something held my finger and I snapped Halt!

Right back came the words 'Lieutenant Moss.'

'Dammit Svenson, what the hell are you doing walking though here like that? That's the way to get killed!' The training officer, still training my men.

'Now we were two, reinforced and ready. We moved toward the river and the bridge. The bridge told me a lot. It had to be held. Our job was to seal off the beaches. We start here. Our armament consisted of one M-1 rifle, one carbine, two hand grenades apiece, ammunition aplenty, sulphur powder and a bandage apiece and-and-and - each of us had a five pound land mine in our musette bag hanging over our bellies. We could stop any tank that tried to cross. Svenson and I found a spot at riverside just to the flank of the bridge. It was hidden by trees but we could see out when light came. Best of all it muffled the sound of fire and better yet, it hid the flash and smoke. We settled in to hold that unnamed bridge.

'Not quite daylight and Svenson was eying the river and I was a few yards back watching our rear when I saw. He was standing about fifty feet away, looking right past us. I saw him first. Now we were three and most confident. That was because we didn't understand the real situation at all. At just about daylight I caught a motion behind us and challenged a Frenchman trying to come around a chicken house. For the first time I could see we were behind a house with a back yard stretching to the river. I showed him the American flag on my shoulder and he seemed pleased. He spoke to me in French - I spoke to him in English. We understood nothing and he signalled and disappeared then returned with a bottle of the great Norman cider we learned to love, plus a boiled egg for each of us.'

Lieutenant Robert Clinton Moss, Jr., Company 'H', 508th Parachute Infantry Regiment.

'In the heart of the Cotentin Peninsula, on my mother's isolated farm, I awoke abruptly. What was happening? I was under the impression that the wall that my bed was against trembled and resounded. Then I heard some voices in the kitchen. Quickly, I got up and discovered an unusual scene. A man, quite bizarre, was seated in a chair in the middle of our kitchen. He wore sort of a khaki uniform, very soft and flexible, with pockets throughout. On his head he wore a helmet covered with leaves, while his face was camouflaged in black. He spoke using words that I could not understand. My mother and my brothers surrounded him and were trying to guess what he was saying. His left hand seemed to support his arm. Without ceasing, he repeated 'broken...broken...' Suddenly, releasing his arm, he pulled out a knife that was contained in a sheath on his lower leg. He then cut a strip from a roll of bandage that had been in a pocket in his pants. And, most wonderfully, he pulled out a chocolate bar that he gave to us. This man, quite strange, was, thus our friend. 'Broken' this first English word remains burned into my memory. The paratrooper of the 82nd Airborne Division was lost in the Norman countryside on this morning and had a broken shoulder. One of my brothers drove him to a place where he was cared for.'

Nine-year old Marie-T Lavieille, born Champel Prétot, Manche. Because of this extraordinary experience Marie became an English professor, often serving as an interpreter during ceremonies of the anniversary of D-Day.

'I was 31 years old and I lived on my stepmother's farm on the Périers Road, near the southwest entrance to the city of Carentan. My fiancée had been captured in 1940 by the Germans and I would not see him again until after the end of the war. Our living conditions were very difficult. We had ration cards for bread, sugar and meat but we were better off for food on the farm than the folk in the villages. My stepmother's farm was requisitioned by the Germans and served as an infirmary. We had to live in the livestock buildings, but the experience of living with the Germans was not too unpleasant for us - we got along OK. As the month of June approached, folk started to worry because there were many aircraft and increased bombing. No one knew what was happening. On 5 June there electrical lines, railroads and at Carentan the bridge of Ste-Hilaire-Petitville over the Taute River was bombed. We saw large numbers of paratroopers to the north and in the direction of the sea. The wounded Germans came to our farm to seek medical assistance. They removed all the hay and the wounded were placed in all available spaces until the whole area was full. Some bled to death; the gravely wounded were moved away. As time passed, the situation became more difficult for me and my stepmother. The Germans became very nervous. Our neighbour, Charles Pigault told us that the farm was no longer secure. We followed M. Pigault to his farm and found a group of 40 other refugees. We were locked in the house and we could not leave, nor show ourselves. If the Germans saw us, they would shoot. The more time that passed, the meaner the Germans became.

'The battle began to unfold around us and artillery rounds continually fell - one hit the chimney. The first Americans that arrived were accompanied by a tank. We had to leave because the thatched roof was on fire. On the road to Carentan were Americans heading to the front and Germans prisoners. During periods of combat we had to descend into the ditches for protection. Those moments brought us great fear. Arriving in Carentan, we went to the home of Madame Lecomte. We had a visit from an American who seemed to me to be drunk. He held his bayonet in hand and continued to drop it. He put all of us in a line and took one of the men to take him through all of the rooms in the house. Once done, he was convinced that there were only civilians there and he relaxed and even provided food. We only slept one night in that house. The area was on fire and the risk was that the house would also catch fire. We moved again, to a small furniture store and stayed for several days. After a last move into another house in Carentan, we finally returned home to the farm that was now far from the front line.'

Marie Madeleine Poisson, Carentan, Manche.

'My parents ran a grocery store and café in Neuville au Plain, which bordered the road to Cherbourg. I was 21 years old and my siblings and I lived at my parents' home. We milked the cows and cared for the animals in the fields. There was no suggestion as to what was about to happen during the night of June 5th. In the middle of the night our father woke us and we then heard aircraft overhead. I opened the window in the first storey room and saw paratroopers descending over fields. They silently entered the village, hugging the walls of the houses as they entered. The Germans had departed and no one remained except civilians. We returned to bed and slept until morning. At daybreak everyone except my father left, as we did not want to remain in the house next to the road. For four days we wandered across fields between Houlbec and Bergeries searching for our animals that had run away. During our search we found dead paratroopers in the ditches, as well as many dead animals. At the castle in Neuville, horses that had tried to get out through the gates were dead, their legs between the bars. At night we slept in barns on hay with other civilians. We returned to our house after five days to find our father there. We helped our neighbour to take care of and milk his animals, which he had locked in so that they could not run away. At this moment my sister was injured by the blast of an artillery shell that the Germans fired from Ecausseville. Later the Americans replaced the Germans at my parent's café and accompanied us in the pastures when we went to milk the animals. We watched their convoys that came from Cherbourg pass and they threw us oranges.'

Denise Lecourtois.

'On the evening of June 5th, when night fell, we saw the first planes. They flew at a low altitude and dropped the first paratroopers. The amount of planes intensified during the night and we found paratroopers throughout, at Blosville, Houesville and Angoville. Parachutes of all colours were then seen strewn about, the nylon and cords hooked onto various objects. We all remained at the farm and didn't move all night. We heard machine-gun fire and explosions and saw flares illuminate the sky. We didn't sleep at all that night and later, planes arrived towing gliders, which landed around Hiesville. At dawn paratroopers of the 101st Airborne Division came to the farm, knocked on the door and asked the location of the Germans. Then they left. Next morning, some of the animals were out in the fields next to the farm and I went to care for them. The hedgerows were filled with paratroopers and they asked me where the Germans were. We were young and unaware and walked everywhere out in the country. During the morning, the Germans, who were holed up in the pastures, tried to escape through the areas that they had flooded. On the border of the flooded area I saw some American paratroopers arrive. I pointed out the escaping Germans to them and the paratroopers fired some shots without hitting them. The Germans turned around and returned with their hands in the air. The paratroopers took them and returned to the village and upon arrival shot them, leaving their bodies in the ditch.'

Roger Lecheminant. Houesville was liberated on the morning of 6 June. During the weeks following the D-Day invasion, Roger had the habit of going for a walk on the road that went to the Grand Vey at the Madeleine. An American officer in charge of the mail went back and forth by jeep to the beach where he met a small, fast boat that carried the mail to and from England. One day, Roger and the mayor's son went along with him to the beach and they were later taken by boat to England and Southampton. The following day they made the return trip to France. Roger then worked for the Americans for four months, assembling prefabricated hangars. This helped greatly because there was no other work in the area.

'Crossing the Channel was uneventful but when we hit the coast of France all hell broke loose. The red light came on to 'Stand up' and after a few minutes we got the Green to jump. When I made my exit from the plane it seemed like a giant hand grabbed me by the seat of my pants and pushed me to the end of the static line. The blast of air was so great that it was as though I had been hit by an anti-aircraft shell. The drop seemed an eternity until I landed in a field surrounded with tall hedgerows. I looked around. I was all alone. My squad's objective was to knock out a particular bridge. In my musette bag I had the explosives along with my shaving gear, K-Rations and a photograph of a girl named Elizabeth, who is now the Queen of England. Finding a way out of the field, I found a dirt road, so I started to walk. I did not know where I was going. A bridge came into view. Was this the right bridge? I walked back and forth over it and then decided it was not. As I was retracing my steps I heard a vehicle coming. It did not sound like one of ours, so I took cover in the hedgerow. When it passed I could see it was a motorcycle and sidecar with two Jerries. Moments later several shots rang out and then it was all quiet again. I learnt later that my mother had a dream about this action. Just as I was about to get on the road again I heard some men coming. They were American paratroopers. I fumbled for my 'cricket' and gave them the signal [one click, which was to be acknowledged by two clicks]. If I had been a German I could have killed them all and I told them so.

'Because I was 505 they put me in command. These men were from the 507 and the 101st. I told them what my mission was so we set out to find the bridge. Further down the road we came across the Germans with the motorcycle. They were both dead. Our attitude changed, now we knew that this war was for real.

'It was daylight by the time we found the bridge. I posted guards on the approaches and it was not long before we heard a vehicle coming and the paratroopers ordered it to stop. The jeep contained an American Lieutenant, his driver and in the back seat was my best buddy, Larry Neipling. Larry told me to get in. As we were driving down the road we were fired on. The officer jumped out on his side and the driver out of the other. Me, I went over the back while Larry got in the front seat and put the 50 calibre machine-gun into action. 'Tony, get me some more ammo' and from that moment on I was his assistant.

'Around midday most of our Battalion was organised into one area. Nearby there were a lot of German prisoners. We were ordered to go to Neuville-au-Plain, but because the Third Battalion was fending off a counter-attack at Ste-Mère-Église the orders were changed. The main body of the Battalion went to help, but forty-four of us went on to Neuville-au-Plain. As soon as we arrived we immediately came under heavy fire. Artillery and 88 shells were coming in like rain. One man received a direct hit, George Ziemski thought it was me and I thought it was him in the confusion. When we got protective covering fire from our 50 calibre machine-gun we ran to the next hedgerow. There on the ground was a beautiful pearl handled German pistol in front of us. Word was passed along that it may be booby-trapped, so we sat there looking at it.

'Climbing through the hedgerow I collided with a smiling German with his hands above his head. It scared the devil out of me. At the next hedgerow I was told to relieve John Zunder with the sniper's rifle, it was a 30 Springfield fitted with a telescopic sight. Zunder pointed out the area where the Germans were and it wasn't long before I saw a German carrying a bucket. I waited until he came back, I took aim and fired. Bullseye. I hit the bucket and the Kraut quickly disappeared.

'Although we inflicted a lot of damage, we came back with only sixteen men. This was the action led by Lieutenant Turner Turnbull which was said later to be of great importance in the first few hours of D-Day. He was resigned to making a last stand, but because of the timely arrival of Company 'E' we were able to pull out.

'Our next major objective was the town of Ste-Sauveur-le-Vicomte. Our last attack was made on Hill 131 which overlooked the town of La Haye-du-Puits. It was raining so hard that you could not see your hand in front of your face. The hill was a hard climb for me carrying a 30-calibre machine-gun up a very muddy and slippery slope. Luckily we did not meet much opposition.

'Several days later we were on our way back to Quorn where I found my girlfriend, Sheila, had got another boyfriend.'
    Pfc Tony DeFoggi, Company 'F', 505th Parachute Infantry Regiment. [22]

'Metallic Christmas cracker 'crickets' had been issued as a means of making contact with each other. We also had a password: The password was 'flash' and the counter-sign was 'thunder'. So when I ran into another fellow, I said 'Flash' and this other person said, 'Jesus Christ, I'm American, don't shoot'. He'd forgotten the password, but it was

22 *Put On Your Boots and Parachutes!: The United States 82nd Airborne Division* written and edited by Deryk Wills (self published, March 1992).

all right - I reckoned no German would say that.

'We all matured well beyond our years that day. We saw not only our own platoon go, but so many others drown in the river. They had so much equipment on them and no quick release 'chutes in those days: if you landed in a flooded river you got drowned... Others got caught in the trees and then [were] shot whilst they were hanging there... they were just left there hanging; when the de-registration people came along, they were still there, just hanging. It was devastating. We'd trained for twenty-one months as a unit and gotten rid of anybody that couldn't cut the mustard so we had a really fine unit. We didn't think that casualties would happen to us, they'd happen to someone else - of course you have to go in feeling that way, war has to be a young man's game, you just figure it's not going to be you, it's going to be the other fellow that gets it.'

First Lieutenant Henry Lefebvre (21), 3rd Platoon 'A' company, 508th PIR, 82nd Airborne Division.

'Dawn on D-Day came clear, cold and tense. Our group was now assembled and pushing toward Ste-Mère-Église. We arrived in the town, but for our particular group resistance was passive, with the exception, of course, of the ever-present snipers. Our Battalion had been given the mission of defending the northern sector of the town. (Through Ste-Mère-Église runs the main road of the Cherbourg Peninsula. It was imperative that the 505th Parachute Regiment hold this road at any and all cost. It was along this road that the Wiley Jerry would try to send his reinforcements. They must be stopped, until the beach landings were completed.)

'Arriving at our company defensive sector, one platoon was dispatched to the town of Neauville Au Plain, 2 miles further north, to act as an outpost line. Everything was quiet, and we wondered where Jerry was.

'For once, nobody needed to prod us to dig in. About noon, we could hear firing to the north and knew our outpost was tangling with the Germans. Then, the shells began to scream their missiles of misery about us. Dirt really flew as we dug faster and deeper into our hedgerow. Small arms fire also began to open, and we knew the Nazi had arrived. Who can explain the terror that strikes one's heart when those shells begin to shatter all around? Small arms and machine guns we can all take, but the deafening roar and the flying shell fragments never lose their terror for even the bravest Airborne Soldier.

'Sometime that afternoon, a breathless runner legged it in from the outpost and told us the platoon was holding off an entire Battalion, and would it be all right to withdraw. Receiving permission, the messenger took off to tell the Platoon leader it was OK. About an hour later, the platoon returned. Gone were many faces that had become so much a part of our life the last two years. We didn't have to question those that were left. One look at their grimy; shocked countenances told more than words can ever tell.

'Night fell, and with it the enemy artillery barrage increased in intensity. Under the cover of darkness, the Germans had moved up to within 100 yards of us, Shells and bullets rained about us like hail on a tin roof back in Iowa, only we had no tin roof. We held our ground. Suddenly, the roar of the old 'sweat-boxes' was heard, and as we looked skyward we could see C-47s, towing and releasing gliders.

'No paratrooper was ever so glad to see gliders before. They were our enemies back in the states, but we were sure glad to see our buddies now. We could use some glider artillery, too. Many of the gliders failed to land near us, but a sufficient number came in to relieve the pressure and alleviate the gravity of our position considerably. All night long, the Kraut artillery broke around us.

'At dawn, the German attacked again. We held our fire until some were only 50 yards away, then layed down such a heavy curtain of fire that any further advance was impossible. When their attack had bogged down, we launched our counter blow, laying down a withering fire as we left our foxholes, driving them a quarter of a mile. A temporary lull came in the battle, and Heinies started streaming out under a white flag to give themselves up.

'In German, they told us our fire was too accurate - there were too many casualties and they were forced to surrender.

'That afternoon, the first elements of Seaborne Infantry came up through our position. Our unshaven men, hollow eyed from lack of shut-eye, cheered the footsloggers and tankers with all the enthusiasm they could muster, and then relaxed for the first time in nearly 48 hours.

'With idle time on our hands, at last we got a chance to look around and take stock in the situation. Dead Jerries lay strewn over the ground, their faces a series of grotesque masks. Smashed Mauser rifles and Mark VI tanks were wrecked too. We did pay a price, also - not a high one by proportion, but it's tough to see your Buddies killed, no matter how few.

'Shaking my head, I returned to my foxhole, sat by my radio and wondered if it was all worth it or not - whether we were fighting for Benny and Frank, or if there was something greater pushing us all. Then, a message came over the radio. It was from General Gavin - 'Slim Jim' we call him. I scribbled the message down on the pad, and after I'd 'Rogered' I took time to read it. It was brief all right. 'Slim Jim' just said, 'A good job, damn well done.' That answered my question.'
Joe Stanger, 505th PIR, 82nd Airborne.

The 82nd Airborne arrived in the ETO on 9 December 1943, battle tested and fresh out of North Africa and Sicily. On D-Day, the 'All American' Division was dropped by parachute and flown in by glider before and after dawn astride the Merderet River. Among other objectives the 82nd was tasked to clear and secure the general area around Neuville, Au Plain and Bandienville and capture Ste-Mère-Église, a key German communications centre for the heavily-defended area of 'Utah' Beach. Preceded 30 minutes by Pathfinder teams, the main body of the 82nd jumped at 0151 hours on 6 June and by 03:12 hours, all paratroopers had landed. By 04:04 hours, the first of 52 gliders landed with artillery, engineers and special troops. The 82nd Airborne had dropped on the fringe of the assembly area of the German 91st Division.

'At 24:00 hours enemy parachute troops made a jump over my command post by the quarry at Hill 69, north of the Quineville-Montebourg road about six miles due north of Ste-Mère-Église. The paratroops were taken prisoner. From the maps in their possession it was evident that the main area for the drop would be Ste-Mère-Église. At 0200 messengers from two nearby battalions arrived at the regimental command post and reported that thousands of paratroops had jumped and their units had been surrounded. Prior to then I had not regarded the situation as so serious because I believed that in this terrain of hedgerows, paratroops would have difficulty in orienting themselves and that some would even land in the wrong places, like those who had jumped near my command post though destined for Ste-Mère-Église. Furthermore, at first I did not believe that it was a question of a drop by complete divisions.'

Oberstleutnant Günther Keil, 1058th Infantry Regiment attached to the 91st Division in the Vire Estuary. [23]

Deeper inland, the 82nd and the 101st dispersed too widely over their target areas because of anti-aircraft fire and inadequate briefings took and held Ste-Mère-Église. Caught by a strong wind about 20 troopers of the 505th Regiment, 82nd Airborne, including Pfc John 'Buck' Steele - a natural comedian with a great sense of humour' - were blown into the Place de l'Église where a house had caught fire and was burning. Steele's risers snagged the church tower in the square and he hung there for more than two hours before he was cut free. By the close of the day, the 82nd had suffered 1,200 casualties, as many as the 101st, which held forward positions in order for the 4th Infantry Division to make shore on 'Utah' Beach; it had captured Ste-Mère-Église and held a general line along the Merderet River from La Fière south to include the eastern end of the causeway over the river.

'That evening on the 5th June, my friends and I were enjoying ourselves trying to break a cycle speed record around the church at Ste-Mère-Église, just to kill time. At 10pm I resumed my post in the steeple - a telephone at my side. Around midnight (2am British time) I heard planes passing overhead and saw 'objects' falling from the sky. During this period a house began to burn. It was the light from this fire that made it possible for me to see hundreds of parachutes falling from the sky as the airplane motors droned on. They fell on the roofs, in the streets and even in the trees of the church square. The sky was studded with parachutes. Suddenly everything in the steeple became dark. Through an opening I saw that a parachutist had fallen on the steeple, hanging by the ropes. He appeared to be dead, but after a moment I heard his voice. There were two of us on duty at the post and my companion wanted to shoot him. 'Are you crazy,' I said, 'if you shoot we'll be discovered.

German soldier, Chief-corporal Rudolph May, who commanded a patrol of ten men, cut the parachute lines with his pocket knife to release Private John 'Buck' Steele, Company 'F', 505th Parachute Infantry Regiment, 82nd Airborne Division, so he could be taken captive. May's brother, a pilot, was killed in 1944. [24]

'When we jumped there was a huge fire in a building in town. I didn't know that the heat would suck a parachute towards the fire. I fought the chute all the way down to avoid the fire. One trooper [Pfc Alfred J. Van Holsbeck] who had joined our Company shortly before D-Day landed in the fire. Privates H. T. Bryant and Ladislaw 'Laddie' Tlapa and Lieutenant Harold Cadish commanding the Second Platoon, were most unfortunate. They were shot in the power poles. My close friend, Pfc Charles Blankenship, was shot still in his chute, hanging in a tree, a little distance from the street. Facing the church from the front, I landed on the right side of the roof, luckily in the shadow side from the fire. Some of my suspension lines went over the steeple and I slid down over to the edge of the roof. This other trooper came down and really got

---

23 See: *D-Day: The Greatest Invasion - A People's History* by Dan Van Der Vat (Madison Press Books Toronto 2003).
24 *Put On Your Boots and Parachutes!: The United States 82nd Airborne Division* written and edited by Deryk Wills (self published, March 1992).

entangled on the steeple (I didn't know it was Steele at the time). Almost immediately a Nazi soldier came running from the back side of the church shooting at everything. Sergeant John Ray had landed in the church yard almost directly below Steele. This Nazi shot him in the stomach while he was still in his chute. (Sergeants jumped with a .45 calibre pistol). While Ray was dying he somehow got his .45 out and shot the Nazi in the back of the head killing him. Sergeant Ray saved my life as well as Steele's. It was one of the bravest things I have ever witnessed.

'I finally got to my trench knife and cut my suspension lines and fell to the ground. I looked up at the steeple but there was not a movement or a sound and I thought the trooper was dead. I got my M-1 assembled and ducked around several places in that part of town hoping to find some troopers, but all of them were dead. I got off several rounds at different Germans before they drove me to a different position with intense gunfire.

'Working my way back past the church, I was the most scared and loneliest person in the world. I thought I was the only trooper alive in the midst of all those enemy soldiers. I was finally spotted again and I believe every German in the area opened up in my direction. Dashing across the street I ran down to a park or wooded area not far away. How the enemy with so much fire power didn't get me I will never know. After I short distance I came to a field. I heard a noise ahead so I started crawling towards it. I got very close and snapped my 'cricket'. A 'cricket' snapped back in return. What a relief! It was a trooper from the 508, a 'live' trooper. We started back towards the trees and came across three more, one from the Third Battalion 50S, one from the 506 and one other from the 508.'

Private Ken Russell, Second Platoon, Company 'F', 505th Parachute Infantry Regiment[25] **Almost as soon as he left his plane Private John Steele of the 505th Regiment, 82nd Airborne was hit by something that felt 'like the bite of a very sharp knife.' A bullet had smashed into his foot. Above Steele, Pfc Ernest Blanchard heard the church bell ringing and saw the maelstrom of fire coming up all around him. The next minute he watched horrified as a man floating down almost beside him 'exploded and disintegrated before my eyes,' presumably a victim of the explosives he was carrying.**

Even with the confusion and with widely dispersed men and material, the paratrooper and glider troops caused the Germans to overestimate the Allied strength and made them uncertain about Allied intentions and rendered them unable to counter-attack during critical and crucial moments of battle.

'I remember thinking at the time, Here it is, the great invasion of Europe; I just made the best jump of my life and I'm caught up in a tree and bouncing two feet off the ground. I looked around. I was completely alone, so I remembered the 'cricket'. I got mine out while I was hanging from the tree and started clicking. Next thing I knew, a voice from behind me said, 'for God's sake padre, stop that noise, or we'll all get killed.'

Chaplain George 'Chappie' Wood. This was his third combat jump. By the afternoon 'Chappie', together with three doctors were busy tending the wounded from both sides in Madame Angele Levrault's schoolhouse. It was 'Chappie' who led the group sent out to cut down the dead paratroopers from the trees around the town square. The son of the Ste-Mère-Église fire chief, Andre Feville, assisted in the gathering of 200-300 American

25 *Put On Your Boots and Parachutes!: The United States 82nd Airborne Division* written and edited by Deryk Wills (self published, March 1992).

dead near the school. Later he was on a burial detail. 'Chappie' Wood went on to become the only United States Army Chaplain in the Second World War to make four combat jumps. The Catholic Chaplain, Father Matt Connelly suffered a broken vertebra on the Normandy jump which ended his parachuting career. [26]

The 101st Assistant Divisional Commander, Brigadier General Don F. Pratt, led the 53-Waco glider assault, carrying 148 men, in Fighting Falcon II. Although all of the pilots managed to land within a two-mile area, only six of them were in the designated zone. Intelligence reports had not mentioned that most fields were bordered with hedgerows, four-foot earthen fences covered with a tangle of hedges, bushes and trees. Because of the darkness and hazards caused by the hedgerows, five soldiers were killed in the glider landings - one of them was Brigadier General Pratt. Ironically, he originally was scheduled to cross to France by sea. Unfortunately, he sat in his jeep with a parachute underneath him and when his glider could not be stopped on the wet, dewy grass of Landing Zone 'E' at Hiesville, Fighting Falcon II collided with a large tree and fallen log in a hedgerow and he hit his head on an overhead strut and broke his neck. The impact from this collision pinned Lieutenant Colonel Mike Murphy the pilot in the wreckage and broke both his legs. Lieutenant John M. Butler, the co-pilot was also killed when a tree branch penetrated the dome of his skull. Only Pratt's aide, Lieutenant John May, escaped uninjured. [27] Pratt was the first American general officer to be killed in the Liberation of France.

Glider troops played an important role during the Normandy operations. As counterparts of the airborne infantrymen, they delivered weapons, equipment, personnel and vehicles to the Division. The first day-light glider operation occurred on the morning of 7 June. Using a heavier cargo glider, the pilots delivered 40 vehicles, 157 personnel, six guns and 19 tons of equipment, which was crucial to the success that the Division had carrying out its objectives. After the seizure of the causeways, the 101st proceeded toward a new objective, the capture of the town at Carentan, the junction point for the two American forces from 'Utah' and 'Omaha' beaches and a key to the success of the invasion. For five days, the 101st waged a bitter fight to dislodge the German 6th Parachute Regiment from the town and to hold it for the arrival of American armour units from the beachhead. During this attack on Carentan, Lieutenant Colonel Robert G. Cole, Commander of the 3rd Battalion, 502nd Parachute Infantry Regiment, wiped out a strategically important pocket of enemy resistance. For his action, Cole became the first member of the 101st to receive the Medal of Honor.

'At approximately 1,500 feet, headed directly for LZW, was a serial of approximately 60 C-47s towing Horsas with CG-4As following. The troop carriers released their gliders directly over what proved to be an enemy position in the woods. As soon as the troop carriers approached, the whole hill on the opposite side opened up with small arms, Schmeissers, and even anti-tank guns, firing at the C-47s and gliders. Despite this fact, the gliders were released right over the landing zone, and many of them landed there, although others obviously realized that something was wrong and landed between our forward tank line and Le Port. Almost all the gliders were forced to make crash landings,

26 *Put On Your Boots and Parachutes!: The United States 82nd Airborne Division* written and edited by Deryk Wills (self published, March 1992).

27 *101st Airborne: The Screaming Eagles in World War II* by Mark Brando (Zenith Press, 2007).

and here it was noted that the Horsa glider seemed to break into many pieces, while the CG-4As' framework was more or less intact. The difference between the two upon impact was visible to me as an eye witness. The Horsa seemed to fall apart. One or two gliders, not making their turn, landed on the hill occupied by the enemy. One of them landed beside what we believed was a pillbox. At least one glider landed beside our still burning tanks, and after its passengers had fled, it burned on the spot. The C-47s then proceeded east and came back low over the landing zone, although some of them scattered and flew back behind our own positions.

'I ordered Major Ingersoll to gather up and assemble all officers and men of the Division, including the glider pilots, near the crossroads, with the hope and intention of collecting enough men to make the breakthrough to Sainte- Mère-Église. By next morning I had perhaps in excess of 200 men, but not more than about 150 of them were trained infantry soldiers. The medical detachment, which evidently had come in on some of the gliders, established an aid station at the crossroads at Le Port, where many of the gliders were assembled. We saw other gliders come in later, and this time I noted that the Germans held their fire until the gliders got in very low and very close.'

Colonel Edson D. Raff. During the afternoon of the 6th, two battalions of the 8th Infantry Regiment that had landed on the invasion beaches had driven the enemy from the southern portion of LZ 'W'. Small seaborne elements of the 82nd Division under Colonel Raff made two unsuccessful attempts later to push the Germans from the rest of the zone. However, when the gliders arrived, the enemy still held approximately the northern quarter. From their lines, southward almost to Les Forges, the zone was a no-man's land, full of snipers, traversed by German patrols and under observed fire from mortars and an 88mm gun on high ground near Fauville. Raff's men did their best to steer the gliders to safety by waving yellow flags and making an F of orange smoke, but the glider pilots either did not see them or did not know what to make of the unexpected signals. About 300 glider pilots gathered at Raff's HQ near Les Forges and 270 of them were evacuated to the beaches on the afternoon of 7 June. About 170 others, who had been guarding the HQ and prisoners of the 82nd Airborne west of Sainte-Mère-Église, left for the beaches with 362 prisoners at noon on 8 June after General Ridgeway had addressed them in a speech which thanked them warmly for their good service in Normandy. [28]

'Six aircrews were detailed to act as 'Flak bait' to cover the paratroop and glider drops in the Cherbourg Peninsular, by drawing searchlights and Flak away from these more vulnerable aircraft. So successful was this that two of the six were hit, one so badly that it crash landed near base and burnt up. The crew ran!'

Flying Officer Bernard M. Job RAFVR, Mosquito navigator, 418 Squadron RAF Holmsley South near Bournemouth.

'On 4 June in the afternoon we were alerted for the Normandy Invasion. I and my ground crew - two other people - had painted alternate white, black, white, black stripes on the aircraft and the reason was to not shoot us down as our aircraft were shot down in the Sicily invasion by our own Navy. The fuselage was marked and each wing was marked and the way I did it was I had put a piece of string around and marked with crayon and filled it in with a flat white and flat black paint. And that was the reason for the stripes.

28 *The Glider War* by James E. Mrazek (Robert Hale & Co 1975).

'Now we were taken back into interrogation (briefing). When we were ready to go we got orders from SHAFE High Command to postpone the Invasion for 24 hours because of the bad weather conditions across the Channel. We were then put into barracks and an MP [Military Police] - each set apart by 10 feet with a Thompson sub machine gun and had orders to shoot to kill if we attempted to flee from the area. And this was because of the fact it was extremely great secret information that we contained.

'On the 5th we got the 'GO' and I came out at pre-flight of the aircraft, checking the para racks. The paratroopers were sitting, standing, constantly relieving themselves - nervous, very nervous and as I'm under the aircraft checking the para racks which I found later on contained mines I knew the reason. We boarded up and set up, took off - an extremely heavy load. We took every inch of the runway and we did get airborne and we formed up and we came out over the Channel. I'm up in the cockpit with the pilot and the co-pilot, checking the instruments, making sure that everything is OK and from there we found the pilot marker and made a turn going in towards the Islands - Guernsey and Jersey and of course, the Cherbourg Cotentin Peninsula. As we were going in I see tracer bullets, but they looked just like Roman candles for sure and as we approached them they were more intensive. We seemed to have been out of range. But the second Island, as we turned, all hell started to break loose...'

Technical Sergeant John J. Ginter Jr., flight engineer and part-time co-pilot of C-47 41-00825 in the 92nd Troop Carrier Squadron.

'Once in the plane... it was beginning to get dark... I can hear the pilots cranking the engines - the cough and firing as they caught and revved up. The pilots pushed the throttles to proper RPMs, checked their maps and gauges. The C-47 shook and vibrated as though eager and we were silent to the man. The ship farthest to our left added throttle, moved forward toward the runway, did a right ninety, and paraded left to right before us as vanguard, moving between us and the runway [as it headed] to the right end of the runway and takeoff point. We watched the flames of exhaust in the growing dark, as the ship filled with 101st Eagle men loaded with tools of war, shadowed past.

'It became our turn; the ship shuddered and moved, turned right and followed the ships in line before us. Our pilot firewalled the throttles and we went as over a bumpy country road, heading toward the skies and Normandy. When the gear cleared the ground, we were airborne, we cheered as one, breaking the silence.

'We were going to war.

'... Inside the other planes I could see the glowing red tips of cigarettes as men puffed away. It was weirdly beautiful, lots of sparks and tracer shells. But I knew that between every tracer shell are four armour-piercing bullets. 'Let's go', shouted Lieutenant. Muir and we began moving in what seemed slow motion towards the open doorway as the green 'go' light spread a glow across our faces. (In the hours before D-Day we were given our objectives - capture the bridges over the rivers and canals around Carentan and secure the exits from 'Utah' Beach - and told to burn personal possessions like letters from home. There were bonfires across the camp. When the ashes could be raked out we used them to blacken our faces for the drops. We looked like raccoons. Several of the guys broke into the Al Jolson Mammy song which helped relieve the tension. Singing might have lightened the emotional burdens, but not the physical ones. If mules were the slave carriers of WW1 then the paratrooper of WW2 was its two-legged equivalent. Our equipment must have weighed over 100lbs). It seemed like forever but in fractions of seconds I was at the door and tumbling into space. Tracers were coming up towards me. As I checked the canopy above I hit the ground backwards so hard that I was stunned, unable to move.' [His aircraft had strayed off course and dropped them nine miles away near Ravenoville. In the light rain of that early morning he crawled on his belly across a field to a thicket…only to hear rustling]. 'I thought it was the enemy and I raised my rifle. Sweat was pouring off me. I knew I was about to kill a human being and it was a terrible thought. Suddenly this guy began crawling towards me. As my finger tightened on the trigger I recognized him as a pal called Hundly. His throat was so dry with fear he couldn't even speak!'

'[After surviving machine-gun strafes across the field from a gun hidden in a hedgerow, Don linked up with several other survivors to begin the march on Ravenoville]. There were about 200 Germans down one end of town and only 20 of us. They began hand-grenading civilian houses. I got a bead on one of them and squeezed. There was a slight vapour that came from his body. He buckled and went down. It was done and it didn't worry me. Another came around the corner. I aimed and shot him in the chest. He fell too. But they killed four of our guys from a heavy machine gun burst from a window in a house. The guys lay there in the front garden.

'The next day we began to march on our objectives but were halted by heavy German machine guns placed outside of town. Several times we tried to break through but were driven back. We decided to march the German prisoners on to the guns, figuring they wouldn't cut down their own. They did. As the Germans screamed, Nicht schiessen, Nicht schiessen, they were cut down. Then they made a break for it and we shot them down from the back. None survived.

'On the road to Carentan a Sherman tank used its tracks to run over three Germans in a fortified trench. Their screams could be heard above the engine's whine. Then we came into conflict with an SS battalion and mounted Cossacks [White Russians on horseback who had deserted Stalin to fight for Hitler]. On the outskirts of the town of Ste-Côme-du-Mont there was another vicious firefight in which the Germans were beaten back before launching an even more ferocious counter-attack. 'The roads, fields, ditches were littered with the dead. I nearly got it from a German except a medic with a long-barreled cowboy revolver got him first. I shot a blond-haired German crawling to a farmhouse to get more mortar shells to lob on to us. I saw his blond hair and it agitated me. Then the whole thing became clear to me: I wanted his scalp. I started crawling towards him. The prize was nearly within my reach when rifle fire opened up and I was forced to dive behind a hedgerow. Twice more I tried to reach him but each time I was driven back by stubborn square-heads. I decided to forget the whole thing. Finally a tank, one of ours, came by and raked the hedgerows with cannon and machine gun fire. When he was out of ammo he said he would be back for more. He took off down the road to make better time instead of crossing the fields. It was a mistake. A German 88 opened up and the tank started to burn. The crew were all killed, the commander burning alive in the turret. We called up artillery and those Germans were wasted in a rain of high explosive.

'The next day we were on the outskirts of Carentan and I was told to go back to regimental HQ with vital information on German positions that they didn't trust being radioed. I had to go back through the heaviest fighting had been the day before. The road was a river of gore. When I came to the end I felt as if I had left a world of darkness for a world of sunlight.'

'Crawling to investigate what lay behind a thick hedgerow I was confronted by a German lobbing a stick grenade into my face. I went after it to return it but it went off inches from my fingertips. It was an orange ball that gave off real furnace heat. I passed out. When consciousness came back I was stone deaf, but otherwise felt OK. I have heard that a person can be just the right place in an explosion and live. I must have found the right spot.

'I was walking to the rear with mortars still exploding around me. Shrapnel from an 88 went into my arm and ripped it open. I didn't lose a teaspoon of blood but my main artery was hanging out like a rubber tube, dangling there as I could put four fingers on the exposed bone.'

'D-Day was the most momentous time of my life. I killed so many Germans I lost count. Would I do it again? It's a hard question. Everyone loses in war, everyone. War isn't like the movies, never will be. It was dirty and de-humanising and disgusting. You never stopped for your buddies in the field, even your best pal. You stopped and they got a bead on you and you were next. You left them behind, dead, dying or just grazed. Hell, war is all politics anyway. We did it to each other because they made us. I just hope that when they make their fine speeches on the beachheads they remember what happened. I do. Every night of the year. The images of the dead always wake me up.'

19-year old Pfc Donald R. Burgett, Company 'A', 506th PIR, 101st 'Screaming Eagles' Division, who left for Normandy in a C-47 of the 439th Troop Carrier Group at Uppottery. *Currahee!* **was the only World War 2 book to be endorsed by General Eisenhower, who called it a 'fascinating tale of personal combat'. Burgett was dropped at less than 300 feet instead of the specified 600-700; the hedgehopping of the pilot 'to save his own ass' in Burgett's view meant that 17 men 'hit the ground before their chute had time to open. They made a sound like a large ripe pumpkin being thrown to burst against the ground... I hope that [dirty SOB pilot] gets shot down in the Channel and drowns,' he wrote bitterly.**

Paratrooper's Equipment

'I was wearing one suit of olive drab, worn underneath my jump suit... helmet, boots, gloves, main parachute, reserve parachute, Mae West, rifle, .45 automatic pistol, trench knife, jump knife, hunting knife, machete, one cartridge belt, two bandoliers, two cans of machine-gun ammo totalling 676 rounds of .30 ammo, 66 rounds of .45 ammo, one Hawkins mine capable of blowing off the tracks of a tank, four blocks of TNT, one entrenching tool with two blasting caps taped on the outside of the steel part, three first aid kits, two morphine needles, one gas mask, a canteen of water, three day's supply of K-rations, two day's supply of D-rations [hard tropical chocolate bars], six fragmentation grenades, one Gammon grenade, one orange smoke and one red smoke grenade, one orange panel, one blanket, one raincoat, one change of socks and underwear, two cartons of cigarettes and a few other odds and ends... Other things would be dropped in equipment bundles that we would pick up later on the ground. Torpedoes, extra bazooka rockets, machine-gun ammo, medical supplies, food and heavy explosives. When all the troops were aboard, a loudspeaker came on and the pilot read us a mimeographed message from the General wishing us Godspeed. A canteen cup of whisky would have been more appreciated....'

Pfc Donald R. Burgett, Company 'A', 506th Parachute Infantry, 101st Airborne Division. He was so weighted down that he had to be lifted bodily by two US Air Force men 'and who with much boosting and grunting shoved him into the C-47 where he pulled himself along with the aid of the crew chief and rode to France kneeling on the floor, which caused a journalist who was flying with the 506th to think that the men spent the crossing in prayer.'

American Paratroopers' Timeline

D-Day begins with an assault by more than 23,000 airborne troops, 15,500 of them American, behind enemy lines to soften up the German troops and to secure needed targets. The paratroopers know that if the accompanying assault by sea fails there will be no rescue. Departing from Portland Bill on the English Coast, 6,600 paratroopers of the 101st Division in 633 C-47s and 83 gliders and 6,396 paratroopers of the 82nd Division in 1,101 C-47s and 427 gliders are dropped over the neck of the Cotentin peninsula. (Force B of the 82nd Division has a strength of 3,871 glidermen).

Night-fighters sweep the way clear and heavy cloud covers the approach of the pathfinders shortly after midnight. They and the first flight of troop-carriers get through without serious difficulty, but later formations lose cohesion in the clouds and many aircraft drift off their courses. By the time they are clear of the cloudbank, the pilots are already approaching the dropping-zones in and beyond the Merderet Valley and it is too late for those who have gone astray to start searching for the pathfinders' beacons, some of which in any case have been set up in the wrong places. Consequently, when the parachutists were due to leap 'many planes were flying at excessive speeds and at altitudes higher than those ideal for jumping.' (After-Action Report, 82nd Airborne Division, June 1944).

The last of the airborne forces was dropped at **0404** hours and they were resupplied between 2053 and 2250 hours in the early evening of 6 June and **0700** to **0855** hours of 7 June by 408 tugs pulling 408 CG-4A and Horsa gliders, in 9 serials. CG-4As were used for night landings and 230 Horsa gliders were used when there was some light.

In total, including 20 Pathfinders, 1,656 sorties are flown; of which 822 are para-drop (of which 805 reach their dropping zone and 21 are lost) and 324 supply drop. 510 of the C-47s tow gliders (397 CG-4A plus 115 Horsa). 46 aircraft are lost (2.78 per cent) while 449 suffer damage. For such losses, 13,215 troops are dropped, with 223 artillery pieces and 1,641,448lbs of combat equipment and supplies. Gliders bring to their zones, 4,047 troops, 110 artillery pieces, 281 jeeps and 412,477lbs of combat equipment and supplies.

Anti-aircraft fire is generally ineffective, for the German guns are not laid by radar and out of 805 C-47 Skytrain aircraft over the Cotentin Peninsula this night, only 20 are lost. Thus Leigh-Mallory's worst fears are not realised, but aircraft losses are reduced only by the bad weather and the wild manoeuvres of the pilots, which combine to endanger and scatter the airborne troops. According to Major-General Maxwell Taylor, commanding the 101st, the anti-aircraft fire 'did have considerable volume and produced an unfortunate effect upon the pilots who had never seen action before.' (After-Action Report, 101st Airborne Division, June 1944). Their evasive tactics 'greatly increased the difficulty and hazard of jumping.' Only one sixth of the men in the 101st Division reach their destination points. Taylor's division was scattered over an area 25 miles by 15, with stray 'sticks' even farther afield. By dawn only 1,100 of his 6,600 parachutists have reached their rendezvous and 24 hours later he had collected less than 3,000. In his opinion, this inaccurate drop was partly due to 'the inadequate briefing of many individual pilots who could not reach their objective by their own pilotage.' Confused by the cloud, thrown off their course in evading the flak, they fly high and fast and spill their troops out of weaving aircraft with little idea where they might come to earth.

The first regiment of the 82nd Division fare better but the second suffer heavy supply losses and much of the division is left without sufficient arms. Major-General Matthew B. Ridgway's leading regiment has the advantage of surprise and three-quarters of the men land within three miles of the DZ. They rally quickly and form smaller improvised squads. By 04:30, two and a half hours after the main drop, the 82nd have taken Ste-Mère-Église, thus blocking the Cherbourg-Carentan road. But then their real difficulties began. Only 22 out of 52 gliders - carrying guns, transport and signals equipment - manage to find the LZ. The enemy forestalls their attempt to seize the bridges over the Merderet and so the division is split by an almost impassable belt of river and swamp.

West of the Merderet, only four per cent of the other two regiments are dropped accurately. The rest are scattered over the eastern half of the area garrisoned by the 91st Infantrie Division, which had been specially trained for anti-air-landing operations. One party of paratroops succeeds in ambushing and killing Generalleutnant Wilhelm Falley, commander of the 91st Luftlande (Anti-Airlanding) Division who is killed in his staff car. The Americans are so heavily engaged in fighting for survival that they cannot proceed to the execution of their principal tasks. Almost a third of each regiment come down east of the Merderet but the remainder, made up of small parties prevent the 91st Infantrie from counter-attacking the American beaches.

1300 101st Airborne Division link up with the US 4th Infantry Division beach landings at Pouppeville, the most southerly exit off 'Utah' Beach, just inland and next to the Vire river estuary.

1900 Merderet crossing at Chef du Pont controlled by 82nd Airborne Division. Elsewhere paratroops are so heavily engaged fighting for their lives they have no chance of blowing the bridges over the Douve or forming a compact bridgehead over the Merderet.

101st Division casualties total 1,240, of whom 182 are killed. 82nd Division suffers 1,259 casualties of whom 156 are killed. Of the 6,396 paratroopers of the 82nd who jumped, 272 or 4.24 per cent were killed or injured as a result of the drop. Of the 6,600 paratroopers of the 101st Division, only about 2,500 had assembled by the end of the first day.

Seventeen Transport Group C-47As are missing over France.

D-Day+1 The 82nd Airborne continues to assemble; re-organize and secure its area against extremely severe enemy resistance. Contact is made with the 4th Infantry Division in the course of the day and the 325th Glider Infantry arrives. Further resupply is carried out in the morning by 320 C-47s and C-53s but is not too successful. Many bundles of the mass drop fall in enemy territory while others fall in areas where it is most difficult to reach them.

By **D-Day+6** The 82nd has secured the area north of Ste-Mère-Église after fierce fighting on the part of the 505th Parachute Infantry with 2nd Battalion, 325th Glider infantry attached, then seizes LeHam and drives the enemy north. By this action, the 82nd Airborne Division considerably delays the German 243rd Infantry Division from contacting the Allied beach assault force.

'Up 21:03, 6 June; down 00:30, 7 June. R/V with transports about 8 miles south of Bill of Portland at 22:05, fighters at 3,000ft, transports at 600ft. Escorted to area over Ste-Mère-Église where gliders were released, at 22:55.Two gliders were observed to blow up on landing. Numerous parachutes seen on ground below. Left transports in this area at 23:05. One FW 190 observed north of Ste-Pierre-Église. Battle line appeared to extend along the railroad running northwest to southeast just west of Ste-Mère-Église. Areas inland from 'Utah' beach appeared flooded. Inaccurate light flak up to 4,000 feet with red, green, white and orange tracers in area between Carentan and Montebourg, believed to be from Allied troops. Observed numerous fires on ground in beach area. Weather at target 9/10 cumulus with base at 4,500ft, visibility poor.'

Report by 363rd Fighter-Bomber Group, XIX Tactical Fighter Command, which dispatched 50 Mustangs on a transport and glider escort mission to Ste-Mère-Église.

'We flew in a V of Vs, like a gigantic spearhead without a shaft. England was on double daylight saving time and it was still full light, but eastward, over the Channel, the skies were darkening. Two hours later, night had fallen and below us we could see glints of yellow flame from the German anti-aircraft guns on the Channel Islands. We watched them curiously and without fear, as a high-flying duck may watch a hunter, knowing that we were too high and far away for their fire to reach us. In the plane, the men sat quietly, deep in their own thoughts. They joked a little and broke, now and then, into ribald laughter. Nervousness and tension and the cold that blasted through the open door, had its effect upon us all. Now and then, a paratrooper would rise, lumber heavily to the little bathroom in the tail of the plane, find he could not push through the narrow doorway in his bulky gear and come back, mumbling his profane opinion of the designers of the C-47 airplane. Soon, the crew chief passed a bucket around, but this did not entirely solve our problem. A man strapped and buckled into full combat gear finds it extremely difficult to reach certain essential portions of his anatomy and his efforts are not made easier by the fact that his comrades are watching him, jeering derisively and offering gratuitous advice.

'Wing to wing, the big planes snuggled close in their tight formation, we crossed to the coast of France. I was sitting straight across the aisle from the door-less exit. Even at 1,500 feet, I could tell the Channel was rough, for we passed over a small patrol craft - one of the check-points for our navigators - and the light it displayed for us was bobbing like a cork in a mill-race. No lights showed on the land, but, in the pale glow of a rising moon, I could clearly see each farm and field below. And I remember thinking how peaceful the land looked, each house and hedgerow, path and little stream bathed in the silver of the moonlight. And I felt that if it were not for the noise of the engines we could hear the farm dogs baying and the sound of the barnyard roosters crowing for midnight.

'A few minutes inland, we suddenly went into cloud, thick and turbulent. I had been looking out the doorway, watching with a profound sense of satisfaction the close-ordered flight of that great sky caravan that stretched as far as the eye could see. All at once, they were blotted out. Not a wing light showed. The plane began to yaw and plunge and in my mind's eye I could see the other pilots, fighting to hold course, knowing how great was the danger of a collision in the air.

'You could read concern on the grim, set faces of the men in my plane as they turned to peer out of the windows, looking for the wink of the little lavender lights on the wing-tips of the adjoining planes. Not even our own wing lights showed in that thick murk. It was all up to the pilots now. There was nothing I could do and I did it. I pulled my seat belt tighter and sat back and closed my eyes, taking comfort from the words of Hal Clark, Commanding General of the Troop Carrier Wing, whose planes transported us.[29]

'Matt,' he had told me before the take-off, 'come hell or high wind, my boys will put you there, right on the button.'

'The cloud and rough air lasted only a few minutes, though it seemed far longer. As suddenly as we had entered the storm, we broke free. All at once, there was the moon again and clear skies and the sharp outlines of the land below, the little fields and hedgerows. But nowhere in the sky, in my field of vision, could I see another plane.

'It was too late now to worry about that. Beside the door, a red light glowed. Four minutes left. Down the line of bucket seats, the No. 4 man in the stick stood up. It was Captain Peter Schouvaloff, brother-in-law of Fëdor Chalipin, the opera singer. He was a get-rich-quick paratrooper, as I was, a man who had no formal jump training. I was taking him along as a language officer for he spoke both German and Russian and we knew that in the Cotentin peninsular which we were to seize, the Germans were using captured Russians as combat troops.

'A brilliant linguist, he was also something of a clown. Standing up, bewilderment on his face, he held up the hook on his static line – the life-line of the parachutist which jerks his canopy from its pack as he dives clear of the plane.

'Pray tell me,' said Schouvaloff, in his thick accent, 'what does one do with this strange device?'

That broke the tension. A great roar of laughter rose from the silent men who were standing now, hooked up and ready to go.

'Are we downhearted', somebody yelled.

'HELL NO!' came back the answering roar.

'A bell rang loudly, a green light glowed. The jumpmaster, crouched in the door, went out with a yell - 'Let's go!' With a paratrooper still laughing, breathing hard on my neck, I leapt out after him.

---

29 52nd Troop Carrier Wing at Cottesmore commanded by Brigadier General Harold L. Clark. General Ridgway would fly with the 315th Troop Carrier Group at Spanhoe.

'The shock of the opening was no worse than usual. I glanced up to see the most comforting of all sights, the spread of my canopy, round and bulging, full of air. Below me, off to the left, for a split second I could see the canopy of the jumpmaster hanging, seemingly motionless, in the dark. Then I was alone in the sky. I saw neither man nor parachute, though I knew that all around me troopers and bundles of heavy battle gear were floating swiftly down. In the stillness of the fall, I could hear far above me the roar of the engines as the following planes sped on to their drop-zones.

'All at once, the ground was very near and I flexed my knees for the shock of the landing. Weighted with his heavy battle gear, a combat paratrooper lands hard. He may strike swinging forward, or sideways, or backward and he absorbs the shock by doing a tumbler's roll, loose-jointed, with springy knees.

'I was lucky. There was no wind and I came down straight, into a nice, soft, grassy field. I rolled, spilled the air from my chute, slid out of my harness and looked around. As I hit, I grabbed for my pistol, for on the advice of the men who had jumped in Sicily, I had got nearly all the division equipped with .45 automatics. In your first moments on the ground, trussed in your tight harness, you are almost helpless. You can't possibly get to a rifle or a carbine and if somebody is after your scalp in these first seconds, you are in bad shape. But in the tussle to free myself from the harness, I had dropped the pistol and as i stooped to grope for it in the grass, fussing and fuming inwardly, but trying to be as quiet as possible, out of the corner of my eye I saw something moving. I challenged 'Flash', straining to hear the countersign, 'Thunder'.

'No answer came and as I knelt, still fumbling in the grass, I recognised in the dim moonlight the bulky outline of a cow. I could have kissed her. The presence of a cow in this field meant that it was not mined, nor staked with 'Rommel's asparagus'. In the days before the invasion, our intelligence agencies had received disquieting word about these fields. They were, we had been told, studded with sharp wooden stakes that would impale a paratrooper and rip the belly out of a glider. Wires connected the stakes, rigged up to mines and a man striking a stake would set off a chain of explosions. The presence of the cow meant that this field, at least, was free of these traps and, if this one was, perhaps the adjoining fields were also clear.

'I found the pistol and started creeping toward the shadows of the nearest hedgerow. Pale as the moonlight was, I felt conspicuous out there in the middle of that field, expecting at any moment to get a burst of small-arms fire. But at least if no friends were visible, neither were any foes and I felt a great exhilaration at being here alone in the dark on this greatest of adventures.

'As I moved cautiously toward the hedge, again I saw a movement in the shadows. I challenged and this time the proper response came back instantly. As I drew nearer, I saw a man lying on the ground in the shadows, his back against the bank on which the tall hedge grew.

'Who are you?' I said.

'Captain Follmer', a voice came back. I could hardly believe what I heard. In the fighting in Sicily, as I had moved out through no man's land, hunting my paratroopers who had dropped inland in front of the troops that were coming in by sea over the beaches, the first man I had found was Captain Willard Follmer. He was sitting under an olive tree, nursing an ankle he had injured badly in the jump. And here, a year later, out of 6,000 men, again my first encounter was with Follmer.

'Well, Follmer,' I asked, 'what's wrong this time?'

'General, I think I've broken my back.'

'Well,' I said, 'I guess you hope to God you never see me again.' [30]

'By now, all over the countryside around us, the Germans were beginning to rouse and shoot. The finest fireworks display I ever saw was going on all around me. Rockets and tracers were streaking through the air and big explosions were going off everywhere. Now and then, glancing up, I could see more C-47s going over, as the formation that had been scattered by the storm got back on course again. Low as they were, they were merely dark shadows against the sky, for a blacked-out plane is very difficult for a man on the ground to see. Even a paratrooper, coming down under a white canopy, is hardly visible until he hits the ground.

'All through the night, by twos and threes, the men in Vandervoort's battallion assembled. They came in slowly, for the clouds over the coast had scattered the formations widely. Many men had dropped in the middle of German concentrations and had been killed or captured. By daylight, though, Vandervoort had enough of his battalion together to move out, hunting the enemy and in the adjacent fields the fragments of two regiments - the 507th and 508th - were assembled, so that by mid-morning we were able to put up some semblance of a division action.

'My own little command group of 11 officers and men set up division headquarters in an apple orchard, on almost the exact spot we had planned to be before we left England. Hal Clark's boys had not failed us. They had put us down on the button.

'The Germans were all around us, of course, sometimes within 500 yards of my CP, but in the fierce and confused fighting that was going on all about, they did not launch the strong attack that could have wiped out our eggshell perimeter defence. This was in large part due to the dispersion of the paratroopers. Wherever they landed, they began to cut every communication line they could find and soon the German commanders had no more contact with their units than we had with ours. When the commander of the German 91st Luftlande Division, Generalleutnant Wilhelm Falley, found himself cut off from the elements of his command; he did the only thing left to do. He got in a staff car and went out to see for himself what the hell had gone on in this wild night of confused shooting. He never found out. Just at daylight, a patrol of paratroopers stopped his car and killed him as he reached for his pistol. The lieutenant commanding the patrol, Malcolm D. Brannen of the 508th, told me the story with great glee. 'Well,' I said, 'in our present situation, killing division commanders does not strike me as being particularly hilarious. But I congratulate you. I'm glad it was a German division commander you got.'

'For a while, had I thought about it, the chances were probably fair that I would suffer the same fate my German counterpart had met. We had nothing but hand weapons with which to defend ourselves: rifles, pistols, grenades and light 2.36-inch bazookas. The guns we desperately needed, the 57mm guns that could stop a tank, were to come in with the glider serials that were to bring 4,000 more men into the zone beginning with daylight. They came just as the first streaks of day began to show in the east, but the morning mist rising from the marshy land hung low over the hedgerows and many a glider was smashed on landing. The fragmentary news that was coming in was both good and bad. By daylight, the division's first objective, the town of Ste-Mère-Église, was in our hands and was never lost thereafter.'

---

30 Willard 'Bill' Follmer, Company 'G's Commander had broken his right hip.

Major General Matthew Bunker Ridgway, Divisional Commander of the 82nd, who had originally intended to land by glider in Normandy, but as D-Day approached he made a sudden decision to jump with his paratroopers. He had only made four training jumps in the past. In the Sicily invasion he came ashore in a landing craft and it is generally believed that he later regretted that he did not jump with his men. His staff got him a parachute and took it back to his house in Leicester where they fitted him out in the privacy of his quarters because he did not want anybody else to see this. Ridgway, who carried a grenade attached to his webbing and a Springfield rifle of World War One vintage, chose to jump with the 505th flying from Spanhoe. He was put in the 'stick' of Captain Talton 'Woody' Long who commanded the 505th HQ Company. It was Long's job to brief Ridgway on the operation. 'It was a rather demanding experience for a young Captain. However, General Ridgway sat there intently following every detail of my briefing. I don't think those piercing eyes left me once. Afterwards, he graciously thanked me and made some comment about seeing me on the ground.'

At the end of the day Ridgway watched his men bury their dead colleagues in temporary shallow graves. With the grim task completed, Ridgway walked back to contemplate the mounds of earth 'where so many of my boys lay,' and saw that little children from the nearby villages had picked wild flowers and were placing them in bunches on the still moist earth. 'I was so overcome that I wept,' confessed the General.' [31]

'As we moved forward we came across parachute equipment, some loose, some in bundles still unopened and a few opened with part of the load removed-part still there. From one bundle we took a bazooka and twelve rockets. We exchanged an M-1 rifle which had a snapped stock - a casualty of the jump for this bazooka. Over more hedges, always bearing to the North we went. All of a sudden we came upon a trail on which were two tents and two motor cycles. We found, after a close and careful investigation, being ever on the alert for booby traps and hidden alarms, that there was nobody there and that it was the CP (Command Post) of some officer of the German army. We destroyed the motorcycles immediate use by slashing all tires and turned the contents of the CP into a pile in the centre of the tent. We then left, continuing on the trail towards a large stone house further along the trail and across a field. Across this field and another road we ran into Lieutenant Harold Richard, Company 'A', 508th Parachute Infantry and his communications sergeant, Sergeant Hall. We were well acquainted, having served together since the activation of the Regiment at Camp Blanding, Florida. It was nice being with two more of our regiment and we were glad to have met at this time. After a conference we decided to ask directions at the large stone farmhouse mentioned above, which was about fifty yards away, we had about 12 enlisted men and two officers in our party now. We split up and surrounded the house. Richard, one enlisted man and I pounded on the door of the house. In a few seconds a very excited Frenchman came rushing or gushing is more like it, out of the door. Several other occupants of the house were looking out of windows on the ground floor as well as from windows on the upper stores of the house. By using our French Guide book and maps we found that

31 *Put On Your Boots and Parachutes!:The United States 82nd Airborne Division* written and edited by Deryk Wills (self published, March 1992).

we were between Picauville and Etienville. Good! We were about midway between the two places and now had a definite location from which we could plan on future moves to get with our own troops. In the house the upstairs windows were alive with little kiddos, wild eyed at seeing the American uniforms instead of the usual German ones. 'I said, 'Here comes a car - stop it!' Lieutenant Richard moved out of the door way towards the side of the house and some of the men went to the stone wall at the end of the house. The house doors shut and I went to the road and put my hand up and yelled, 'Stop!' But the car came on faster. When the car went by me I ran to the other side of the road and I guess that all of us fired at the car at the same time as a dozen or more shot rang out and I, on the far side of the road, found myself in line of fire from the others in our group. I fell to the road and watched the car as it was hit by many shots and saw the car crash into the stone wall and possibly the side of the house as the driver lost control of the car as he slouched in the front seat trying to avoid being hit by the bullets that filled the air around the car. The car was full of bullet holes and the windshield was shattered. The chauffeur, a German corporal, was thrown from the front seat of the car and was trying to hide in a cellar window, or trying to gain entrance into the cellar of the house, but couldn't make it. An officer sitting on the front seat of the car was found later, slumped onto the floor with his head and shoulders hanging out the open front door, dead. The other occupant of the car, who had been riding in the back seat of the Mercedes Phaeton, was in the middle of the road crawling towards a Luger pistol that had been knocked from his grasp when the car hit the stone wall and house. I had crossed the road after the car sped past me as I tried to halt its forward progress, climbed upon a hedge row six or more feet above the road bed and had a perfect view of the immediate situation, including the road, the house, the car and the personnel - German, French and American.

'From my position above the dusty, dirty road I saw the German Corporal trying to escape by crawling into the cellar of the house and I fired my .45 Colt pistol at him - grazing his shoulder and saw him sit down beside the house, where our enlisted men attended his slight wound.

'I also watched a German officer crawling in the road towards his Luger lying in the road several feet in front of his position. He looked at me as I stood on the hedge above him and 15 feet to his right and as he inched closer and closer to his weapon he pleaded to me in German and also saying in English, 'Don't kill, Don't kill.' I thought, 'I'm not a cold hearted killer, I'm human - but if he gets that Luger, it is either him or me or one or more of my men'. So I shot! He was hit in the forehead and never knew it. He suffered none. The blood spurted from his forehead about six feet high and, like water in a fountain when it is shut off, it gradually subsided. Upon examining the personnel that we had encountered we found that we had killed a Major and a Major General (later learned that he was a Lieutenant General) and had as a captive, a corporal, whom we made carry two brief cases that were full of official papers that we had found in the car and our intention was to turn the papers in to our headquarters when we rejoined the 508th Parachute Infantry Regiment.

'As we left the scene, I tore the General's hat apart, looking for further identification of name or unit to which he was assigned. I found only a name printed in it. The name was 'Falley'. I thought, 'I have a Steve Fallet in my light machine gun platoon'.

1st Lieutenant Malcolm D. Brannen, HQ Company, 3rd Battalion, 508th Parachute Infantry Regiment.

'All went well until arriving near the DZ 'O'; the C-47s did not slow up for the drop. Everyone in the Second Battalion agreed that it was the highest, fastest jump ever made. Eyeballs had to be screwed back into their sockets. The Second Battalion landed on or near the DZ. Except for one stick from Company 'F' and they headed for the centre of Ste-Mère-Église.'

Don McKeage of Company 'F', 505th Parachute Infantry Regiment, 101st 'Screaming Eagles' Division. In the first few minutes low cloud obscured the target areas and the Second Platoon mortar squad of Company 'F', 505 mistimed their exit and landed in the Square of Ste-Mère-Église. Thirty minutes before, two sticks of the 101st Airborne's 506th Parachute Infantry Regiment had jumped across the east side of the town. The German guards killed four and this alerted them to the 505 error.

'We were about four hundred feet up and I could see fires burning and Krauts running about. There seemed to be total confusion on the ground. All hell broken loose. Flak and small arms fire was coming up and those poor guys were caught right in the middle of it.'

Lieutenant Charles Santarsiero, 506th Parachute Infantry Regiment, 101st US Airborne, standing in the door of his plane as it passed over Ste-Mère-Église.

Private David Webster, Easy Company, 101st Airborne Division whose objective was to eliminate the German infantry company at Ste-Marie-du-Mont, as well as the platoon on the gun batteries at Ste-Martin-de-Varreville.
'I fell a hundred feet in three seconds, straight toward a huge flooded area shining in the moonlight. I thought I was going to fall all the way, but there was nothing I could do about it except dig my fingers into my reserve and wait to be smashed flat. I should have counted one-thousand, two-thousand, three-thousand - the general would have had me shout 'Bill Lee', but that was expecting too much - and yet all I could do was gape at the water.

'Suddenly a giant snapped a whip, with me on the end, my chute popped open and I found myself swinging wildly in the wind. Twisted in the fall, my risers were unwinding and spinning me around. They pinned my head down with my chin on the top of my rifle case and prevented me from looking up and checking my canopy. I figured that everything was all right, because at least I was floating free in the great silence that always followed the opening shock.

'For several seconds, I seemed to be suspended in the sky, with no downward motion and then all at once, the whole body of water whirled and rushed up at me.

'Jesus, I thought, I'm going to drown.

'I wrenched desperately at my reserve-chute's snap fasteners as the first step in preparing for a water landing. I also had to undo two leg snaps, my chest buckle and the bellyband. The next step would have been to drop the reserve and work myself into the seat of my harness, so that I could fling my arms straight up and drop from the chute when I was ten feet above the water. I didn't even have time to begin the procedure.

'We had jumped so low - about three hundred feet, instead of the scheduled seven hundred - that while I was still wrenching at the first reserve snap, I saw the whole immense sheet of water rushing up at me twenty feet below. I've had it, I thought. That goddam Air Corps. I reached up, grasped all four risers and yanked down hard, to fill the canopy with air and slow my descent. Just before I hit, I closed my eyes and took a deep breath of air. My feet splashed into the water.

'I held my breath, expecting to sink over my head and wondering how I was going to escape from my harness underwater - and hit bottom three feet down. My chute billowed away from me in the light wind and collapsed on the surface. I went to work to free myself from my gear. Immensely relieved at the safe landing, I undid the reserve and discarded it, yanked loose the bellyband, unsnapped the leg straps and chest buckle, detached my rifle case and let the harness sink into the swamp. I was on my own at last.

'The silence ended abruptly with a long, ripping burst, burrrrrrrrp; that made me look around in fright.

'That's a German machine gun I told myself. They've seen me. The bullets cracked and popped in the air above and as I stared open-mouthed and paralysed with fright, I saw whip-like tracers darting at me from some far-off place. I dropped to my knees in the cold, black water, which tasted old and brackish, as if it had lain still for a long time and passively waited to be killed.

'Somebody wants to kill me, I thought. So this is what war is really like? I couldn't believe that somebody wanted to kill me. What had I done to them?

'I wanted to go up to them and tell them that I didn't want to kill anybody, that I thought the whole war was a lot of malarkey. 'I don't want to hurt anybody', I would say. All I ask of the world is to be left alone.

'The machine gun fired again, a longer burst that held me motionless. It was like a bad dream.

'I shook my head to make sure it was true and it was. The bullets were not in my imagination; they were real and they were seeking me out to kill me. The gunners wouldn't even let me get close enough to talk it over with them. They wanted to kill me right here in the swamp.

'The machine gun searched the area again. Far off in the night, others burped and spluttered. Enemy rifles added their popop ...pop...popopop.

'I waited about five minutes for someone to walk up and kill me and then my courage returned when I noticed that the shooting was all quite far away. I rose from the water, assembled my rifle and loaded it and rammed on my bayonet. I was ready to go. 'Burp...burrrrp...burrp... crackle-crackle-crackle...popop...burp... popopop.

'Lost and lonely, wrestling with the greatest fear of my life, I stood bewildered in the middle of a vast lake and looked for help.

'I shivered convulsively and started to cry, then thought better of it. The hell with everything! I'm here for keeps; make the best of it. At least I can try to get out of this swamp before sunrise.

'I took the little brass compass from my pocket and looked at it in the next spell of moonlight. The needle was frozen in position. I shook the compass and cursed and, holding it close, saw that it was filled with water. 'Sonofabitch,' I hissed, throwing it away. A wise-guy probably made a fortune off those compasses in the States. And now men will die because somebody gypped the government and made a fortune. Sonsofbitches.

'A flare burst over the water several hundred yards away. I bowed my head and waited for the bullets to hit me like a baseball bat, but there were no bullets. The flare died out with the afterglow of a burnt match and I looked around in the moonlight. I sought an orchard, three white lights, a crossroads village named Hébert, five hundred men from the 2nd Battalion and all I saw was water and flares and tracers. I listened for our bugle call and all I heard was enemy rifle and machine-gun fire.

'Suddenly the whole thing struck me as ludicrous: the preparations and briefings, all the maps and sand tables. For all the good they did, the Army might as well have yanked us out of a pub and dumped us off helter-skelter to find our own way to the Germans. Instead of a regiment of over 1,500 men carefully assembled on a well-defined drop zone, D-Day was one man alone in an old swamp that the Air Corps said didn't even exist.'

The Ste-Martin-de-Varreville battery consisted of four 122 mm guns in open emplacements. It was shelled by HMS *Hawkins* **and taken from an inland assault by paratroopers of the 101st Airborne Division soon afterwards. The battery crew (1/HKAR 1261) were billeted in about a dozen nearby houses, some of them quite large with many rooms. Staff Sergeant Summers of the 502nd Parachute Infantry attacked these one by one and mostly single-handedly, save for the occasional assistance of one or two other paratroopers, over a period of several hours, killing about 50 of the enemy and capturing another 50 or so. No doubt this act, which merited the award of the Medal of Honor (he received the Distinguished Service Cross) helped the battery to surrender.**

'At 4am there was a knock at the door. When I opened it, two Americans walked in. They pulled a printed message in French from their helmets, which read 'My comrade is wounded. Please help.' They led me to a para with a broken leg and we carried him to my house. By dawn we had found another six. For two weeks they hid in my attic, but then the Germans came to arrest me. Someone had informed on me. An Austrian captain interrogated me. He knew who I was but protected me by pretending I was someone else. He told me, 'If we find the owner of this farmhouse he will be shot.' He saved my life by letting me escape. That night my wife and I crossed the German lines, got through an American minefield and were taken directly to American HQ. I warned them my farm was a German base and asked them to shell it. Half an hour later there was nothing left of my house... and nothing left of the Germans.'

Pierre Huet, a farmer living with his young wife in Prétot near Ste-Mère-Église.

'Alerte! A great number of low-flying planes fly over the town - shaving the roof-tops, it is like a thunderous noise, suddenly, the alarm is given; there is a fire in town. In the meantime the Germans fire all they can at the planes. We go into hiding, what is going on? Thousands of paratroopers are landing everywhere amid gunfire... We are all huddled in M. Besselievre's garage with our friends. Our liberators are here! It is real hell all over with the firing of guns, machine guns and artillery. Around 3 am we risk a peek to see what is going on. The Americans are the only ones in the streets of the town, there are no more Germans. It is an indescribable joy. I was never so happy in all my life.'

André Mace.

'We were about 400 feet up and I could see fires burning and Krauts running about. There seemed to be total confusion on the ground. All hell broken loose. Flak and small-arms fire was coming up and those poor guys were caught right in the middle of it.'

Lieutenant Charles Santarsiero of the 506th Regiment, 101st Airborne Division, standing in the door of his plane as it passed over Ste-Mère-Église.

British manned Sherman tanks await the off at Gosport on 3 June.

A GI with full kit and
machine gun climbs
aboard a C-47

British commandoes with bicycles set off to board their transport to a south coast port.

Passing is such sweet sorrow: *Sorry Joan Had To Go - Johnny.*

Wrecked railway line in Normandy.

Opposite page: British soldiers hold up their mugs and give thumbs up before leaving for Normandy.

Brigadier General 'Slim' Jim Gavin (right), assistant division commander, 82nd Airborne. Gavin, an orphan who joined the Army as a Private in 1924 and who was nicknamed 'Slim Jim' by his men because of his slim, boyish looks, assumed command of the 82nd Airborne on 15 August 1944 at the age of 37, the youngest American division commander in WWII and the youngest since the Civil War. (US Army via Deryk Wills)

A Horsa in Normandy after landing near a French road.

A British 6th Air Landing Brigade jeep passing a wrecked Horsa glider on the evening of 6 June.

Second Lieutenant James J. Coyle, a platoon Leader in Company 'E', 505th Parachute Infantry Regiment, 82nd Airborne Division. (US Army via Deryk Wills)

Paras unload a Horsa glider affectionately known as *'Charlie's Aunt'*.

A wounded GI on a stretcher evacuated from Normandy by the 313th Troop Carrier Group is taken away for medical treatment after arriving back at Grantham. (D. Benfield)

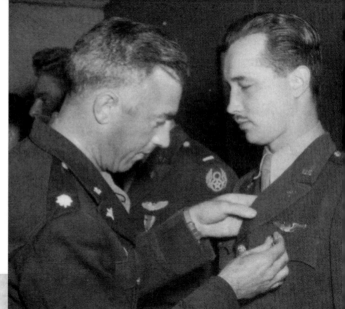

Lieutenant Colonel Clarence A. Shoop (left), a Lockheed test pilot, who had been flying with the 55th Fighter Group while in England reviewing and making modifications to P-38 aircraft. He was given orders to report to 8th Air Force HQ on 5 June where he learned that he was to take over the 7th Photo Group. (USAF)

Colonel Wilson Wood, CO, 323rd Bomb Group at Earl's Colne, Essex. On D-Day 'Wood's Rocket Raiders' flew three 18-plane formations instead of the usual 36 to bomb targets near the beach-head. (USAF)

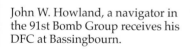
John W. Howland, a navigator in the 91st Bomb Group receives his DFC at Bassingbourn.

GIs treat injured French children in the battle area near Utah Beach. The little girl, Genevieve Marie was wounded in an attack on a gun battery near the beach on the night of 5/6 June. (US Navy)

375th Fighter Squadron , 361st Fighter Group Mustangs at Bottisham led by the Group CO, Colonel Thomas J. J. Christian in Lou IV IV/Athlene. The second P-51D in the formation is E2-S, being flown by the Group's third-ranking ace, 1st Lieutenant Urban Drew. (via Tom Cushing)

Robert 'Punchy' Powell, pilot, P-51B Mustang West "by Gawd", 352nd Fighter Group at Bodney, Norfolk

P-47D Thunderbolts of the 82nd Fighter Squadron, 78th Fighter Group. (USAF)

B-26 Marauders of the 599th Bomb Squadron, 397th Bomb Group (Medium) at Rivenhall on a bombing sortie.

British paras with their RAF flight crew.

GIs line up ready to depart in their Waco glider for Normandy.

B-24 Liberators of the 487th Bomb Group at Lavenham, Suffolk taxi out on D-Day.

Loading stores aboard a USAAF IX Troop Carrier Command C-47 at Spanhoe. (R. Baker via D. Benfield)

Opposite page: Two German soldiers pass a wrecked Allied glider in a field in Normandy.

B-26 Marauder 42-96078 *Slightly Dangerous of* the 599th Bomb Squadron, 397th Bomb Group, which was destroyed a few days after D-Day. (USAF)

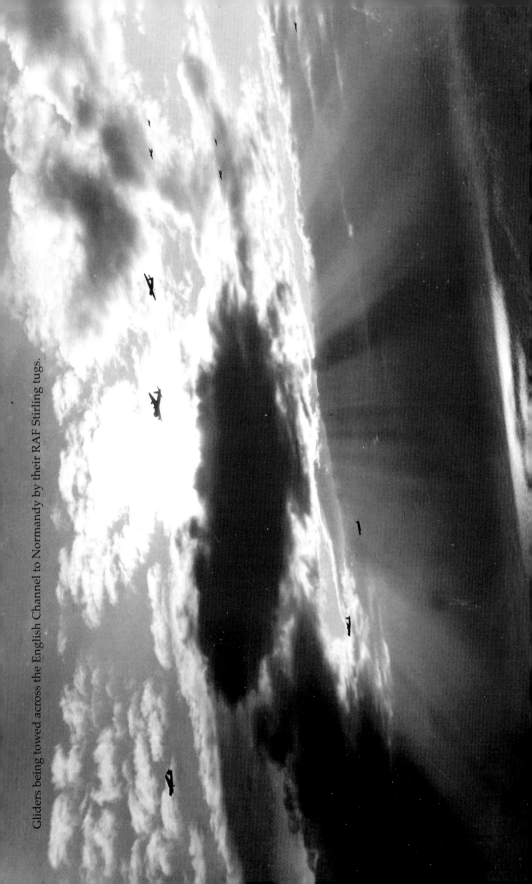

Gliders being towed across the English Channel to Normandy by their RAF Stirling tugs.

Bazooka

Commonly known among US troops as the 'Bazooka' after the wind instrument played by Bob Burns, an American comedian in the 1940s, the 2.36 inch Rocket Launcher M1A1, or the later two-piece M9, was based on a pre-war, shoulder-fired recoilless weapon. A trigger produced an electric impulse that fired a 3.4lb fin-stabilized rocket. The development of shaped charged warheads turned the rocket launcher into a potent tank-killing weapon for the infantry. The launcher was 5 feet long, had an effective range of about 450 feet and the warhead could penetrate up to 8 inches of armour at 90°. The launcher could also fire HE and White Phosphorus rockets. As a rocket weapon it had a low muzzle velocity of 270feet/second. During WWII, 476,628 Bazookas and 15,603,000 rockets were produced.

'A fire broke out in a house at about 10pm (midnight British time). A German sergeant gave Mayor Alexandre Renaud permission to rouse the populace and for Abbé Roulland to ring the church bell. The people set up a bucket brigade in the light of the flames. As they were fighting the fire, American planes appeared low overhead, so low that I could see their open doors. Paratroopers began jumping out by the hundreds. I saw one paratrooper drop on the road, but a German killed him before he could get untangled from his parachute. Another was killed near me. I will never forget the sight. After the parachute jump, as I was coming back in the darkness from the house which had burned in the square, we found in the middle of the street, twenty metres from our home, a parachutist of the 82nd Airborne who appeared dead. We carried him a few metres away to the edge of the square and covered him with 'his parachute. The next morning I was amazed to discover that there was no body under the parachute. Nearby a parachutist was sitting on the steps of a truck left behind by the Germans the night before. He spoke French and told me he was from Louisiana. I told him that the night before we had carried one of his friends who had been killed. He burst out laughing and told me that it was him. He had been wounded in the shoulder by a bullet and that he had shammed death in order not to be killed by the Germans. When he heard us coming, without knowing if we were French or German, he kept playing dead. We spoke a long time together and I did not see him again.'

20-year-old Frenchman Raymond Paris, who lived in Ste-Mère-Église. M. Alexandré Renaud was proprietor of the chemist's shop in the Place de L' Église. A veteran of the great days of the French army, he was proud to have fought at Verdun. The house that was on fire was M. Hairon's villa on the opposite side of the square. Renaud had dressed quickly and leaving his wife Simone to look after their three children he crossed the familiar square, beneath the chestnut and lime trees in front of the church. Nobody knew how the fire had started. It might have been just an accident, but the sky was full of aircraft and it seemed more likely that a flare had fallen on the roof, which was well alight. The firemen in their bright brass helmets were trying to save the thatch of a barn nearby which was threatened by sparks and volunteers were carrying water in canvas buckets from the pump in the cattle market. Renaud joined them. He remembered that the aeroplanes cast 'great shadows on the ground and red lights seemed to be glowing inside them'. He watched a paratrooper plunge into a tree 15 yards from him and almost immediately, as he tried frantically to get out of his harness 'about half a dozen Germans emptied their sub-machine

guns into him and the boy hung there with his eyes open, as though looking down at his own bullet holes.' The flames lit up the bell-tower of the church, where German machine-gunners, posted on the roof, were shooting aimlessly at the aircraft overhead, filling the sky with arches of tracer bullets. Other men of the anti-aircraft unit, waiting the order to fire, watched the firemen from their positions in the square.

'The church bell continued to ring, urgently and quickly: the tocsin, the ancient signal of alarm. M. Renaud stopped on his way to the pump, with a new clutch at the heart as he asked himself what more disaster the clamour of the bell fore-told. He instinctively looked up towards the tower and so he saw what was coming: low over the rooftops and the trees, almost in silence, a host of aircraft sweeping across the town, their lights burning, their wings and bodies black against the moon; and then as the first of the waves of them receded, the giant confetti which drifted in their wake. M. Renaud and the firemen stood amazed, neglecting the fire, unable to believe that the thing which they had thought about so long was really happening and was happening in Ste-Mère-Église itself. High up, the parachutes were seen in silhouette against the sky; as they fell, the men on them were also seen, in the light of the fire. The machine-gunners on the church tower and in the square saw them too and fired lower. The watchers, horrified, saw the convulsion of a man who was shot as he was falling. They saw a parachute which draped an old tree: the parachutist began to climb down; the machine-gunners saw him and left him swinging limply in his harness. They also saw a man fall into the fire and crash through the burning roof. Sparks spurted out and the flames blazed up afresh. More squadrons of planes were passing over: the bell still ringing; shots cracking through the square. The German soldiers ordered the Frenchmen indoors and M. Renaud, anxious for his wife and children, hurried home. A German beneath the trees, pointing at the body of a parachutist, shouted to him with satisfaction: 'Tommies - all kaput.'
    Dawn Of D-Day. [32]

'I jumped with the Second Platoon. It was commanded by Second Lieutenant Harold Cadish. I don't remember all the stick in our plane but I know Private H. T. Bryant, Private Ladislaw 'Laddie' Tlapa and Lieutenant Cadish were most unfortunate. They were the fellows who were shot on the power poles. My close friend Pfc Charles Blankenship was shot still in his chute, hanging in a tree, a little distance down the street. When we jumped there was a huge fire in a building in town. I didn't know that the heat would suck a parachute towards the fire. I fought the chute all the way down to avoid the fire. Facing the church from the front, I landed on the right side of the roof, luckily in the shadow side from the fire. Some of my suspension lines went over the steeple and I slid down over to the edge of the roof. This other trooper came down and really got entangled on the steeple. I didn't know it was Steele. Almost immediately a Nazi soldier came running from the back side of the church shooting at everything. Sergeant John Ray had landed in the churchyard almost directly below Steele. This Nazi shot him in the stomach while he was still in his chute. While Ray was dying he somehow got his 45 out (Sergeants jumped with a 45-calibre pistol) and shot the Nazi in the back of the head killing him. He saved my life as well as Steele's. It was one of the bravest things I have ever witnessed.

32 By David Howarth (The Companion Book Club 1959).

'I finally got to my trench knife and cut my suspension lines and fell to the ground. I looked up at the steeple but there was not a movement or a sound and I thought the trooper was dead. I got my M-1 assembled and ducked around several places in that part of town hoping to find some troopers, but all of them were dead. I got off several rounds at different Germans before they drove me to a different position with intense gunfire.'

Private Ken Russell, Company 'F', 505th Parachute Infantry Regiment. Van Holsbeck died falling into the house, which was on fire on the south side of the town square. The Germans allowed the villagers, under guard, to break the curfew to fight it.

'It was a very secret mission and at one time we were prepared to board the aircraft on 5 June and then they sent us back because of the weather and then on 6 June... sometime around midnight of 5 June, we boarded the aircraft and took off for Normandy... It was a full moon night when we left England. You could see the fighter aircraft all around the plane until we finally hit the coast of Normandy and all of a sudden it was just black. I thought it was cloud but it was smoke from German ack-ack fire and I believe our plane was hit two or three times, it was shaking all over and I was scared to death.

'We were wearing the authorised American jump suit which consisted of a jacket and a pair of pants with many, many large pockets... and we had a main chute and a reserve chute and about everything else you can imagine we carried into battle. We even carried land mines in on our persons, grenades... the only place we could find to put our gas mask was the bottom part of a leg and it was the first thing we got rid of when we hit the ground. We were so heavily loaded that the crew chief on the plane had to come around individually and pull each man up. He couldn't rise up by himself. We had twelve men on each side I believe and we had a cable going through the aircraft and we used static line. When the red light came on it meant stand up and hook up and then we would wait for the green light to go on and when that went on the first in line on the door side went out. Each person should check the man in front but on the Normandy jump I don't think anyone checked anything we were all so... in a big hurry to get out of the plane.'

Trooper Howard 'Goody' Goodson. Company 'I', 3rd Battalion, 505th Parachute Infantry Regiment, 82nd Airborne Division, who dropped near Ste-Mère-Église.

'I honestly don't remember the opening shock. I remember the sky was being criss-crossed with tracer bullets and flak. The noise was terrible. I looked down and immediately went into a state of shock. I was over water. My first thought was that that SOB pilot had dropped us over the English Channel. I looked to my right and saw a herd of dairy cows grazing. About that time I landed in water up to my chest. I was in a salt marsh. It seemed like an eternity before I could get out of my harness and wade to dry land. All this time, the gunfire was deafening and the planes kept going over. I saw one plane take a direct hit and explode in mid-air. Every man in that plane died a quick and merciful death.

'I was only able to find one other man from my stick. We picked up another stray paratrooper and went off in search of a fight. We had no idea where we were and which way to go. After checking our compass, we decided to crawl towards a hedgerow approximately a hundred yards west. As we crawled up to the hedgerow, we could see a sunken road on the other side. Then we heard voices - German voices. It was a patrol of about fifteen or twenty soldiers approaching from the south. Can you believe that the German patrol was marching in formation? After whispered conversation, we decided that each of us would throw a grenade at the same time and then take off north at top speed. As they drew abreast of us, we each pulled a pin and threw our grenades. The three grenades exploded at the same time and then we took off. After running for about 150 yards, we came under machine-gun fire and had to go to ground. We could hear the screams and moans back down the road, but didn't go back to finish off the survivors.

'For the next hour, we crawled up and down hedgerows, looking for some of our buddies. Machine-gun and rifle fire was all around us. You could tell the difference between German and American machine gun, because the German machine guns fire at a much more rapid rate. We finally located two more troopers and were shocked to find out they were from the 82nd Airborne which was supposed to land ten to fifteen miles west of us. Then we realized there were American paratroopers scattered over many, many square miles.

'As it began to get light, we found three more from my platoon. We started moving west and shot three Germans who had been sleeping in a barn. Up ahead of us we could see a familiar church steeple. We knew that we were approaching Ste-Marie-du-Mont. Then we ran into a group from my company. We must have had a force of about seventy-five men in all, a general hodge-podge of people from the 506th, 502nd and a few from the 82nd. We had no idea how many Germans were in the town, but our training paid off. We played the leapfrog by squads as we moved into the town. One squad would dash forward, while the other squad provided covering fire. A machine gun was on each flank, also giving covering fire. Two fellas with a bazooka dashed down the street, stopped, aimed and blew the front door off the church. Shortly after that a white flag appeared and a dozen German soldiers surrendered. We cleared the town in less than an hour. We found one of our buddies hanging in a tree. His parachute got caught in a tree and he was still in his harness.

'A lieutenant and two GIs found a battery of three 88s about a thousand yards east of town. Two of their guns had been wrecked. The third one was still serviceable. They turned the gun around and sighted on the church tower. One round was fired and the church tower disappeared with all the snipers. In the meantime, we had found two equipment bundles in a pasture outside of town and we replenished our supply of ammo and grenades.

'The naval bombardment had long since stopped and we were wondering about the beach, the beach named 'Utah'. Colonel Sink, our regimental commander, finally arrived in a Jeep. He conferred with Colonel Turner, our battalion commander and soon learned that the beach people were finally making their way inland.'

Robert Flory, 506th Parachute Infantry Regiment, 101st Airborne.

'It was 22:00 in the evening of June 5 and it was nearly time to go. The officers and men of our First Platoon joined hands and prayed that God guide us. I took my 'stick' of 18 men· on to the aircraft. Our equipment was so abundant and binding that we could scarcely move. We took off just after 22:30 and all the planes circled above the airfield and waited, then began forming up in Vs. It took us an hour to get into formation. The

V was so perfect that I could have pitched a grenade at the plane just outside the open cargo door of the C-47. Then our formation turned inland and the sky erupted in fireworks - flak. All around my plane the others were jinking and diving, but my pilot - I never did learn his name - flew the course without a tremor. He flew directly into a fogbank and all the other planes disappeared. When we came out of the fog, we were all alone.

'I stood at the cargo door with the equipment bundle of machine gun and ammunition, ready to kick it out when the jump light came on. I saw the proper landmarks come up, but felt no tap from the No 2 jumper, Private Thurman Day, or from Sergeant Adams. Then I saw the ground disappear and then whitecaps - we were back over the sea.

'Private Day pulled me back from the door and shouted that the pilot wanted to see me. He looked worried. 'Lieutenant', he said, 'we missed the drop zone and are over the Channel, headed back to England. What shall we do? I told him to take us to land and we'd get out. The pilot dived, came around and headed for the French shore again. He took us down just above the waves to evade the flak and as the plane reached the shoreline, he put it into a climb so steep that it threw several men off their feet.

'I decided it was now or never. I pushed out the equipment bundle, hooked up my chute ring and followed. I was jerked by the ring and my parachute opened automatically just before I hit the ground.

'After I landed hard, I cut myself loose from the parachute. I found the equipment chute in a low tree, a part of one of the Normandy hedgerows - thick, nearly impenetrable lines of trees and bushes. I pulled the red light attached to the pack, which was showing clearly and pulled it down and turned it off. Then I pulled out my carbine. I crawled into a hedgerow and waited and listened. Finally Private Day came up.

'We had no idea where we were. I pulled out my flashlight and map. I studied the map but could not find any points of terrain that matched - we'd obviously jumped off the map. We waited some time, but no-one else showed up and we decided we'd better take the machine gun and two boxes of ammunition out of the bundle and head south. After about half a mile, we were exhausted and had to stash the gun and ammo.

'Finally we met up with some other troopers and I really felt as if I had an army, with the 34 men I collected. Soon we approached a village and saw a light in a house on the outskirts. The others surrounded the house while I went to the door and knocked. A woman came to the door and as she opened it. I could see another woman sitting at a table in the kitchen; three empty chairs, bread on the table and two bottles of wine. The woman was not very friendly and she seemed monstrously stupid, but she told me we were in Foucarville, near the fourth causeway that led the beach road - about three miles from 'Utah' beach and about ten miles northwest of Ste-Côme-du-Mont, where I thought I could find some of my battalion. I asked the woman the way and she didn't understand, or said she didn't. I repeated my question. She became sullen and when I told her I was an American paratrooper, her eyes widened and she shouted something and tried to run out the door. I stuck my carbine in her belly and she stopped. I didn't know if she was a German collaborator, or just frightened. I told her to sit down at the table and when she did not, I went out, closed the door firmly and motioned to the men to come with me, back to the road. We had just rounded the bend when we ran into our first enemy fire. Had there been men in the farmhouse and had they run off to warn the Germans? A burst from a German light machine gun swept over the road. It sounded like someone tearing paper. We dropped and crawled off the road to the left and moved into a field of grain. The noise started up again.

'I got up and started to run. I saw a ditch ahead and got ready to jump it. Just then, a German soldier stood up in the ditch and raised his hands. I could not understand what he was saying. Private Nick Denovchik came up and said the German was speaking Polish, which he understood. They began to talk and the firing suddenly stopped. They must have decided that we had moved on.

'The Polish German told Denovchik that he and his buddy were manning an aircraft listening station. He shouted and his buddy stood up about 50 yards away. After some more talk, they led us to a pillbox buried underground in a grove of trees, in which was a big radio set and enough ammo to withstand a minor siege.

'The two prisoners helped us destroy the listening device, four large instruments perfectly camouflaged in the trees. We blew up the ammo dump and wrecked the radio. We accepted these two soldiers as our allies and they showed us the way to the causeway. We were still a long way from our assigned objective, the locks of the Douves. It was nearly time for the troops to be landing on 'Utah' Beach, I could only hope and pray that someone else had taken the locks at La Barquette.

'They had and a vast armada of ships were in the English Channel - the invasion of Normandy was on.'

Lieutenant Sumpter Blackmon, leader of First Platoon, Able Company, First Battalion, 501st Parachute Infantry Regiment, 101st Airborne Division.

'On the jump as I went out the door I watched two planes going down in flames that had already dropped their troops and two more planes were going down in flames that hadn't dropped their troops yet. Our plane made a successful drop, but there was quite a ground wind and I landed in water up to my knees. A friend of mine flattened my parachute so I could get up and walk. When we went out the door it was 1:32 in the morning. Trenches had been dug and these had barbed wire fencing. We got caught in them and either had to go over or under them to get off the drop zone. We got to a house and an officer came and asked for volunteers for a 50 man patrol to go seize the locks about three miles from this town of Basse Addeville, which was one of our main objectives. I volunteered for this patrol but the locks had already been opened and the area was flooded. We came under intense artillery fire from Germans on a hill. I had a mortar with me and two guys were carrying the mortar shells and my assistant gunner was in the patrol. We jumped down behind the bank of the canal, right in front of a German machine gun. The other 46 guys in the field could hear the gun but they didn't know that it was firing down the canal at us. The man on my left and the man on the right were hit and went down. The assistant gunner and I got around a small bend in the canal but the gun kept firing to keep us from coming back at them. By this time we had 15 men on the locks and the other 31 headed for us. We didn't know whether they were American or German troops until they got closer. The officer in charge told us to go back to Colonel Johnson, the Regimental Commander's CP. I dug a fox hole near his CP and spent the afternoon of D-Day capturing troops that were being driven back from the beaches. We probably captured 150 to 200 of them that afternoon and we put them in a barn. And then the Germans with an 88 gun started shelling this barn. They didn't even care about their own troops. We stayed all night in the swamp on D+1 and then went back to near where Division Headquarters were to get ready for the attack. On D+6, 501 and 502 and 506 and 327 gliders that had landed captured Carentan, the largest city in the peninsula. Then we pushed out of Carentan for the next 20 days or more. We held positions on outpost. I was on outpost with about 12 other guys. We stayed in that until our duty in Normandy was over and then we returned to England.'

George Eugene Willey 2nd Platoon, Company 'D', 501st Parachute Infantry Regiment. Maurice Duboscq, a railwayman who managed Level Crossing 104 and better known as 'Papa Maurice', used his small boat to rescue paratroopers in the flooded fields and turned his signal box home into a sanctuary for American wounded. A year later his son Claude was killed by an unexploded land-mine.

'Our Drop Zone was 'DZ C'. Our objective was to provide security for the 101st HQ and to be held in ready reserve for any situation that might arise. Very likely we were dropped too soon, far enough south of the line from Le Port to Hiesville so as to arrive at the south bank of the Douve River. This accounts for the 16th man in our jump-stick ending up on the other side of the river! The Germans seemed to have been on the alert because our scout, Lavern French, was captured. Then we received machine-gun fire while we were crossing a road, the upshot of which, our squad was divided. As the sun was just beginning to bring light that morning we saw a German patrol walking beyond a short hedgerow. We walked along it until we found a gap. I, McMullen and Paraseau had just emerged on the other side when another German patrol came along. We froze and hoped we wouldn't be seen in the faint light of dawn, but it wasn't to be! We were not to start any 'little wars' but the moment we were spotted, McMullen opened up with his sub-machine gun. I saw the patrol hitting the ground and threw a grenade. I guess Mac felt we had them neutralized because he said, 'let's get out of here'. I waited a couple seconds and threw another grenade. I waited for it to go off and then I headed for the gap, only to find Mac struggling to get through the hedge with his sub-machine gun. I gave him one mighty shove and Mac fell forward. His feet were above my face and a German opened up with his burp gun. I felt my carbine being wrenched from my hands and a burning, stinging on the right-side of my cheek. I fell all over Mac and panicked! I got up on the run, feeling my bloodied cheek with my right hand. I ran faster than my feet, stumbling all over myself. I tore off my helmet and kept feeling for the hole I just knew must be in my head. After a couple of hundred yards I slowed down for Paraseau to catch up. He said, 'you'd better bandage that wound'. In the dim morning light it I could see a gash running along the inside of my right wrist, with blood still spurting out. I realized that the bullet that stung me in the right cheek must also have gashed the blood vessel in my right wrist. Relieved that it wasn't my head I reached around with my left hand to retrieve my First Aid kit off my cartridge belt. But I was not having any luck getting hold of it so I looked at my left hand and was startled to see at the rounded bone of the first joint of my thumb! The fore-finger was dangling on one side of my hand and the middle finger down the other! I guess it was dumb of me but I tried to put them back to where they belonged, only to find the bones had partially been blown away!

'I took my shot of morphine out of my First Aid kit and we went to work bandaging my hands, only to be interrupted by 12 or so Germans. They stripped us of everything we had except for our dog tags and uniforms. They made us put our hands on our heads and marched us off to a CP, or medical station a mile or so away. They had a couple of their own guys there with shrapnel wounds so we had quite a party wrapping wounds. I must have passed out and when I came to, they had one of our medics try giving me blood plasma, but they couldn't get it in my veins and they finally gave up on me. Later, they brought in Mike Kinzer, who had been separated from our group when they had fired on us crossing the road earlier in the morning. That afternoon they loaded Kinzer, Paraseau and the medic and me on an open truck and dropped the medic and me off at a Field Hospital and took Kinzer and Paraseau on to Germany as PoWs. Although I was pretty well out of it, I got the impression the field hospital had been established in a school house or seminary. They took the medic and me to a room on the second floor which had a wounded RAF airman in it. The next morning they sent the medic on to the rear. On Thursday the 8th an artillery shell exploded just outside our room. It blew a hole in the wall and sent a piece of shrapnel into the room. Later that day they tried to take me downstairs to examine my wounds. I passed out on them and kept drifting in and out of consciousness.

'On Friday, 9 June they took me downstairs. My hand was swollen about the size of my head and the bandages that had been on since D-Day were all crusted to where they had to use scissors to cut them off. They pointed to the streaks running up my arm and suggested the hand be amputated. I vigorously shook my head so they shrugged their shoulders and wrapped my hand back up. Saturday the 10th they brought us all downstairs to a courtyard where we now totalled 21 PoWs altogether. The Germans were evacuating the facility, loading their own wounded on trucks. A few of the wounded were 101st and 82nd troopers, but most were off 'Omaha' Beach and some British or maybe Canadians off their beaches. A horse drawn wagon with straw mattresses on it but no horse, was provided, so some of us were pushing and pulling it with those who couldn't walk were riding. They also provided six guards. Three were teenagers and three were older, maybe 40 or 50 years of age. The guards were I believe eastern Europeans. Five of them were riding bicycles. We didn't get started until afternoon. So we didn't get far before we stopped for the night and stayed in a barn for the night. On Sunday 11 June we came to a fork in the road. The guards didn't know which way to go, so half of them went one way and the other half the other way. They abandoned us! Some French people took us to a slate mine. The next day, Monday 12 June, elements of the 1st Infantry Division took us back to 'Omaha' Beach where we were loaded on an LST. We landed back in England the morning of 13 June.

'My D-Day jump was my 13th and final jump.'

Dale Q. Gregory, 1st Platoon, Company 'H', 501st Parachute Infantry Regiment.
'In England they put a cast on my left arm and hand. I never got back to the 101st Airborne area. I ended up in a hospital in Scotland where I ran into McMullen on crutches. He had received a wound in his knee from the blast of the burp gun that got me. He, Houston and the medic took off and hid in a low-lying area until mid morning on D-Day and then they waded the river where they joined up with Colonel Johnson and the others at the bridges. Houston suffered a shrapnel wound to his foot before the Normandy campaign was over. But he went on

through all the operations the 101st was involved in and he was awarded a battlefield commission before the end of the war. I was put aboard a C-54 Hospital Ship as an ambulatory patient and landed in New York on 3 July 3 at about 3 am in the morning.

'During the battles one does not have time to look around to see how others are doing. We were told that when we took up our position by the bridge we would have to hold it at all cost until the men from the beach arrived, for if the Germans broke through they would have a good chance of going all the way to the beach. Our job was to be in the forward position by La Fière Bridge with our bazooka to stop any German tanks from advancing over the bridge and onto Ste-Mère-Église and the beaches. This we accomplished all the while the Germans were continuously firing everything they had at us. After I went across the road and found more rockets for the bazooka and returned, the third tank was put out of action and the Germans retreated. When the Germans pulled back, we looked around but did not see anyone. We then moved back to our foxhole. Looking back up the road toward Ste-Mère-Église, we saw that the 57-millimetre cannon and the machine gun were destroyed. Looking down the pathway across from the Manor House we could not see any of our men. We were thinking that we were all alone and that maybe we should move from here; then someone came and told us to hold our position and he would find more men to place around us, for the Germans might try again to breach our lines. We found out later that of the few who were holding the bridge at this time, most were either killed or wounded. Why we were not injured or killed only the good Lord knows.'

Marcus Heim, Able Company, 505th Parachute Infantry Regiment. Heim and his four-man team were awarded the Distinguished Service Cross.

'We boarded the planes at about 22:30 on 5 June. With two chutes and full combat equipment, we could hardly walk. Some of the men looked like they were scared to death. I was certainly uptight but had no thoughts of being killed. I had the feeling we were part of a big chunk of history. Out of the window, there were planes in every direction and, below, hundreds of ships. As we crossed the French coast, a plane on our right was hit by flak and blew up, wiping out 18 to 20 men. Welcome to the real war.

'The green light came on and we jumped. I hit a road and went head first through a wooden fence, knocking out two teeth. Then I took cover in a hedgerow. A minute later 40 Germans came marching past. I could have reached out and touched them. Being alone behind enemy lines is a unique experience. You feel so helpless, so alone. After a bit I ran into John Gibson, our medic and Charles Lee, a mortarman. It was as if I had found a long-lost brother.

'I looked up and there was a C-47 transport plane at about 800 feet with the left engine on fire and troopers bailing out. The last one bailed out at not more than 200 feet and the plane went right over the top of our heads, hit the adjoining field and burst into a million flaming pieces. From the direction of the crash, four men came running towards us. We discovered they were from our troop - Phil Abbie, Francis Swanson, Leo Krebs and my high school pal Francis Ronzani. The downed plane had damn near got them.

'We now had an army of seven but we ran into about 100 Germans as daylight was breaking. Abbie and Ronzani were killed and the rest of us were pinned down in a field.

Bullets were flying all over the place and Leo Krebs remarked, 'God, these guys are lousy shots.' A German officer was running back and forth and Krebs said, 'What the hell is wrong with that guy? Is he nuts?' We shot at him and he went down. But we were in a hopeless position and were captured in no time.

'Lee had got away into a wood and, a short time later, began shooting at the Germans who were guarding us. I told Leo I still had a hand grenade the Germans had missed. If Leo hit one of the guards I was going to throw the grenade at the other one. But the Germans circled behind Lee and killed him. I left the grenade in the ditch.

'Ronzani had been hit in the chest three, four, five, or six times. I'm sure he never knew what hit him. When I returned to the States after the war and visited his mother and father, one of the things that seemed to be of great relief to them was that Francis had not suffered.'

George Rosie, 101st Airborne. Captured, he spent eleven months in PoW camps before being liberated by the Russians south of Berlin.

'As we neared the drop zone we encountered heavy fire from the ground. All hell broke loose. We were only flying at about 800 feet and the anti-aircraft fire broke loose and the ground fire; it was really a fireworks display from there until jump time. In the confusion we were dropped in the wrong place. I landed at 1.24am on June 6. I came down in this field and there were about 15 German soldiers firing up at our planes. That turned out to be a blessing because they were making so much noise that they couldn't hear me coming down and they were blinded by their rifle fire. I realised I was alone. That feeling will be etched in my memory forever. Eventually I met with about 25 fellow Americans who had also been dropped in the wrong place. Their mission was to secure bridges over a river. By 11am my unit ran into fierce German resistance. We had had resistance all the way down but not real heavy. We took some casualties.

24-year-old Captain Sam Gibbons, 101st Airborne Division.

'A stick is one string of men that jump on one command. Normally, a C-47 maximum stick would be sixteen men. Going towards France, there were twenty-two in our stick. I remember how helpless I felt at the time while sitting in the airplane. There was absolutely nothing you could do to improve your situation in the event that you were fired upon. Absolutely nothing you could do. You were completely helpless.

'It took considerable effort to get up. I hooked up and then we started out the door and just as I approached the door, the top of the airplane opened up. It had been hit by some type of explosive shell. As I turned into the doorway, the plane started a right wing dip, as it was going into its death spiral. It took everything I had to get over the threshold and out as the threshold was coming up. I managed to roll out. It seems to me the threshold was just a little bit more than chest high as I rolled over and got out. I was the last man out of the plane.

'When I felt the opening shock of the chute, more by habit than anything, I looked up to check the chute and I remember seeing clusters of tracers going through it. I then reached for my trench knife, but having taped it to the sheath, I couldn't get it loose. I hit the ground with one leg up trying to get the trench knife out and fortunately didn't break anything.

'I landed on the ground and lay there momentarily, fully expecting a German to run up and stick me with a bayonet. But nothing happened, which quite surprised me. I had landed in front of a German bunker, which was about thirty yards away, but someone who had hit the ground before me dropped a gammon grenade on it and put it out of order.

'I immediately grabbed my trench knife and with all my strength, I tore it loose from the tape that was holding it and started cutting all the straps that were binding me. I grabbed my carbine in one hand, trench knife in the other and I ran for the hedgerow, dove over it and lay against the bank for a short while.

'I saw two Germans approaching on the other side of the hedgerow. We had orders not to load our weapons until we were organized, so my carbine was not loaded. As the Germans approached I fully intended to let them go on by but just in case, I unscrewed the cap on my gammon grenade. When they got just opposite me, they noticed me and ducked. I sat there and waited as one of them started slowly rising. I saw the top of his head and when I saw his shoulders, I threw the gammon grenade and he fired. I had not seen the rifle, but the bullet passed through the crotch of my outside pair of pants. The muzzle blast knocked me out and when I came to, my face was in the bank, in the dirt, my mouth was open, blood and spit was trickling out. I could hear, but I couldn't move. I thought I was dead and that this was the way people died.

'I heard moaning on the other side of the hedgerow, so I knew that my grenade had had some effect. While on the airplane, I had some English coins in my pocket, so I took out all the English coins and I lined them around the outside of the C2 under the cloth skirt of the gammon grenade, making a fragmentation grenade. Those two Germans would have been buried with British coins imbedded in them.

After a while, it got quiet on the other side of the hedgerow. I don't know how long I was out to begin with and I don't know how long it took before I could move. I heard and saw someone approaching on my side of the hedgerow and it turned out to be a couple of paratroopers and I told them that my ears were ringing and I couldn't hear. Anyway, we talked for a while and noticed someone else approaching us. They ducked down behind me. I knelt down and waited the approach of this other person and when he got within range, I shouted, 'Flash!' He came back with 'Thunder!' and I thought that everything was OK. But the next thing I saw was a ball of fire and a bullet hit my helmet between the eyes and glanced off. Fortunately, I have a small head that fits quite deeply in the helmet. I rolled to my left and started swearing and the next bullet caught me in the hip pocket and went through a couple of layers of two paper maps I had folded in my left hip pocket, ODs. He then quit firing when he heard my swearing. Swearing turned out to be one of the best passwords. No one can swear in American like an American, or in English like an Englishman.

'We talked for a minute and then we saw some movement off to one side, somewhat in the same direction this person had come. So we lay down and waited. The next time I looked up, I was all alone again. The guy had moved on and it was about that time that I decided it was kind of useless to move around in the dark, as it was too difficult to identify anyone.

'I noticed a kind of a brush-filled gully some short distance away, so I ran for that and dove into it. I was lying on my back in the dry brush, my trench knife was under me and my carbine was off to my left, unloaded when I heard two Germans approaching. You could tell Germans by the amount of leather they wore. You could hear it creak as they walked. They stood over me and looked down at me. There wasn't anything I could do, just play dead. I waited. I had to go to the bathroom very badly and I went. It's quite possible the Germans mistook what they saw for blood. After a while, I opened my eyes and saw they had gone, so I crawled deeper down to the bottom of the gully and lay there and later went to sleep. While lying there, I heard a glider coming in through the trees. It seemed like it would never stop. It must have had something heavy in it, because it just kept crashing through the trees.

'I went to sleep and then when it was daylight, I woke up and heard someone approaching. Just as the person got within about five or six feet from me, I challenged him with 'Flash' and he took one more step and when he took that one more step, I saw his paratrooper boot through an opening in the foliage and I looked up and saw his face and recognized him and he had a very perplexed look on his face - he was trying to remember what he was supposed to say, but couldn't remember. And I hollered out, 'That's OK, Malcolm. I recognize you.' He and I embraced each other and jumped up and down. We were so happy to see somebody. He and I then started to move in the direction in which we thought our objective was.

'We met three other troopers and the five of us approached a hedgerow. As we looked over the hedgerow, there was a German truck with two Germans sitting in it. One of the guys threw a gammon grenade and hit the windshield. It exploded, the Germans tumbled out, one on each side of the truck and began running up the road. We were firing at them, but in the excitement we forgot to aim. They kept running and we kept firing and they reached a turn in the road and continued on out of our range. Then someone threw an incendiary grenade at the truck and set it on fire and it burned with black smoke spiralling up into the air. One of the boys stated that there was a German battalion approaching down this road that the two Germans had run up, so the five of us decided that we would ambush this German battalion and we crossed over into the hedgerow and lined up along this road. We spread out far enough to what we thought was far enough to cover a battalion of Germans. All we had were carbines. There were five of us with five carbines and I think we were all out of gammon grenades. I still had my two fragmentation grenades. We waited and waited and suddenly, German machine gun opened up behind us. We were taken completely by surprise. We vacated the area in a hurry. One of the boys got hit in the leg and we were helping him out of the area. We never got to ambush our German battalion. I think it was them who ambushed us.

'We continued on looking for other troopers. We reached a point where we couldn't carry the wounded guy any further and it seemed kind of hopeless anyway, as we didn't know where we were going really and we didn't know whether we were improving our position or not. So, we figured he would be just as well off if we hid him in the brush and if possible, we could get back to him later, whenever we found our unit.

'About a hundred yards further on, we joined a group of about thirty men. There was a sniper firing on us and it hit one of the boys in the belly and he was laying there. There was nothing we could do for him and we remembered the story at that time, that if he lived an hour, he would live. Well, one of the other guys decided to dispatch the sniper. He went over the bank toward the sniper, hit the dirt and when he did, the sniper killed him. Someone then told us that there were a group of our boys stranded on an island and that the Germans had them pretty well surrounded, so we decided to go join them. We went for quite a while before we saw them and they saw us. But there was quite an open space in between. We stayed where we were and waited for them to come to us. They had to cross this opening and the Germans had a machine gun, zeroed in on the opening. As they ran across the opening, the machine gunner fired at them. I borrowed a pair of field glasses from someone and looked over and located the machine gun and then I went away from the troops so I wouldn't draw fire toward where everyone was congregated. I started shooting at the machine gun and he started shooting at me and while we were so occupied, the boys on the island were able to come across and join us. My carbine got so hot I couldn't even see the sights anymore. It was smoking, but the machine gun quit firing altogether.

'We were roughly about a hundred strong now, just about company strength. Our senior officer there was my battalion commander, Lieutenant Colonel Shanly. We began hiking toward our objective, which was a bridge across the river, somewhere near Ste-Mère-Église. The Germans shelled us for a while, but they would fire all their guns at once and when you heard them coming in, you hit the ground and after they quit exploding, you could move away from the area.

'We kept marching that night. We moved and then we would rest and then we would move some more. Another guy and I fell asleep and when we woke up it was daylight. We were surprised, because we were still alive. We went in the direction we were hiking and it turned out that our unit was only a hundred yards away, that they had set up a defensive position on the banks of this river. We joined them there.'

Harold Canyon in the 82nd American Airborne was number six man in his stick.

'Over our drop zone flak hit a plane and it went down burning. Everything from the ground was coming our way. It looked like Fourth of July. When I hit the ground I was about 200 yards from a house. I could hear Germans yelling 'muck schnell toot sweet americanos'. They started their motorcycles and went inland. I fought with some of 101st Airborne fellows and that afternoon we took about 75 prisoners down to 'Utah' beach. I stayed on the beach that night. The 507 went in with about 2,000 men and came out with about 800. My company had around 75 left out of about 230 men. We had the worst drop of all paratroopers on D-day why I guess because we were the last ones and the fellows before us had stirred up the bees (Germans). After 33 days of fighting without any replacements we were finally sent back to England.'

21-year old Pfc Howard Huebner, Charlie Company, 507th Parachute Infantry Regiment, 82nd Airborne.

'I couldn't see much of the ground, it was more or less of a blur but I watched all these tracers and shell bursts and everything in the air around me and I watched one stream of tracers - obviously a machine gun - which looked like it was going to come directly at me. Intellectually, I knew that I could not be seen in the air under this camouflage chute. But that stream of tracers came directly up at me. I lost three shroud lines that were clipped by bullets from my parachute and it obviously had punctured some holes in it. In an obviously futile gesture (but normal, I guess) I spread my legs widely and grabbed with both hands at my groin, as if to protect myself. Those machine gun bullets traced up the inside of one leg, missed my groin, traced down the inside of the other leg, splitting my pants on the insides of both legs, dropping two cartons of Pall Mall cigarettes to the soil of France.

'I set up my radar beacon and went around the periphery of a small field and I heard

German voices on the other side. I sneaked up through the brush and stuff on top of the hedgerow and I saw two German officers talking to each other, apparently totally unaware that we were in this field right next to them. Well, I couldn't shoot. We were ordered not to shoot unless it was totally in self-defense, but just to be as quiet and as secret as possible. And of course, the main thing was to keep the beacon in operation as long as possible. But when I saw those two German officers, in my mind's eye I saw two beautiful Lugers, a souvenir that I wanted very badly. Since I couldn't make any noise I tossed a white phosphorus grenade down at their feet through the hedgerow. This makes a small pop when it goes off, very little noise. And of course it can't be put out. It burned the two officers to death. I got back out of the way and waited until the thing was finished burning. When the fire died down I went back to collect my Lugers; not thinking what damage the white phosphorus grenade would have done to them. Well, of course, both Germans were burned to death and hardly recognizable as humans. Unfortunately, the ammunition had exploded in the clips of the Lugers. It had blown them apart and they were totally worthless. So that was not the best idea that I'd ever had, but at least it got rid of those Germans, my first two Germans.

'We accounted for quite a number. We had orders to take no prisoners for the first nine days. The reason for this was that the paratroops, when they land behind enemy lines, are all by themselves, even if they are in a group. They can't afford to set up a PoW compound, use personnel to guard prisoners, or anything like that. It's just totally impossible. So even though some of the Germans surrendered, or thought they were surrendering, of course, they were disarmed and killed. In fact, we used bodies for roadblocks. We'd stack them up like cordwood in some of the road junction - German corpses.

'For the next two or three days we gathered up other small groups of paratroops. There were no officers with us, but fortunately we were trained to live on and fight either alone or with one or more of our paratroops buddies. So, this was no big deal. In fact, it was kind of fun not to have some officer telling you what to do.'
Frank Brumbaugh, a radar operator in the 101st Screaming Eagles.

'Our C-47 had been hit by both flak and machine-gun fire. We were off target. The green light came on and the troopers started out of the plane. The fifteenth man had equipment trouble. After some delay trying to fix his rig I, being the sixteenth and last man to go, bailed out on a dead run. My opening shock was terrific. First, I saw all the tracers coming my way. Second, I tried to guess how high I was. Third, I checked my chute. I also saw flame from a fire ahead of me which was reaching as high as I was in the air. A tracer had gone through my chute canopy like a cigarette hole in a silk handkerchief, smouldering and fiery red. The hole was getting bigger by the instant. I grabbed my front risers and brought them to my waist. I was in a hell of a hurry to get down before my chute became a torch. The bullets, in which tracers intermingled, were still snapping all around me. It seemed as if they would curve to one side just as they were going to hit me. I became so fascinated by this that I forgot to release my risers and I was plummeting to earth extremely fast. Just as I checked the burning hole in my chute and saw it was now about eighteen inches in diameter, I hit the ground, ploughing through the limbs of a tree. I bashed into the ground. I took most of the shock with my hind end. My chute then draped lazily over the tree.

'I could hear shooting and yelling all around me and saw a glow of light from a huge fire to my front and left of where I was laying. From this glow, I could see troopers coming out of the C-47s only three or four hundred-feet high. As I started to sit up to get out of my chute, I promptly slid flat again. After two or three more attempts and a sniff of the air, I finally discovered that I was lying in cow manure. I even snickered at my own predicament.

'Suddenly from my right front, three men came running towards me, the first one about 100-feet away. I could see the coal-bucket helmets and thought, 'Oh hell, out of the frying pan into a latrine - now this.' As my Tommy gun was strapped to my chest, I gave up trying to get it out and reached for my .45 automatic that was strapped to my right thigh. I always keep a round in the chamber and seven in the clip. I thumbed back the hammer and started firing. The third man fell with my eighth round right at my feet. I gave a huge sigh of relief and tried again to get up. This made my chute shake the tree. Then from my direct right about seventy-five yards away, a German machine nest opened up at me. I could hear the rounds buzzing and snapping through the leaves of the tree and into the ground beyond me. Again, I thought: 'Dammit; is the whole Kraut army after me, just one scared red-headed trooper?' I tried once again to rise up and bullets ripped into my musette bag and map case strapped to my chest, rolling me on to my left side. I rolled back and tried to unstrap my Tommy gun. Just then a loud boom came from the area of the machine gun and all I could hear was the shooting and yelling coming from the direction of the glow of the big fire about 300 yards away.

'I finally got out of my harness, grabbed my Tommy gun and started moving for the scene of action. All this took place within five minutes and hearing a sound behind me, I dropped flat and tried to see what or who was there. Taking a chance on a hunch, I snapped my 'cricket'. An answering two clicks came back at once, then up crawled a trooper, whom I didn't know but I could have kissed him for just being one of us. His first words were: 'I got those Kraut machine-gunners with a grenade, but it blew off my helmet and I can't find it. Holy cow, you stink! '

'Moving to the edge of the orchard, we came to a hedgerow. As we were attempting to get over through this grove, we heard a click and answered it at once with two clicks. Another trooper, ready to go. Assuming a hedgerow to be about four-feet high, I slid through and dropped about ten feet down to a narrow roadway.

The three of us prepared to move across fields to the fight going around the fire about 250 yards away. We figured it to be quicker than trying to follow the road and running into some kind of a roadblock. Just then to my left, coming down the road towards us, was a noise of hob-nailed boots running. We crouched down along the bank and I could hear the other two move to my left and fan out. I told them to wait for an opening burst before firing. The runners had to come around a slight curve in the road and I wanted to make sure all of them had rounded the curve before firing. We then saw there were three of them strung out, the first one now only about forty feet away. I started firing short bursts at the last man, then the second one. All three fell.

'We then scurried over the hedge into another orchard. A large two-storey house was to our right, so we circled around it and moved closer to the action, now only a very short distance away. One of the men with me had an M-1 rifle; the other, a Tommy gun, same as mine. Hearing running and shouting to our left, we dropped down as about ten Krauts came crashing through what looked like a garden. They were almost on top of us when we opened fire. All fell. Also, the trooper with the M-1 fell. We then moved on.

'Suddenly, two figures loomed out of the shadow of a building. I almost fired before I recognized them as being in civilian clothes. The man with me could speak French, so crouching low, we held a hurried consultation. I could understand some of the talk and the trooper told me the rest. All of us had bailed out right on top of Ste-Mère-Église, when the townspeople were trying to put out a fire and being 'chaperoned' by a hundred or more Krauts. Our planes were so low that the troopers bailing out were perfect targets and were being slaughtered.

'We thanked them, told them to get back in the building and then moved on.

'About seventy-five yards further on, we entered the edge of a large square with a church at our left side. There were troopers lying everywhere, almost all of them still in their chutes. One was hanging from the spire on the church. There was a stone wall around the church. We dropped behind this, just as a troop-carrying vehicle came down the street towards us. We were sitting ducks, so we both started firing, hoping to take as many of them with us as we could.

'Out of the corner of my eye I also noticed firing coming from a building across the street at point blank range. One of us got the driver of the truck and it stopped and out of it, the Krauts came. I had to put in another clip. I had just accomplished this and began to fire again when I heard my buddy grunt and saw him fall. Suddenly, the firing from the vehicle stopped.

'I shot out the building's window area and raced back behind the church, circling around it. I reloaded with just one clip, as I had no more taped together. I had started out with twenty clips, ten on my belt, seven in my knapsack and three taped together, staggered and reversed. At thirty rounds to a clip, I had 600 rounds. The three taped together, gave me ninety rounds for speedy reloading. I had already emptied six clips.

'Starting out again down the opposite side of the square from where we had met the troop carrier, I almost tripped over a Kraut lying on the ground. He had a burp gun. As he rolled to bring his gun around, I fired.

'Then in the building behind me, a Kraut carbine let go and numerous Kraut voices began to yell something. Somehow, the one lying on the ground missed me, the bullet hitting the K-ration in my right pocket. I emptied my clip at the front of the building and moved out fast, reloading as I ran. It was now about one hour and thirty minutes since I had bailed out.

'Hearing some firing immediately ahead I ran on, figuring on being some help to someone in need. Plus I wanted some company of my own people. I came upon four Krauts undercover, firing in the opposite direction. Sporadic fire came from the direction they were firing. As I looked, one fell, so I dropped the other three. One thing about a Tommy gun: it's just like a garden hose. You aim it in the general direction of your target, hold on the trigger and wave it back and forth. You waste some ammo, but you just can't hardly miss.

'There were eight troopers behind a low stone wall and among some bushes. I held a hurried conversation with a sergeant and was told there were six members of the 505th Regiment, also one from the 508th and one from the 101st Division. Two of the 505 men were seriously injured. One man had some TNT.

'I then explained my mission to this sergeant and asked him to help. We checked the two wounded. One had died and the other lad was past help. We made him as comfortable as we could and moved out towards Chef du Pont. The sergeant told me it was only a couple of miles away. It was then somewhere around 3 o'clock in the morning.

'We skirted a road, keeping to the second hedge from the road; three men to the left side of the hedge and four to the right. We saw eleven dead troopers, all in their chutes, four hanging in trees. Somehow, we managed to reach the edge of Chef du Pont with only two short battles and without losing a man. We ran into a group of Krauts at the edge of the village. There must have been a platoon. For some reason, they thought we must have been at least a company, because they broke and ran, maybe because of our numerous automatic weapons, two BARs, three Tommy guns and two M-1s. I was now down to nine clips.

'We passed a building on the left side of the street with lots of German writing on it. A heavy machine-gun opened up from behind a low stone wall. One 505 man circled behind and threw two hand grenades and cut loose with his Tommy. The nest was silenced.

'Across the street was some kind of an important building and it was flushed out by two of the men, two from 505 and the other 508 trooper. Then one of the men peeked around the corner and reported a train depot just to the left of a long narrow courtyard. He took off for it, with a word to cover him. At the far end of the courtyard or square, a machine gun cut loose and he fell. Then directly ahead of us along each side of the road and across the track, more Krauts opened up. One more man fell.

'We concentrated our fire on them and then dashed towards them. They ran, going on down the street, house to house, room to room, we proceeded on towards the river. When we got to the edge of the town, there were only three of us. I had two-and-a-half clips left, so I took the remaining clip from the last man to fall that had a Tommy gun. I picked up four more clips. Of the three men left, one was from the 505, one from the 101st and myself from the 508. When I jumped, being a demolition man, I had ten pounds of TNT. The man from the 101st had six pounds, plus his BAR. The trooper from the 505 had an M-l. That was our fire power.

'Each one of these TNT quarter-pound blocks were tremendous, if set right, packed right and detonated correctly. Starting across the causeway, I noticed it was flooded on both sides. Suddenly from our right, from an old factory-looking type of building about 400 yards across the flooded area, heavy fire power poured on us. We dove to the left of the offside of the causeway for protection. We immediately drew fire from across the bridge in the middle of the causeway. The 505 man fell.

'The other man and myself moved on, firing in bursts at the ones ahead of us. When we came to the bridge, no more fire was coming at us from that direction. However, from the old factory, heavy fire was still coming. We then noticed some rifle fire from the other end of the causeway and to our right. I directed the 101st man to give me his TNT and keep firing at the factory.

'I dropped below the left side of the bridge. I laid my gun down, set my eight pounds of TNT, then hand walked under and to the other end of the bridge, set the other eight pounds - and was promptly knocked into the water. I came up and swam back to the starting point, fire from the factory hitting all around me. I retrieved my gun and then noticed my side and my head were bleeding. It was then I noticed my BAR man wasn't firing. He was dead.

'At the same time I heard firing going on again in Chef du Pont. Crawling along the offside of the causeway, I set my short fuses to my charges, connected them with primer cord for instant detonation to the end of the regular two-foot fuse and continued along the offside of Chef du Pont. I had gone about fifty yards when the roadway vibrated terrifically from my charges. I went on into Chef du Pont and met up with fourteen paratroopers, most from the 505, a couple from the 101st and three from the 508. I told the officer in charge what had happened and he sent six men back to set up a roadblock.

One had a bazooka and I was sure he was glad to have him stay with us.

'The others headed back to Ste-Mère-Église. Within five minutes, they were shooting at all kinds of vehicles trying to come through Chef du Pont, get over the bridge and get away from the invasion of the paratroops. We knocked out a big truck just as it reached the causeway and another small one that tried to get by him. We now had a very effective roadblock. Within the hour, about twenty more troopers came up from behind us and almost the same number entered the scene from the Chef du Pont side. In the meantime, I lost three more men, as almost that whole hour had been one continual roar of guns. I had fifteen rounds left.

'I joined the troops in Chef du Pont and sent eight men back to the causeway to keep the roadblock active. Not seeing any of my men, we returned to Ste-Mère-Église. I ate, drank a bottle of wine, had the blood washed off my minor wounds and joined in the civilian celebration that was going on. I was so happy that they were happy. I cried with them.

'It was now late in the afternoon and almost dark. An officer from the 82nd came up and told me my group were assembled at Hill 30 and I was to join them. He had another mission scheduled for that evening. I joined what was left of my people at the edge of Hill 30 and after one hell of a battle, we captured it. This lasted until the wee hours of the morning. After the hill was secure, we set up a perimeter defence and by morning light, June 7 had beat off four counter-attacks. We had started with thirty men for this particular mission; six were left.

'I said a silent prayer and slept.'

Paratrooper James Eads, who landed just outside Ste-Mère-Église.

Paras Equipment

Paratroopers carried an average of 70lbs of equipment, officers 90lbs. With the parachute, men weighed between 90-120 lbs over their body weight. The items carried were:
Standard Parachutist Pack:
M-1 Garand Rifle with 8-round clip
Cartridge belt with canteen
Hand grenades
Parachute and pack
Anti-flash headgear and gloves
Pocket compass
Macheté
.45 calibre Colt automatic rifle
Flares
Message book
Officer Pack (British, but similar to American officer pack):
Sten gun
Spare magazines with 9mm ammunition
2 lb plastic high explosives (HE)
2-36 primed hand grenades
Two full belts of Vickers .303 ammunition
Wire cutters

Radio batteries
Small-pack
Basic equipment webbing
48 hours worth of rations
Water
Cooking and washing kit
Spread throughout pockets:
Loaded .45 automatic pistol
Medical kit
2 additional lb. HE
Knife
Escape/survival kit
Toggle rope
Additional personal items
Emergency Rations
4 pieces of chewing gum
2 bouillon cubes
2 Nescafe instant coffees, 2 sugar cubes and creamers
4 Hershey bars
1 pack of Charms candy
1 package pipe tobacco
1 bottle of water purification (Halazone) tablets

'My glider made a beautiful landing at Ecoqueneauville and I made my way south to my assembly point at Les Forges crossroads. Here I got the bad news that I had lost half of my six-man team in glider crashes. The good news was the others had already eight German prisoners for interrogation. I started off with German but with little response, so I switched to Russian with the question, 'Vj Russkij chelovek?' (Are you a Russian?). Their reply was immediate, 'Da, ya khochu ekhat' na Ameriku' (Yes, I want to go to America). I slapped both my hands on top of my helmet and shouted at them, 'Durak, durak. Ya tozhe!' (Crazy, crazy. Me too!).'

2nd Lieutenant Leon E. Mendel, Interrogation Officer, proficient in seven languages, 325th Glider Infantry, Mission 'Galveston' on D+1 at Landing Zone 'W'. (The enemy included 'volunteers' from Eastern Europe and Soviet Russia. The Seventh Army had 13 'Ost' battalions made up of non-Germans).

'The original plan was that we would hold Ste-Mère-Église for one day. Then the outfits that hit the beaches would come in and relieve us. Two days later, they still haven't showed up. So General Ridgeway asked for volunteers to go toward the beach head and look for help and find out what happened since we had lost all radio contact with the beachhead. Five of us took off through the German lines with this message from General Ridgeway. Troops strength down to 50%. Ammunition down to 50%. Perimeter around Ste-Mère-Église closing in. Germans realizing we had no big guns to fight off their tanks. Our patrol made it through the German lines. We captured one German soldier who we made walk down the middle of the road while we strung out through the woods. About 5 miles down that road, we found a whole gang of American tanks sitting along the hedgerows eating their lunch. Our Lieutenant really reamed the Major out who was in charge of these tanks. The tanks wound up real fast and headed up the road to Ste-Mère-Église. We jumped up on the tanks and rode the tanks back to town. We broke the circle of Germans around the town and Ste-Mère-Église was ours again.'

Technical Sergeant Howard Hicks, 505th Regiment, 82nd Airborne Division.

'The paratroops dozed, or pretended to. They were the Army's elite, the tough boys - lean and wiry men clad in green camouflaged battledress, faces stained with cocoa and linseed oil. ('We'll have something to eat if our rations run out!')

'One paratroop lieutenant survived to return and tell how the Germans 'were machine-gunning us all the way down'. Another officer told of seeing German tracers ripping through other men's parachutes as they descended. In one plane, a soldier laden with his go pounds of equipment got momentarily stuck in the door. A 20 mm. shell hit him in the belly. Fuse-caps in his pockets began to go off. Part of the wounded man's load was T.N.T. Before this human bomb could explode, his mates behind him pushed him out. The last they saw of him, his parachute had opened and he was drifting to earth in a shroud of bursting flame.'

Time **magazine.**

'When we jumped, it was 01:14. Thank God with a bag strapped on my leg, I was the 3rd man out the door, because our plane was hit and a wing was on fire. We were so low that when my chute opened, I swung twice and hit the ground. I know that all the men didn't get out. If they did, they were too low and their chutes never had time to open. When my chute opened, it opened with a jerk and the bag that I had strapped on my leg took off and I never did find it. After landing, I crawled out of the field to the edge of the road and used my cricket. Every man was given a cricket to make contact with each other after landing, that way the Germans didn't know what was going on until we hit them. When I cricketed, I got an answer from across the road and a Mexican boy came over to me. He asked me where I landed and I pointed over my shoulder and he said, 'Jesus, how lucky can you get.' I turned and looked where he pointed and there on the fence was a big sign – 'Achtung Minen'. I had landed right in the middle of that field, took off my helmet and threw it away because I couldn't hear anything with it on and I crawled out of there without setting a mine off.

'About 20 minutes later, we met Bill Hayes and the three of us set out Kraut hunting. About a half an hour later, while we were lying in a gully figuring which way to go to meet up with our company, we heard some noise and about eight or ten Krauts came running towards our gully. When they got to the gully, they split up and ran up both sides. We had pulled the pins on our grenades, so we just waited until they got pretty well past us and then we threw the grenades and took off in the other direction. I know we got a few of them, because of all the screaming and hollering. A little later, while walking across the field, someone hollered, 'Halt!' I was in the lead so I pumped a few shots in the direction from where the yell came from and we three hit the swampy ditch that we were walking along the side of. We got out of there and kept moving.

'Whenever we'd come across any wires, we'd cut them. If it would have been daylight, the Germans could have followed us very easy just by following the cut lines. We had a few more running fire fights until daybreak and then we spotted a farm house. A few French kids came out from the house to the barnyard where they had seen us and brought us some bread and wine. We didn't know French and they didn't know English, but they saw the American flags that some of the guys had sewn on their jackets and they knew who we were. We got out our maps and they pointed where we were and which direction would be best, but we didn't trust them and we went another way, but we soon realized that we should have listened. We got out in the middle of a field and a shot went by my ear. I said to Hayes and Sanchez, 'Let's keep going and see if we can spot the guy.' When the second shot rang out, we hit the ditch filled with swamp water. We spotted from where the shots had come from, so we returned the fire. After a few shots, we find out it's another trooper. Well, the four of us started out of there and we ran into what looked like the whole German army in front of us. Between the four of us and the Germans, we had quite a battle till we ran out of ammunition and the Mexican boy got hit three times. We were taken prisoner and they stripped us of everything. They took us to a farmhouse where we saw some other wounded paratroopers and some of our boys hanging in trees still in their chutes with their privates cut off. That was the final straw. We had our minds made up then that if we got out of there, there would be no prisoners taken by us nowhere.

'From there, they walked us about three miles to a small village and threw us into a pig pen with a couple of pigs. The pigs looked at us and went over in a corner and lay down. I don't blame them. I guess we did look a little rough. We had our hair cut like an Indian and real short, had stove-black all over our faces and we stank worse than the pigs from being in all that swamp water. We stayed there about two hours and then they walked us to St. Lô where I met Joe Dolo and Chuck Cunningham. They held us in a big barn next to a very large cathedral or a church. That night, St. Lô was bombed and I thought that was the end of about six or eight hundred prisoners. The next morning when the Germans took us out of the barn, we looked around and everything was flattened except the church and the barn where we had been held. The Germans then marched us about ten miles to a monastery of some kind. By this time, we were getting pretty hungry. The Germans were also short of food, so they shot and butchered a few horses.

'As a manner of getting to see one another, we got together in groups and there were 11 men from Company 'B' there. The Germans also gave us some hot water and some leaves of some kind and told us it was soup. We were marched out of there and went to a regular prisoner of war camp.'

Bill Oatman, 506th Parachute Infantry Regiment.

'Upon landing, we discovered the source of the ground fire which nearly got me. It turned out to be a bunker containing about a dozen conscripted Polish soldiers with one German in charge. After the glider infantrymen from several gliders, including ours, directed a hail of rifle fire at the bunker, the resistance ceased. There was silence in the bunker and then a single shot. Then there were shouts and laughter and the Poles emerged with their hands held high and surrendered. They weren't about to fight the Americans so they simply shot the Kraut sergeant.

'We took refuge in a thatched roof farmhouse nearby to get ourselves organized and were surprised to find an American paratrooper in bed. He had jumped and had fallen through the thatched roof. He broke his leg. He simply had crawled into bed and was awaiting the outcome of the war. We left him there after awhile, but at the time, he was being aided by a young French lady and didn't seem to care whether the war continued or not. I hope he made it back home.

'By nightfall, we were looking for somewhere safe to, maybe, catch a few winks. We came upon several Americans busily digging holes in one small field, so figuring out that misery loves company, several of us sunk our shovels at the edge of the field. 'Hey, you guys can't dig in here.' 'Why?' we asked. 'Because we're starting a temporary American cemetery here.' That did it. We went elsewhere.

'Following two days of confusion where there were no battle lines and the war was actually small engagements between groups of Americans and Germans, we glider pilots assembled and began a 3 mile hike which took us back to 'Utah' Beach. Having drunk all the canteen water, I was thirsty by that time. I sighted a canvas bag of water being guarded - no kidding, this is the truth - by a Lieutenant Colonel from the Army. He gave me a half a can of water and that included seaweed.

'Once we were at the beach, glider pilots were given a job of herding German prisoners on to an LCI (Landing Craft, Infantry) ship, for the start of their trip to prison camp in England. From the LCIs they were put into larger LST boats for the short trip back across the English Channel. My own personal experience in this aspect of my duty had a strange beginning. After an American major turned over a group of Krauts for the boarding of the small craft, he asked us for our rifles. He overruled our protests by telling us that the rifles were where they were needed and there was no logical reason for us to take them back to the land of plenty, England. Also, because we were officers, we still had our trusty 45 revolver on our hip. It all made sense so we surrendered our rifles. It developed, however, that once we did get back to our home base in England our supply officer couldn't see the wisdom of the whole thing and actually threatened to take action to make us pay for them. Luckily, our commander vetoed this idea.

'Roy Samples and I were successful in getting our group of Germans onto the LCI and then in the LST for the trip back to England. The LST was anchored next to an American oil tanker which later attracted the attention of a German E-boat which fired one torpedo into the tanker which exploded and sank almost immediately. One sailor who was on top of the mast as lookout was the sole survivor. The LST crew fished him and his dog out of the water. The E-boat's luck ended with the sinking, because at practically the same second as the American ship's sinking, a British ground attack aircraft swooped down with rockets and machine gun fire and destroyed the German attacker. At the end, it was like watching a newsreel as we observed the whole drama, from the deck of our LST.

'One of our Kraut prisoners was an over-aged German major who had been stationed in Normandy to recover from wounds received earlier on the Russian front. When we passed out the dreaded K-rations for a midnight meal, the major refused to eat. We asked an English-speaking German corporal what The major's complaint was and we were informed that the major was used to good meat and dairy products of Normandy and didn't appreciate our canned product. One of my friends told the corporal to inform the major that it was K-ration or nothing and if he didn't eat that we might stuff them right down his throat, cans and all.

'The LST was a mess. We had 1,200 German prisoners on the main tank deck and only four GI cans to serve as toilets. Among the 1,200 were several officers who were pretty well subdued, except for one Nazi storm trooper. This lieutenant insisted that every German prisoner passing by him give him the Nazi salute. One glider pilot finally tired of this and told the corporal to tell the lieutenant - without the preliminary Nazi salute - that if he, the Nazi, saluted one more time, he, the glider pilot, intended to emphasize his point with a bayonet on the end of his rifle. That was the end of the saluting.

'I got fairly well acquainted with the prisoner that was a corporal after using him for two days as an interpreter. I discovered he was the son of a German father and a British mother. At the outbreak of war in 1939 when he was still a youngster, the family was visiting and got stuck in Germany. He was eventually drafted into the German Army. I believed his story enough to give him a note of appreciation to take along with him to his eventual prison camp in England. I hope he was able regain his English citizenship, because that's what he wanted.

'A couple more incidents on the boat: The German commander of the E-boat was taken from the water suffering from a wound in his leg. I helped carry him to the operating table below deck where an American medic got ready to work on the wound. When the medic indicated that he wanted to cut apart the officer's prized sealskin pants, the latter raised all kinds of hell. It seemed he prized the pants above his well-being. 'If he wants them that bad, let him keep them,' the sympathetic medic said. So he pulled the pants off of that wounded leg. It must have been dreadfully painful, but the Kraut never uttered a sound. And that reminded me of another German who caught his ring on a nail while descending on a ship's ladder. The ring tore into his flesh so badly that the same medic had to take a surgical saw and remove the ring. He did it without painkiller, which, for some reason the German refused. Again, the pain must have been terrible, but again, no sound. Most German soldiers had guts, but so did a lot of Americans I knew during the war. Glider pilots and German prisoners made it back to England okay on my ship and we were glad to be there and I imagine the Germans were glad to be there too.'

Flight (Warrant) Officer 'Chuck' Skidmore Jr., combat glider pilot, 91st Troop Carrier Squadron, 439th Troop Carrier Group.

'The flights coming back strung lights all over the sky in sharp contrast to the perfect wingtip patterns of out-going craft. Warmwell was the first stop on the way home for crippled aircraft. Here they brought in their wounded and dead. They landed aircraft that by every law of man and God could not be flying. They flew back looking like sieves, trailing control cables and flopping ailerons, engines coughing and flaming, flat tyres making a soggy slapping sound on the runway. Yet they came back. The dead man's ship circled the airfield in an eerie holocaust of red and white flares. It groped down through the darkness and hit the runway. The big ship turned on the runway, wheeled towards us... it suddenly stopped. 'Doc' Collins was talking to the co-pilot. His voice was soft and calm. 'He's dead'; he said matter-of-factly. 'I didn't have time to examine the wound too closely, but it was a big chest wound.' One of the crew members came up. 'We had to go around twice, two paratroops wouldn't jump. We had to go round again for them. We talked to 'em. One guy said the slipstream was too strong. I helped to shove him out the door. The German fire was coming up thick as hell. Just after the last man jumped, the pilot caught it.' His face was bitter. 'If those goddam guys had jumped it wouldn't have happened.' He must have been the first casualty to return... this dead man.'

HQ History, 474th Fighter Group, 9th Air Force at Warmwell, Dorset.

'La Bataille Suprême est Engagée! After much fighting, furore and pain the decisive shock has come, the hoped for shock. Of course, it is the Battle of France and it is the Battle of the French!

'We are told that an immense assault force has begun to leave the shores of Old England to aid us. Before, this last bastion of Western Europe was stopped for a short time by a sea of German oppression. Today it is the departure point for the offensive of liberty. France, submerged for four years but at no time reduced nor vanquished, France is arising to do its part there.

'For the sons of France, it goes without saying, the obligation is simple and sacred, to fight with all the means at their disposal. They shall destroy the detested enemy, the dishonourable enemy.

'The Battle of France has commenced. There is nothing more in the nation, in the Empire, in the armed forces but one and the same will, one and the same hope. Behind the clouds, if heavy with our blood and with our tears, there is that which will restore the sunlight and our grandeur.'

General Charles de Gaulle, Broadcast to France, June 6.

'On D-Day the teacher turned on the radio at school and there was John Snagge saying that we had invaded France. We didn't discuss it. There was no feeling of celebration. We just got back to our books. A week later the Doodlebugs started.'

Bill Tomlinson (14) who lived in the East end of London.

'This is London, London calling in the Home, Overseas and European Services of the BBC and through United Nations Radio Mediterranean. And this is John Snagge speaking. D-Day has come. Under the command of General Eisenhower Allied naval forces supported by strong air forces began landing Allied armies this morning on the north-western face of Hitler's European fortress'.

BBC Home Service Report, June 6. The first official news of the Allied landings was flashed to the world at around 9.30am (British time) on D-Day.

'We can only wait for bulletins and pray for success. It is the most exciting moment in our lives.'

Mayor Fiorello H. La Guardia of New York.

'This is Robert St. John in the NBC news room. Ladies and gentlemen, all night long bulletins have been pouring in from Berlin claiming that the invasion of Western Europe has begun. D-Day is here...!'

'When we stumbled sleepily down the hall to answer the ringing telephone we made a mental note that it was shortly before 3am. We picked up the receiver thinking it was Sherriff Roberts calling to say that there had been an accident. Instead, it was Miss Lloyd-Long playing the feminine counterpart of Paul Riviere, saying 'get up and listen to the radio; the invasion has started.' We sat by the radio for over an hour, listening to the breathtaking announcements. And then we went to bed to lie there for a long time, wide-eyed in the darkness, thinking what Rock County boys are landing on French soil tonight.'

Al Mackintosh, *Rock County Star Herald.*

U.S. Hears News Soberly; FDR Pens a Prayer
President Sits Up Late to Follow Action; Lights Blaze in Pentagon

NEW YORK, June 6-Prayers were said in churches and homes throughout America today as the nation grimly and soberly heard the news at last that its sons were embarked on the great invasion.

President Roosevelt, closeted alone ill in his bedroom, spent the early hours before dawn composing a national prayer for the victory of the Allied liberation forces.

Time was reserved on all the radio networks at 10 o'clock tonight (4 AM in the ETO) for the Commander-in-Chief to read his prayer and for listeners all over the land to join in it.

Other prayers were offered during the day in the various states in accordance with D-Day proclamations issued by the governors. In New York, Mayor Fiorello H. LaGuardia arranged a mass prayer meeting at Madison Square Garden.

Times Square Nearly Deserted

It was half-past midnight in New York and the theater crowds had departed from Time Square when the first German announcements came and the endless belt of lights around the Times building, spelled out the news and the radios of the taxicabs along the curbs broadcast cautious bulletins. SHAEF's confirmation did not come until three hours later, when most of the East was asleep.

It was still Monday in Hollywood-the day before D-Day-when the first News reached the movie colony. Bands stopped playing in the night clubs and dance halls while the glib MCs, not so glib for once, announced the opening of the invasion. The gaiety went on - but somehow it was not as gay as it had been. At the Clover Club many prominent film stars bowed their heads while an Army chaplain offered a prayer.

In war plants from coast to coast, men and women on the night shift heard the main landings reported over public address systems. In some plants they cheered, in others they listened silently - in all of them theykept right on working.

Lights Blaze in Pentagon

There was no sign of anything unusual in Washington before the news broke but soon after 1 AM lights flared up in windows all over the War Department's sprawling Pentagon Building and officials began arriving by taxi and private car.

At the White House, President Roosevelt sat up with a few intimates listening to the radio and receiving direct reports from the War Department. Gen. George C. Marshall, Chief of Staff, had remained at his desk all night but other officials, including Secretary of War Henry L.Stimson, were at home.

Chapter 4

'Gentlemen in England now a-bed shall think themselves accurs'd they were not here.'

'You will remember Henry V's words when he briefed his types for the famous sortie on Agincourt 'and gentlemen of England now abed, shall think themselves accursed they were not here.' I was not there.'

Wing Commander Bill Anderson OBE DFC AFC (*Pathfinders*, Jarrolds 1946) who saw a film of the Battle of Normandy. 'No mention was made of the bombing of the beachhead batteries by Bomber Command on D-Day. But that is how the RAF would have it. For years we had been given the limelight. D-Day was the turn of the 'Brown Jobs' who had been training ever since Dunkirk. It was enough for us to know that we played a part, even though a small one compared with theirs, in the dawn of the day of victory.'

'The thunderous roar of engines and the buffeting of the wind filled Danny Lyons' ears, as the aircraft bounced its way through the windy night! Orders and objectives whirred back and forth in his anxious and racing mind! His head was spinning, his stomach churned, there was so much to be remembered, so little time left before he had to put it into practice. Then in the odd brief silences when the wind turned and drove the engine noise away, a droning mumble filled the fuselage as muttering lips recounted orders. On either side of him his comrades pressed shoulder against shoulder and space between their legs was non-existent. Every inch of the Short Stirling was crammed with kit bags and the specialist equipment that was needed to launch a war. Nor was there was any concession to comfort in a Stirling. The floor was hard, the fuselage dark and it wasn't particularly warm. Danny squirmed, rolling his shoulders and stretching a little as his parachute harness pulled tight into his clothing and pressed the torturous knotted-string vest deep into his skin! Whichever way he turned the vest dug in all the more and any efforts to make life easier only brought rebuke from fellow sufferers cramped in their own private hell. So he stayed put, soon he'd have all the space he could ever want.

'Then the telltale rhythm of the Bristol Hercules engines faltered as the pilot slowed the aircraft, the order was given to stand and the aperture door opened. Danny instinctively reached to check his static line and the line of the man in front and then he checked his own line again. And all around the aircraft two hundred fingers and thumbs moved in the semi darkness acting out ingrained routines. Checking buckles Checking straps. Tugging and tweaking. Hooking on kit bags and other bits of extra equipment. Then it's the red light followed by an interminably endless minute of fidget and uncertainty. And when Danny thought it would never come, when he thought the pilot had forgotten and was going to take them all home again, 'sorry lads, just our little joke', it was green light on and go, go, go!'

The 'stick' shuffled towards the rectangular hole in the floor, stooping beneath the low ceiling, their thirty pound kit bags hooked to the front of their webbing, pulling that stoop into a toppling lean. Danny felt the urgency to get out, pressed from behind and driven by the momentum of the occasion. Then someone in front stumbled and this rippled domino like back down the line. Now others stumbled and with each successive man the lean forward became more and more acute until Danny had little option but to dive headlong out of the aircraft and into the swirling night sky! It was H-Hour plus 50 minutes, ten minutes before 1 am. Somewhere in that black night, eight hundred feet below on the green fields of Normandy, D-Day awaited the men of the 6th Airborne Division.

Danny fell for a five second eternity whilst his last connection with England and safety, his static line, snatched setting into motion the series of events that would pull his parachute clear. One second. Two seconds. Three seconds. Four seconds. Five seconds. Then his harness grabbed him like an iron fist and the silken canopy tautened as it swallowed the rushing air. For few seconds, he just hung there as he tried to get his bearings. But he saw nothing in that pitch black night and only heard the quickening beat of the Stirling's Hercules engines as the aircraft climbed away.

Into The Night by Snoltz.

'The first aircraft that is going to lead at the very front in the early hours of tomorrow morning is turning at the end of the tarmac to make its take-off. A graceful machine... its wing-tip lights shining red and green over the heads of the small dark figures of people watching it take off... taking off from here loaded with parachutists and taking with it perhaps the hopes and fears and the prayers of millions of people in this country who sleep tonight, not knowing that this mighty operation is taking place. There she goes now. The first aircraft leading the attack on Europe.'

Richard Dimbleby speaking from RAF Harwell on 5 June, describing the departure of the first wave of paratroops for Normandy.

'At last the big day came. On D-Day minus one, 5 June, we checked our kites and ground-tested them ready for the aircrews to marshal the aircraft on to the runway. As the day went on, in came the Paras who eventually boarded the aircraft after writing all sorts of slogans on the fuselages. It was at 23.00 hours that they began to take off. The doors of the aircraft were still open and you could hear the lads singing *Shoo Shoo Baby*, a popular song at the time.'

Fred Baker, an engine fitter on 'A' Flight, 299 Squadron at Keevil in Wiltshire. [33]

'We took off from Lyneham aerodrome on the night of 5 June. Somebody - I think it was the Padre - had the bright idea of getting a piano to keep the lads amused while we were waiting. A driver, called Jack Young, found one from somewhere and brought it in his truck to the airfield. As I could play a bit I was detailed to play a few tunes and we had a sing-song alongside the waiting planes, When the time came, we climbed into the aircraft and flew off to France to play our part in the invasion, leaving the piano in

33 *Stirling Wings: The Short Stirling Goes to War* by Jonathan Falconer (Sutton Publishing Ltd, 1995).

the middle of the airfield... it seems that next morning Jack Young went back to the airfield to collect it, but the piano had completely disappeared, He searched' everywhere but could not find it. He said 'I must have taken it to France and flogged it...'

Sergeant A. G. Reading MM, 8th Parachute Regiment.

'Soon we were flying over the Channel and what a sight that was! It seemed that everyone in England was on an excursion to the shores of Normandy. The noise from the engines of the towing planes made conversation difficult but people did not seem to have much to say except, 'This is it' and that summed up the total conversation.

'Soon we were crossing over France, then the towing planes released their tow ropes and the gliders were on their way down; the silence after the planes left us made the soldiers feel as if they were in a new world. The next thing I recall was the glider landing. The tail of the glider fell off and I was struggling in a bed of poppies. I wondered whether I was in this world or the next, then there were things to do and I was off.'

Sergeant-Major Scriven, of the 195th Field Ambulance Division.

'We made our way to a prearranged rendezvous, thence to Ranville where villagers in the dark (approximately 0350 hours) whispered 'Bonjour' from bedroom windows.

'Arrived at a château (picked previously from aerial photographs). Our second-in-command knocked and asked if there were any Germans inside. There were and four or five surrendered and were made prisoners. We then entered and set up our various departments. I was in a surgical team and we started operating about the time of the main seaborne landing, which was announced to us by a thunderous barrage from the Navy.'

E. Purchase, 225 Parachute Field Ambulance.

'A few minutes after one o'clock in the morning of 6 June 1944 Monsieur Georges Gondrée, a Norman innkeeper, was awakened by his wife Thérèse. 'At that time we slept,' he explained, 'in separate rooms; not because we wanted to, but because that was the best way of preventing German troops from being billeted upon us. She said to me, 'Get up. Don't you hear what's happening? Open the window.' I was sleepy and it took me some little time to grasp what she meant. She repeated, 'Get up. Listen. It sounds like wood breaking.' I opened the window and looked out. '

'The window which Gondrée opened was on the first floor of a cafe on the outskirts of Bénouville, a village in Normandy. It is situated a few yards from the western end of the steel swing bridge which there crosses the Canal de Caen and which by decree of the French Government will always be known as 'Pegasus Bridge.' 'It was moonlight,' he continued, 'but I could see nothing, though I did hear snapping and crunching sounds.' A German sentry was standing at the bridgehead a few yards away and Gondrée, whose wife is an Alsatian and speaks excellent German, suggested that she should ask him what was happening. She leant out of the window and did so, while her husband observed his face, clearly visible in the moonlight. His features were working, his eyes wide with fear. For a moment he did not speak and 'I then saw that he was literally struck dumb by terror. At last he stammered out the one word 'Parachutists'.'

'What a pity,' said the wife to her husband, 'those English lads will be captured,' for they both thought at that moment that what the sentry had seen was the crew of a bomber baling out. Almost immediately firing broke out and tracers began to flash across the night sky. Having two small children, the Gondrée's took refuge in the cellar, where they remained for some time listening to the spasmodic sounds of battle outside. Presently there was a knock on the front door and a voice in German called on them to leave the cafe and walk in front of German troops. This German version of 'Dilly dally, come and be killed' did not appeal to them and they remained where they were' until Madame Gondrée, clad only in her nightdress and shivering with cold, urged her husband to go up and see what was happening. Gondrée did so. 'I am not a brave man,' he said 'and I did not want to be shot, so I went upstairs and on all fours and crawled to the first-floor window. There I heard talk outside but could not distinguish the words so I pushed open the window and peeped out cautiously... I saw in front of the cafe two soldiers sitting near my petrol pump with a corpse between them.'

'Somewhat unnerved by this sight, Gondrée could not clearly understand the reply of the soldiers to his hail in French, but he thought one of them said: Armée de l'air and the other 'English flieger'. 'I still thought that they belonged to the crew of a crashed bomber, but I was worried by the clothes they had on and also by the fact that they seemed to be wearing black masks. 'This was scarcely reassuring, but the innkeeper, mindful of the danger in which he and his family appeared to stand, determined to continue his investigations. He went to another window, this one giving on to the canal hank which, runs at right angles to the road crossing the bridge. Peering out, he saw two more soldiers who 'lifted their weapons and pointed them at me. By then there were a number of flares burning in the sky, so that I could see quite plainly. One of the soldiers said to me, Vous civile? I replied' Qui, Qui and added something else which I don't remember. The soldier answered Vous civile? and after a moment I realised that these were the only words of French he knew. I was for twelve years a bank clerk in Lloyds Bank in Paris and I therefore speak good English, but I did not wish to let that fact be known at that moment, for I was not sure who they were. One of them then put his finger to his lips and gestured with his hands to indicate that I should close the shutter. This I did and went back to the cellar.'

'Nothing more happened for some time, till the Gondrée's heard sounds of digging in their vegetable garden outside. They looked through a hole in the cellar and 'there was the wonderful air of dawn coming up over the land.' Vague figures were moving about. They seemed peaceful enough and to Gondrée's astonishment 'I could hear no guttural orders, which I always associated with a German working-party. I turned to my wife and said: IIs ne gueulent pas comme d'habitude. The light grew stronger and I began to have serious doubts whether the people I could see were in fact the crew of a bomber; their behaviour seemed to me to be very strange. I told my wife to go to the hole in the cellar, listen and tell me if they were speaking German. She did so and presently said that she could not understand what they were saying. Then I in my turn listened and my heart began to beat quicker for I thought I heard the words 'all right.' 'Presently there were further sounds of knocking and this time Gondrée opened the door, to be confronted by two men with coal-black faces. He then realised that it was paint, not masks, which they were wearing. They inquired in French whether there were any Germans in the house. He answered 'no' and brought them in to the bar and thence, with some reluctance on their part, which he overcame by smiles and gestures, to the cellar. Arrived there, he pointed to his wife and two children. 'For a moment there was silence; then one soldier turned to the other and said: 'It's all right, chum.' At last I knew that they were English and burst into tears.'

'Madame Gondrée and her children at once kissed the soldiers and as a result were immediately covered with black camouflage paint.

'Monsieur and Madame Gondrée were, in all probability, the first French civilians to see British airborne troops, harbingers of freedom and victory, when they landed by parachute and from gliders on the morning of the Allied invasion of Europe.'

The Wonderful Air of Dawn; By Air To Battle, the official account of the British Airborne Divisions HMSO 1945. On 27 May British agent 'Red' Wright was among a group of scouts who went ashore, four at a time in rubber dinghies, to link up with the French Resistance, don old clothes and receive false papers and armed only with pocket pistols, casually walk several times across the two bridges over the Canal de Caen and the Orne River memorizing the local landscape and defensive features. [34]

'The Hun thinks that only a bloody fool will go there. That's why we're going.'

Major-General Richard Nelson 'Windy' Gale DSO OBE MC commanding 6th Airborne Division, 4 June 1944. Brought up in Australia, Gale - ruddy faced, six foot three in height, ramrod straight with a bristling white moustache - served in the Machine Gun Corps in the First World War, being awarded the Military Cross but he was only a lieutenant colonel in 1940. Promoted to head Britain's first airborne brigade, he was director of airborne forces at the War Office before taking command of 6th Airborne Division as a major general.

Oberstleutnant Hoffmann had just glanced at his watch. The time was forty minutes past midnight. June 6 was less than three-quarters of an hour old. For the past hour there had been a continuous drone of aircraft above the battle headquarters of III Battalion, 919th Grenadier Regiment east of Montebourg.

Another wave was approaching. The roar grew louder.

Hoffmann stepped outside the bunker. He gave a start. Six giant birds were making straight for his battle headquarters. They were clearly visible, for the moon had just broken through the clouds. 'They're bailing out.' For an instant Hoffmann thought the aircraft had been damaged and its crew was going to jump. But then he understood. This was an airborne landing by paratroops. The white mushrooms were floating down-straight at his bunker.

'Alarm! Enemy paratroops!' The men at III Battalion headquarters had never pulled on their trousers so fast before.

'Alarm! Alarm.'

The sentries' carbines were barking. They were firing at the parachutes floating down from the sky. Then the moon hid itself. Darkness enveloped the descending enemy. Hoffmann grabbed a rifle. Then the darkness was rent by the first burst of fire from an American sub machine-gun.

The battle for Normandy was on.

Fifty miles south-east of the battle headquarters of III Battalion, 919th Grenadier Regiment, on the far side of the Orne, things were also fairly noisy. The German sentry on the eastern end of the bridge over the Caen canal a Bénouville jumped as some 50 yards in front of his concrete sentry-box a spectral aircraft swooped towards the ground without any engine noise. A moment later there was a crash and a splintering sound, then quiet.

The sentry snatched his carbine from his shoulder and loaded. He held his breath,

34 See: *D-Day: The Greatest Invasion - A People's History* by Dan Van Der Vat (Madison Press Books Toronto 2003).).

listening. 'A crashed bomber,' was his first thought. After all, enemy bomber formations had been roaring overhead in from the coast for well over an hour. From the Caen direction came the noise of explosions. Anti-aircraft guns were barking from the neighbourhood of Troarn.

'They've had it,' thought Gefreiter Wilhelm Furtner. Then a searing flash blinded his eyes. He no longer heard the burst of the phosphorus grenade.

His comrades in the dugout by the approach to the bridge leapt up. They raced to their machine-gun. They fired a burst at random. They saw nothing. Suddenly they heard voices calling: 'Able-Able.' They did not know that this was the recognition signal of A Detail of a combat team of the British 6th Airborne Division, one of whose gliders had just crash-landed there in front of them. The lance-corporal of the guard was about to lift up the telephone to give the alarm to his platoon commander on the far side of the bridge. But there was no time. Two hand-grenades came sailing in through the aperture of the pill-box. Finished.

There was no point now in keeping quiet. The hand-grenades were bound to have roused the guard on the far side. With shouts of 'Able-Able' the Tommies galloped across the bridge.

They heard other gliders crashing. They also heard the rallying cries of B Detail: 'Baker-Baker.' And a moment later they could hear C Detail as well: 'Charlie-Charlie.'

The German machine-gun was blazing away over the bridge. The first Tommies were falling. But the bulk of them got through. A short skirmish. The guard on the bridge was overwhelmed. The crossing of the Caen Canal at Bénouville was in British hands. Only Lance-Corporal Weber got away. He tore through the village to the commandant. 'British paratroops have seized the canal bridge.' What he did not know was that the nearby bridge over the Orne at Ranville had also been seized by men of the British 5th Parachute Brigade in a surprise attack. At 2nd Battalion, 192nd Panzer Grenadier Regiment at Cairon the field telephone rang: 'Launching immediate counterattack against enemy paratroops in Bénouville bridgehead.'

'Quickly Danny Lyons unclipped the kit bag and paid out its attachment line through his gloved palm. With nothing to gauge his descent, with no horizon to fix his position, this kit bag dangling twenty feet below would be the only thing to tell him where the ground was. Automatically he ran through his checklist to, everything was where it should have been, then once again he strained for the familiar, a house, a tree, anything. Suddenly the dangling line slackened! Instinctively he braced for impact- bent his knees and hit the soft-ish ground, rolling to his left. The months of repetitive training now kicked in. Before he knew it the harness was off. The chute made safe. His equipment out of the kit bag and onto his back. And he was stooped low so as not to present a target!

'After about half an hour of trotting back and forth across the surrounding fields Danny found someone he knew and together they worked towards higher ground. Their eyes were growing accustomed to the poor light; they could make out fences and trees. Then near to the top of a low hill they saw a range of buildings, probably a farm and the furtive movement of familiar outlines. As they approached Danny called out 'Ham' and was answered by the word 'Jam', it was their side. They were paras, infantry men of 5 Para Brigade who'd taken refuge in the farmhouse where one of their number, injured in the drop, was laid on the kitchen table and receiving first-aid from the farmer's wife. Other paras rallied on farm and the stick commander set about fortifying their position. They had a Vickers machine gun and Danny and his mate joined the task of setting it up to cover any approach from the passing lane. At about 0330-0400 the sky started to lighten and at last they were able to pick out landmarks and plot them on their maps. Danny and his mate should have landed close to the village of Le Bas de Ranville, but the wind and their search for a vantage point, now had them about two miles from where they should have been. They waited for the light to improve a little more, then at approximately 05:00 they left the relative comfort of the farmhouse and made their way cross country to join up with the rest of Division HQ at the Château du Heaume.

'The better light brought blessings and they were able to pass through the landscape a lot easier knowing that gate posts topped with rounded foliage were gate posts and not the outline of a German sentry or that protruding logs or fallen glider poles were just that. Not the barrels of tanks and mobile guns. But the better light had its downside too, sobering up any elation of a safe landing or the joy of serving a purpose at last. Danny was now within yards of where he had floated to earth a couple of hours before and his blood froze. He saw his rolled up chute, the empty kit bag, his tell tale boot prints in the soft earth and a wooden sign bearing a 'skull and cross-bones' accompanied by the chilling words 'Gefahr Miner'! He had landed slap bang in the middle of a minefield, thank god it had been dark and he'd had the luck of blind ignorance.

'Quickly they moved on and a bit further down the road they came across the remains of a fire fight. Slumped against a wall was a young German soldier, perhaps a little younger than themselves, he was in a poor state, a British officer lay dead on the other side of the wall. He'd been someone they both knew. They disabled the body taking his dog-tags, pay book, cigarettes and revolver. Then gave the smokes to the wounded German and continued on their way, arriving at the château around 06:00.

'Stragglers had been arriving all through the early hours and the process of digging in was well under way. Danny was tasked with digging a slit trench on the south side of the château, where he would install and operate a No. 22 Wireless Set until relieved. Digging in was hazardous work, neighbourhood resistance was considerable and the château was under sporadic small arms fire. The paras had stirred up a hornets' nest and although the local military had been surprised by Major Howard's successful glider assault and his capture of the bridges over Orne River and the Caen Canal, the defenders were now wide awake and speedily organising. But the Allied surprise had been total and those very same German defenders believing all was well, had confidently gone about their evening activities, just a few hours before, happy in the knowledge that they were safe behind Rommel's Atlantic Wall. They'd had a very rude awakening as hundreds of armed men appeared out of nowhere! Suddenly their own surprise airborne strategies had been successfully used against them! And scenes reminiscent of the German assault on the Belgian fortress at Eben Emael, were being re-enacted all around them. But instead of a single isolated action involving 78 Fallshirmjägers (paratroopers) as in 1940, these hapless defenders were now confronted with who knows how many men. They seemed to be everywhere! And with every passing minute more and more armed invaders were emerging from the shadowy countryside. Then as if to compound their confusion, a rolling rumble of big guns could be heard out at sea. Something big was in the offing and they could only hope they were up against another poorly planned raid like the 1942 raid on Dieppe! Never in their wildest dreams could these defenders have imagined that behind that distant rumble of guns, 5,000 ships were preparing to land 133,000 troops and that another 22,000 others were already coming from the skies above!

'Danny made himself comfortable in the newly dug trench, flicked the switch, the valves warmed and the 22 set hummed into life. Bullets were still flying back and forth across the lawn and a couple thudded into the château wall whilst others ricocheted off the stonework balustrades. Instinctively he hunkered down hoping the Norman earth would give him just a few inches more. More bullets clipped the walls and loose masonry pattered onto the groundsheet covering their metre deep trench. Then Danny was handed his first signal of the day. This was it; a year's training would now be put to the test. He made his beret comfortable, clamped the head-phones to his ears and flexed his fingers as do concert pianists before they strike the first note, positioned his Morse key and sent out a stream of code. It was 0700 and it had already been a very long day for Danny, the longest he could ever remember. It was well over twenty four hours since he'd had any real sleep. It would be many more hours before he and his mates were to get any more sleep. Because having achieved all they had set out to do the 6th were now prisoners of their own success. Now was the time for 'guts'! And until they were relieved by the troops pushing up the beaches, the men and boys of the 6th Airborne Division would have to hold the front line. They had to prevent German re-enforcements bolstering up their beleaguered Atlantic Wall defences.

'It was now H+7 hours and 19-year old Danny Lyons and the Divisional HQ Signals Section would continue at their posts for the next sixteen hours without a break!'

Into the Night by **Snoltz.**

'All over Normandy German headquarters were empty of senior officers. The practice alert for the night of the 5th/6th had been cancelled. A number of senior officers were on the road to Rennes where there, was to be a kriegspiel the following morning. Prophetically, the theme for the 'staff war game' was 'enemy landings in Normandy, preceded by parachute drops'. At Caen, earlier that evening, a weekly staff conference ended with 52-year old Generalleutnant Wilhelm Richter, who commanded the 716th Division from a series of bunkers in a quarry on the outskirts of Caen, jokingly informing his officers of that the wires were buzzing with a rumour that an invasion was imminent. They had, he said, suffered so many false alarms that they could certainly expect it to happen that night! But Generaloberst Friedrich Dollmann, the tall and gangly Commander of the Seventh Army, had an afterthought that evening; worried about the exodus of officers for Rennes, he ordered them not to leave Normandy before dawn. It was too late. Many had taken the opportunity to snatch an evening off duty.

'In St Lô a midnight 53rd birthday party in honour of General der Artillerie Erich Marcks commanding LXXXIV Corps was under way. One of his staff officers was present: 'He disliked all forms of celebration, so he looked surprised; his gaunt strong-willed, deeply lined face might have been that of a scientist or scholar. He had lost a leg in Russia and the joint of his artificial limb creaked as he stood up; he raised his hand in a friendly, but nevertheless cool gesture.

'We each drank a glass of Chablis standing and the little ceremony was over in a few minutes.' [35]

'As far as I know', said Marcks, 'the British, they will go to church on Sunday and on Monday they will come here but our division is the only one here and we are here to protect the big steel factory and Caen...' Rommel had proposed that Marcks, who was born in 1891 - the same year as Rommel - be given command of the Seventh Army

35 See *D-Day* by Warren Tute, John Costello and Terry Hughes (Pan 1974).

but Hitler preferred his Nazi sycophant, the inept and indolent 62-year old Generaloberst Friedrich Dollmann (who on 6 June, despite his concerns over the exodus of officers for the war games at Rennes, was one of its attendees, as was Obergruppenführer 'Sepp' Dietrich commanding 1st SS, whose HQ was at Rouen[36]). On 29 June Dollmann apparently committed suicide after failing to stem the tide of Operation 'Epsom' when he committed the entire II SS Panzer Corps. Hitler was told that Dollmann had died of a 'heart-attack'.

'At the Dives Bridge on the Varaville-Grangues road another sentry was peering into the night. The watch at the bridge was mounted by II Battalion, 744th Infantry Regiment, which was barely a platoon in strength. The men had every reason to curse the bridge. Four weeks previously III Battalion had organised a night exercise without warning neighbouring units and staged a dummy attack on the bridge: The sentry, of course, could not have know that the shots that suddenly came from the approach to the bridge were blanks. He had thought the balloon had gone up in earnest and opened up with his machine-gun. There had been several wounded and two men killed. There was a terrible rumpus and some very unpleasant investigations. All that flashed through the mind of the sentry on the bridge when, shortly after midnight, he saw three men with blackened faces charge up the embankment. 'Silly fools,' he called out to them contemptuously. But then he jumped. Too late. He was given no time to call out or to scream. Without sound he collapsed, stabbed by a long paratroop knife. From then onward it was an easy matter for the Tommies, Five minutes later the bridge was blown sky high.'

Invasion-they're coming! by Paul Carell.

It was exactly 0111 hours '- unforgettable moment -' when the field telephone rang on General der Artillerie Marcks' desk at his HQ at St Lô. Marcks and his staff officers were still sitting over their maps. Something important was coming through and the general himself picked up the receiver. The call was from chief of operations, 716th Division. Whilst listening, the General stood up stiffly, his hand gripping the edge of the table. With a nod, he motioned Admiral Hoffmann his chief of staff to listen in. Hurriedly the words tumbled out of the earpiece: 'Enemy paratroops have landed east of the Orne estuary. Main area is Bréville-Ranville and the northern edge of the forest of Bavent. Main objective apparently the Dives bridges and the crossings over the Orne. Countermeasures are in progress.'

'Was this, at last, the invasion, the storming of Festung Europa? Someone said haltingly 'Perhaps they are only supply drops for the French Resistance.'

These were the questions to be answered. After a little hesitation Admiral Hoffmann shook his head. 'Too close to our front line. The Resistance people would never risk that.' His conclusion was: 'This is the invasion.'

General Marcks nodded. 'Let's wait and see.' [37]

At 0200 on the 6th June Marcks persuaded Seventh Army to issue an alert. Feldmarschall Gerd von Rundstedt, Commander-in-Chief West, ordered Panzer Lehr and 12th SS Divisions ready to move at 0400 but all movements of armour were subject

36 The first indication that 1st SS Panzer Division Leibstandarte in Turnhout received of the Allied landings was in the afternoon of 6 June when the Chief of Staff was told by OKW to put the Division at two and a half hours' notice to move. Lehmann & Tiemann, *The Leibstandarte IV/I*.

37 See *Invasion-they're coming!* by Paul Carell (George Harrap & Co. Ltd 1962) and *D-Day* by Warren Tute, John Costello and Terry Hughes (Pan 1974).

to Hitler's approval (which was not forthcoming until 1600 that same afternoon. However, von Rundstedt dispatched half the 12th SS to the coast north of Lisieux to deal with parachutists and a reported seaborne landing near Deauville). At 0925 Marcks reported to Generalmajor Max Pemsel, Chief of Staff, Seventh Army: 'The situation on the left bank of the Orne is dangerous; enemy tanks have reached the artillery positions; 84th Corps has no mobile reserves equipped with anti-tank weapons.' Marcks asked for 12th SS to be dispatched at once to the area west of Caen, since 21st Panzer was already committed to the east of the Orne.

'They were still arguing the pros and cons when Oberst Hamann, acting commander, 709th Division, came through on the telephone: 'Enemy paratroops south of Ste-Germain-de-Varreville and at Ste-Marie-du-Mont, A second group west of the Merderet river and on the road at Ste-Mère-Église, Headquarters of III Battalion, 919th Grenadier Regiment, holding prisoners from the US 101st Airborne Division.'

'The time was 0145 hours. Five minutes later, at exactly 0150, the telephones were also ringing in Paris, in a big block of flats on the Bois de Boulogne. The chief of operations of Naval Group West, Hauptmann Wegener, summoned his officers to the situation room. 'I think the invasion is here,' he said calmly.

'Admiral Hoffmann, the chief-of-staff, did not even wait to dress. He grabbed a dressing-gown and rushed into the situation room. The reports from the radar stations under Leutnant von Willisen were unanimous: 'Large number of blips on the screens.'

'At first the technicians thought the huge number of blips must be caused by some interference. There just could not be so many ships. But presently no doubt was left. A vast armada must be approaching the Normandy coast.

'This can only be the invasion fleet,' Hoffmann concluded. He ordered: 'Signal to C-in-C West. Signal to the Führer's headquarters. The invasion is on.'

'But both in Paris and in Rastenburg the news was received sceptically. 'What, in this weather? Surely your technicians must be mistaken?' Even the chief-of-staff of C-in-C West scoffed: 'Maybe a flock of seagulls?' They still would not believe it. But the navy was certain. Naval headquarters alerted all coastal stations and all naval forces in port: 'The invasion fleet is coming!'

Invasion-they're coming! by Paul Carell.

While the 1st Airborne Division was engaged in the campaigns of North Africa, Sicily and Italy, those in authority at home had been busy organizing the expansion of airborne forces; but when in May 1943 the 6th Airborne Division was formed, its training and expansion were again limited by the number of aircraft available. It was placed under the command of Major-General R. N. Gale DSO OBE MC. Major-General R. E. Urquhart DSO was the other Divisional General, having taken over command of the 1st Airborne Division from Major-General Down. Lieutenant-General Browning assumed command over all airborne forces and subsequently established a Corps Headquarters. With them, as an indispensable part of the organization was 38 Group RAF but many of its aircraft and crews were still in Africa. It was not until the summer and autumn of 1943 that its whole activity could be employed in the training of troops destined to play a part of the highest significance in what was hoped and believed would be the opening of the war's final stage - the invasion of the Continent of Europe.

It is possible that development would have been hastened if the full number of enthusiastic and skilful officers had been there to continue their long association with airborne troops. Unfortunately for those troops, for England and for the Allies, they had already laid down their lives. Squadron Leader Wilkinson, who with Group Captain Cooper was an expert in the art of glider towing, had met death over the inhospitable hills of Sicily, flying a Halifax with a Horsa on tow to the attack on the Ponte Grande. Four days later Major Lander, commanding the 21st Independent Parachute Company, who was an expert in the difficult business of dropping in advance of the gliders and making flarepaths to assist their landing, had been killed in the expedition against the Primosole Bridge. Wing Commanders P. Day and W. S. Barton DSO DFC closely connected with the work of 38 Group, were also dead and to these losses must be added the deaths, already recorded, of Rock, Norman and Hopkinson. When a new arm is being developed, it is usually those intimately associated with its beginnings who run the greatest risk and pay the highest penalty. So it was in the early days of flight; so it was again when airborne troops began to play their part in war. Fortunately, ready to take the places of the pioneers were men endowed with the same enthusiasm and very soon the same degree of skill.

Glider training went on slowly and steadily; larger and larger formations presently took the air. By November exercises in which as many as forty gliders took part were being successfully mounted and the methods of marshalling larger formations and putting them on the right route for their objective were being worked out and could now be tried on a reasonable scale. In these unceasing labours the 9th United States Troop Carrying Command, by then in the United Kingdom, played a considerable part and their enthusiastic help made possible a policy of expansion on a more generous scale than had at first been hoped or contemplated. In January 1944 Air Vice-Marshal L. N. Hollinghurst CB CBE DFC, a most experienced officer, was appointed to command all the squadrons of the Royal Air Force now formed into several groups. Stirlings and a number of Halifaxes no longer needed by Bomber Command were diverted to airborne work and the training of their crews in the use of special devices to enhance the accuracy of navigation was put in hand. Such progress was made that on 24 April 1944, an entire airborne division, the 6th, was taken into the air by the united efforts of the Royal Air Force and the United States Troop Carrying Command. On that day and the two following, it carried out an exercise which, though those who took part in it did not know it at the time, was a dress rehearsal for the invasion of Normandy six weeks later.

Throughout this long period, the lessons learnt by all three Services in Africa and Sicily were being studied and applied. One thing soon became very clear. No successful invasion of Europe could take place without airborne forces able and ready to leap over Germany's vaunted west wall and thus bring its formidable defences to no account. Every invasion plan, therefore, made provision for the use of parachutists and glider-borne troops.

The chances that they would succeed seemed in the spring of 1944 to be high, certainly high enough to justify the risk of using them. To begin with, the country in which they would operate was inhabited by people friendly to them, from whom aid of one kind or another might reasonably be expected. Then, too, it was known that the quality of the German troops and equipment in France was very mixed. Some of it was good, but much of it was not. Most important of all, air superiority and, very possibly air supremacy, would be ours. This dominion over the enemy in the air was the determining factor in planning airborne operations which, if successful, would greatly lighten the heavy task of those who must invade by sea.

It was as far back as August 1943 that the use of airborne troops in the Caen-Bayeux area of Normandy was being studied. At first the dropping of an airborne division immediately in front of the seaborne invaders was considered; but it was soon realized that, if they were spread over a wide area, they would be unable, lightly armed as they were, to offer serious resistance to the enemy's armour should he choose to use it in any strength against them. When General Montgomery, fresh from the triumphs of the 8th Army in the Mediterranean, arrived to take command of the invasion forces under the direction of the Supreme Commander, it did not take him long to decide that they would be best used in helping the 1st Corps to hold and protect the left flank of the British sector. How they were to do so will shortly become apparent.

Planning proceeded in detail through the late winter of 1943 and the spring of 1944. As information concerning conditions in Normandy flowed in, it became obvious that many of the landing zones tentatively chosen for gliders would not be suitable, for, as the reconnaissance photographs showed, the enemy was engaged in the erection of stout poles designed to over-set gliders at the moment of touching down. Consequently, wherever possible, parachute troops were substituted for glider borne, the first to be reinforced by the second when daylight revealed the best places where gliders could land with a reasonable chance of survival.

Many of the plans had been devised by a staff of Army and Air Force officers working in an unobtrusive house hiding among trees on Salisbury Plain. The precautions to maintain secrecy were elaborate and effective - almost too much so. There was but a single key to the house and, when one day the officer who possessed it was delayed, he found on arrival a throng of eager planners, most of them of field rank, in a state of high indignation, far the door was fast locked and entry by any other means was impossible, since all the windows were barred. For an hour the planners had had 'to fleet the time carelessly' in silence or in talk on more trivial matters, the nature of their occupation making it impassable far them to discuss what was uppermost in their minds outside in the churchyard which, *absit omen,* stood next to the house.

During the last weeks before the day of the invasion, the volume of training increased. It was during this period that Major-General Gale issued to his officers a general instruction on the conduct of the coming battle, in which he summed up the whole duty of the airborne soldier. 'You must,' he said, 'possess tactical ability, you must take care of your men and you must have a sound and properly working system of supply and maintenance of equipment.' The first duty of every commander, whatever his station, was to know what was expected of him. 'It is not a question of what he wants to do but what he is wanted to do.'

The degree of freedom allowed to subordinates in the method of carrying out their task was next emphasized. 'You must remember' urged the General 'that it is your plan and it must be your duty to ensure that it is your plan which is being carried out. Your responsibility in this is not one that you can be permitted to shirk. Your natural tendency may be to fight shy of it. You cannot; for ultimately the edifice is yours and its foundation and cornerstones must be laid by you.' Gale then laid down, or rather reiterated, the principles on which an assault upon an enemy must always be based and was especially emphatic on the manner in which the inevitable counter-attack must be met and defeated. 'At night hold your fire,' he advised 'and beat your enemy by guile. By day or by night you must lay traps for him. Laugh quietly at him if he falls into your snares and when you have him, kick him in the pants.' How best to do so was contained in a number of suggestions or maxims and the General ended with a pregnant phrase, 'What you get by stealth and guts,' he said, 'you must hold with skill and determination.'

As May gave place to June the main anxiety of the airborne commanders - one which they shared with their naval and military colleagues - was the weather. Its importance to any enterprise of great pitch and moment needs no emphasis; but the fact that the invaders of Normandy were to be taken to their destination in aircraft as well as in ships made suitable weather even more essential. When the revised plans for the raid on Dieppe, carried out not quite two years before, were being drafted, it had been found that weather favourable to the Navy might be unfavourable to the airborne troops. For that reason commandos, not parachute battalions, had attacked the two main coastal batteries guarding the port. The attack on Dieppe was only a raid and, as is always so in such an operation, the hardest problem was not how to put the troops ashore but how to take them off again. What Ramsay, Montgomery and Leigh-Mallory were planning to carry out under Eisenhower was not a raid but an invasion. Provided, therefore, that weather conditions suitable for the airborne part of the task were not too unfavourable for the Navy, the operation .could be launched with a reasonable prospect of success. Meteorological experts, whose task no man envied, gave it as their opinion that, with due regard to the state of the tide - a vital factor where the Navy was concerned-two days, the 5th and 6th of June, would be suitable. If the invasion did not take place on one of them, it would have to be postponed for at least a fortnight, so that the tide might once more be of the height and speed required.

All was ready for June 5th, but the forecast on the 4th was unfavourable and the order to start could not be given. The further outlook was unsettled - so much, so that the chief German meteorological officer gave it as his professional opinion that no invasion could take place on that day or the next. The Allied experts were of another view. Conditions on the night of June 5th/6th and for twenty-four hours later, though not very good, would be possible.

For General Eisenhower that was enough. In the slowly gathering dusk Air Chief Marshal Sir Trafford Leigh-Mallory, commanding the Allied Expeditionary Air Force, flew from airfield to airfield to speak to the pilots and crews and take leave of troops, many of whom were to go into action for the first time.

Their equipment, if not perfect, had been devised and constructed in the light of experience gained by their predecessors at the risk and loss of many lives on the stony fields of Africa, the dusty olive yards of Sicily. The aircraft and the gliders in which they flew, though not so numerous as they might have hoped and expected after more than four years of war - there were not enough to carry the whole Division in one lift - were manned by well-trained and for the most part experienced crews. The officers and men themselves were most resolute and determined; upon their right flank American Allies as well, if not better, equipped and twice as numerous, were also to go into battle and to share with them the peril and the glory.

Sunset had faded from the sky when Air Vice-Marshal Hollinghurst took off in the first aircraft carrying the pathfinders. The invasion of Europe had begun and the airborne troops were in its van. The first men of them to land were Captains Tate and Robert Midwood and Lieutenant Robert de Latour. They touched French soil between ten and twenty minutes past midnight, the foremost of the 22nd Independent Parachute Company. Their task, which they duly, if with some difficulty, accomplished, was to mark with lights the landing and dropping zones.

The 3rd and 5th Parachute Brigades, comprising the parachute element of the 6th Airborne Division, landed together and fought side by side. How they did so is best described by recounting the exploits of each brigade in turn. It was the duty of the 5th Parachute Brigade, under the command of Brigadier J. H. N. Poett, to land in the area north of Ranville and there to accomplish three tasks. They were first to seize the crossings over the River Orne and the Caen Canal near the villages of Bénouville and Ranville. For this purpose six gliders carrying a special coup de main party were to be used. They were also to secure and hold the area surrounding these two villages and the village of Le Bas Ranville. Finally they were to clear and protect landing zones near Ranville and Bénouville on which the gliders carrying the rest of the Division, on the evening of the first day, would touch down.

The part of Normandy in which these operations were to be carried out consists of high ground interspersed with valleys through which flow the rivers Orne and Dives. Separating them is a belt of ground well provided with woods, of which the largest is the Bois de Bavent. The pasture in the valleys is lush and the rivers are bordered by reeds and thick, long grass. There are a considerable number of open spaces in the form of fields devoted to pasture or tillage. The country depicted in the landscapes of Sisley and Monet, though belonging to a different part of France, closely resembles that in which the parachute and glider borne troops were to land.

The first and all-important task, the seizure of the two bridges, was to be accomplished by a force of six platoons of the 2nd Battalion of the Oxfordshire and Buckinghamshire Light Infantry, helped by a detachment of the Royal Engineers. Three of them were ordered to land within fifty yards of the east end of the swing bridge across the Caen Canal and three within the same distance of the western end of the bridge across the River Orne. The bridges were to be seized immediately and half an hour later the attackers would be reinforced by the 600 strong 7th Parachute Battalion, who were to land near Ranville, 1,000 yards from the bridge over the Orne. To make certain that the parachute troops dropped in the right place, it was decided that pathfinders should land a short time before them and set out navigational and other aids for the use of the parachutists.

Training for this very difficult .and dangerous operation began in April and Colonel George Chatterton, in command of the Glider Pilot Regiment, was fortunate enough to discover a part of England bounded roughly by the four villages of Aston, Bampton, Buckland and Hinton, which is very much like that part of Normandy where the two bridges were situated. 'Some weeks before the show we did an exercise,' reports Major R. J. Howard DSO who led the attack on the swing bridge over the Caen Canal, 'during which we 'pranged' the bridges at Lechlade. This was a tremendous help, for the place was very like the part of Normandy we subsequently attacked.' [38]

38 On the River Exe, where a road crossed both the river and a canal, Howard spent a week drilling his men in the bridge attack over and over, night and day, complete with live grenades and explosives, as the local citizenry watched the show. Each platoon was given a letter designation and each platoon as it went into action was trained to shout this letter at the top of its collective voice. The tactic was designed to keep elements of the assault force from shooting each other in the darkness and confusion of the initial attack. Howard trained his men for this operation so thoroughly that the soldiers of any platoon could perform the tasks assigned every other platoon. Although he had driven his men to the point of complete exhaustion in training, they had complete confidence in themselves and in him. 'If Johnny Howard said we could do it,' said one soldier long afterward, 'we could do it.' The assault force had been visited by Field Marshal Bernard L. Montgomery himself on June 3. 'Can you do it?' asked Montgomery. 'We can,' said Howard. Monty added quietly, 'Get as many of the chaps back as you can.'

RAF and 6th Airborne Division Operations 5/6 June

38 Group

295, 296, 297, 570 Squadrons	Albemarle
190, 196, 299, 620 Squadrons	Stirling
298, 644 Squadrons	Halifax

46 Group

48, 233, 271, 512, 575 Squadrons Dakota

1665 HCU had sixty trained reserve crews on stand-by.

38 and 46 Groups RAF had undergone many weeks of intensive training which culminated in Exercise 'Mush', carried out on 21 April over an area stretching from the Severn estuary to the borders of Wiltshire and Oxfordshire. Such exercises, of which the frequency increased as D-Day drew nearer, were difficult and dangerous; but both Lieutenant-General Sir Frederick 'Boy' Browning, commanding the airborne forces and Air Vice-Marshal Hollinghurst, commanding the air transport groups, took the view that it was better to run considerable risks rather than to send half-trained and inexperienced soldiers and air crews into battle. This decision was abundantly justified, for the task facing the Groups was heavy. Not only must the 6th Airborne Division be taken to the right place, it had also to arrive at precisely the right moment, if surprise, essential to success, was to be achieved. All turned therefore on correct timing. 'The interval between take-offs' said Hollinghurst 'was of paramount importance, as we were working with very little margin of range. The use of different types of aircraft and different types of combinations complicated matters because of the different speeds'.

Dusk had fallen over England when the first aircraft, piloted by Squadron Leader Merrick with Hollinghurst on board took off from Harwell at 2303 hours. The pathfinder aircraft, six Albemarles, carried the 22nd Independent Parachute Company to the three main dropping zones in the neighbourhood of the Orne. All went well until the areas were reached, when one of the aircraft mistook its own zone and dropped its passengers on the south-east corner of the neighbouring zone, where they erected lights and beacons. The result was that in the main drop fourteen 'sticks' of the 3rd Parachute Brigade arrived at the wrong zone and the situation was for a time confused.

Out of the three zones chosen, the third, known as 'V' was situated in a valley with a wet and treacherous surface, for the River Dives, which ran through it, had overflowed its banks. [39] At this zone the advanced guard composed of part of the 3rd Parachute Brigade was dropped from fourteen Albemarles of 295 and 570 Squadrons. One, unable to find the dropping zone after seven unsuccessful runs, was hit by anti-aircraft fire and returned to base with Major W. A. C. Collingwood, the Brigade Major, jammed in the exit hole. There was a 60lb kit-bag attached to one of his legs, but despite this handicap his men heaved him on board and he arrived in Normandy later in the day by glider. Other aircraft loosed their cargo of parachute troops too soon. In the event, 106 out of 140 of the men of the advanced guard were dropped accurately.

The main body of the 3rd Parachute Brigade was carried into action thirty minutes

---

39 The Dives is a small river, which winds gently among the water-meadows and willow trees; but the Germans had flooded its valley as part of their scheme of defence and made an impenetrable marsh from half a mile to two miles wide. *Dawn Of D-Day.*

later in 108 Dakotas of 46 Group. Seventy-one of these conveyed the principal group to zone 'V' by the River Dives, but only 17 aircraft dropped their passengers on the correct spot, nine within one mile and eleven within 1½ miles. Two-thirds of the strength of the brigade were dissipated over a wide area and its most vital task, the destruction of a battery of four coastal guns believed to be of 5.7-inch calibre, near the village of Merville, which had been allotted to the 9th Battalion, was thus rendered even more hazardous than had been expected.

The 5th Parachute Brigade, taken into action by 129 aircraft, found their dropping zone correctly marked. 123 aircraft dropped their loads accurately, though a high wind scattered the parachute troops far and wide. 2,026 out of 2,125 parachute troops of this brigade were dropped and 702 out of 755 containers.

A total of 264 aircraft and 98 glider combinations were despatched. Altogether 4,310 paratroops were dropped and gliders carrying 493 troops, 17 guns, 44 jeeps and 55 motor cycles successfully released. Seven aircraft and 22 gliders were lost. One of the lessons learnt and applied in future operations was the importance of maintaining a steady course when near the dropping zone in face of anti-aircraft fire. There is abundant evidence that 'jinking' threw many of the parachute troops off balance at the critical moment when the red lights had been switched on and they were preparing to jump.

The operation to secure the two bridges over the River Orne and the Caen Canal began at 22.30 hours on 5 June when six Horsa gliders were towed off from Tarrant Rushton by Halifaxes from 298 and 644 Squadrons. At 2250 hours Dakotas of 233 Squadron towed six Horsas into the air above Blakehill Farm. Seven Horsas left Down Ampney at 2249 hours behind the Dakotas of 271 Squadron. From Harwell a further four Horsas carrying paratroops and medical staff left at 2310 hours towed by Albemarles from 295 and 570 Squadrons. More Horsas left Brize Norton at 0230 hours on 6 June, towed by Albemarles.

'Each time an explosion took place we bounced a couple of hundred feet or so and it was on one of these occasions that the leader of our paratroop stick - still waiting for the order to jump with the red preparation light on - was jerked through the hole head downwards and completely blocked it.

'I could hear through the intercom the verbal and physical efforts of my wireless operator and gunner to pull him out but he was solidly stuck. We reached home some three hours after take-off with the unfortunate paratroop leader still blocking the hole.

'The problem remained as to how I could land, there being a very real danger that the landing itself might throw him out of the aircraft. After three orbits of the airfield, a triumphant shout from my crew indicated that they had managed to pull him back inside the aircraft.'

D. S. C. Brierly, 570 Squadron RAF.

'We met heavy flak over the DZ and I was wounded in the left leg but we did drop our paratroopers in the right place as I was to learn later. We had both tyres punctured by flak and cannon fire and had 150 holes in the aircraft and a hole in the port tailplane, but we landed safely on the rims of the wheels and pulled the undercarriage up on touching down. This shows what punishment a Stirling could take.'

Warrant Officer Leonard Brock, flight engineer on Stirling EF243/S on 299 Squadron flown by Flying Officer 'Gib' Goucher which took off from Keevil at 23.35 hours on 5 June.

We dropped the paratroops in Normandy at about 02.00hrs and returned and tried to sleep, while the ground crews worked hard to refuel all the aircraft and line them up, closely packed, at the eastern end of the main runway, with tow ropes attached to the Horsa gliders.'

Flight Lieutenant George Copeman, wireless operator on Squadron Leader D.W Triptree's crew on 299 Squadron.

'After the aircraft were clear of the 'drome we went back to our flight dispersal to fill empty petrol cans with engine oil ready for the return of the aircraft for refuelling. Having only one 450-gallon oil bowser it would have been a big job topping up the oil tanks on the aircraft, so we formed a chain up through the fuselage, through the hatch and on to the mainplane. In the meantime the petrol bowsers were going from plane to plane topping up the fuel tanks while other lads were clearing out the sick bags. It was a very quick turn-around and we got the aircraft marshalled back on the runway ready to take off again with the Horsa gliders that evening.'

Fred Baker, engine fitter, on 299 Squadron. Shortly after 19.00 hours on the evening of D-Day 33 Stirling crews at Keevil flew back to France for their second trip across the Channel in less than 24 hours, towing Horsas containing Divisional Troops of the 2nd Ox & Bucks Light Infantry. The first of the Horsas began to land in France on LZ 'W', west of the Caen Canal, at 21.30 hours. George Copeman on Stirling 'G' skippered by Squadron Leader Triptree, recalls:

'We took off in the early evening of the 6th and formed up for the flight over the Channel, flying at a steady 1,000 feet. After casting off our glider those who could, watched intently as the gliders dived steeply down and smashed their way through the poles on the landing zone. There was more heavy machine-gun fire than during the previous night when the tracer looked pretty, but it was very effective.

'It was a magnificent sight with ships everywhere, landing craft, aircraft and HMS *Warspite* firing its 16-inch guns over the top of our troops, big black belches of smoke with each salvo. When we turned and went out to sea we passed near the Warspite. Shortly afterwards Tosh Truelove, our tail gunner, happened to mention one of our Stirlings hitting the water near the Warspite and I knew instantly that it was Bob Clark's aircraft. As I looked back it was already half submerged and burning furiously. Nothing could be identified.

'When we got back, Clark's aircraft was certainly missing but how could I have known it was his aircraft near the *Warspite*? Some weeks later when the 299 Squadron adjutant, Roy Fischel, was on leave, I was sitting at his desk trying to keep his job under control, when in came a letter from the Admiralty. It said that on D-Day a Stirling had hit the water near the Warspite, which had put out a boat and picked up the body of a Flying Officer Boyce. He was Clark's navigator.'

Flying Officer J. H. Clark and his five-man crew in Stirling 'K' had successfully cast off their Horsa glider, piloted by Sergeant Richardson of the Glider Pilot Regiment and carrying nine troops, but as Boyce gave Clark a course for home their Stirling IV was hit by flak and within minutes it had crashed into the sea in flames.[40]

40 *Stirling Wings:* The Short Stirling Goes to War by Jonathan Falconer (Sutton Publishing Ltd, 1995).

'...on D-Day evening - of course it was coming up to Midsummer, so it was light for quite a time - there was such a commotion. Everything started firing; people got their Stens out and rifles and everything. And two Junkers Ju88 bombers came over. They could only have been 40 or 50 feet up and both of them were on fire. The nearest one to me, I could see the pilot clearly. And they swept over our heads, hit the sea and blew up. Later the same evening there was another British glider landing and as they were coming back we saw a Stirling had been hit. It's a frightening sight, to see a big aircraft burning in the sky. And of course the whole little bay at Lion-sur-Mer and Ouistreham was absolutely packed with craft waiting to get in to 'Sword', or lying off. And this Stirling, even though it was burning badly, was still manoeuvring so that it didn't hit anything... Then when it hit the sea there was an almighty explosion. You suddenly realised you were in a war...'

Stan Leech, B10 Beach Signals; one of the units formed specifically to provide the beach-master with communications in the early stages of a landing. 'We were his servants' he says.[41] No-one survived the crash of the Stirling and only two bodies were recovered from the sea by the air-sea rescue service. They were later identified as Flying Officer F. A. Boyce and Warrant Officer E. H. Shrump. The glider that Triptree's crew had cast off over the LZ, piloted by Lieutenant Martin and carrying eight fully equipped troops, crashed on landing, killing the pilot. [42]

'On the night of 5/6 June we took off for France taking Captain George Holland and a medical team. Shortly after take-off the Gee equipment went on the blink and as we approached the Channel it packed up altogether. The weather wasn't all it might have been with quite a lot of low cloud. As we came up to the French coast the most positive landmark we could see was Le Havre. We decided to make this point our landfall and make a direct run from there to the DZ where we got rather a warm reception from the defences but got away with it. Three or four weeks after the drop I received a letter from George Holland thanking us for dropping them on the right spot. All had landed safely and we were all very touched that he had found the time to drop us a line in what must have been hectic days just after D-Day.'

Pilot Officer Den Hardwick, 299 Squadron, who took off from Keevil at 23.55 hours in Stirling IV EF267 'The Saint', carrying twenty troops from 225 Parachute Field Ambulance, Royal Army Medical Corps and nine equipment containers, under the command of Captain George Holland. Hardwick dropped the troops at 0050 hours on 6 June at DZ 'N', ¾ mile east of the River Orne.

'At eleven o'clock we took off from Tarrant Rushton to spearhead the invasion into Europe. It was rather like being picked to play for your country at Lords. The exhilaration buoyed us up and kept us going. We were all scared stiff, of course, but we'd been waiting and waiting for this stage from 1940 onwards and none of us had even been in action before.'

Lieutenant 'Tod' Sweeney 2nd Battalion, Oxfordshire and Buckinghamshire Light Infantry

41 *Invaders: British and American Experience of Seaborne landings 1939-1945* by Colin John Bruce (Chatham Publishing 1999).
42 *Stirling Wings: The Short Stirling Goes to War* by Jonathan Falconer (Sutton Publishing Ltd, 1995).

'The seizing of the crossing intact is of the utmost importance to the conduct of future operations. As the bridges will certainly have been prepared for demolition, the speedy overpowering of the bridge defences should be your first object. They must therefore be seized by a coup de main party, landed in gliders as near to the bridges as is humanly possible. You must accept risks to achieve this.'

Major General Richard Gale, 6th Airborne Division Commander's, orders to Brigadier J. H. Nigel Poett, 5th Parachute Brigade for the capture of the parallel bridges over the Canal de Caen at Bénouville and the River Orne at Ranville. Major John Howard commanded the coup de main party of 150 men - 4 platoons of 'D' Company and two attached platoons from 'B' Company, 2nd Battalion, Oxfordshire and Buckinghamshire Light Infantry and 30 men of 249 Field Company (Airborne) Royal Engineers. After capture their task was to hold the bridges until relieved.

The German today is like the June bride,' the general said. 'He knows he is going to get it, but he doesn't know how big it is going to be.'

Major General Richard Gale.

'The noise of the Halifax bombers that had towed us across the Channel faded away and, at 6,500 feet above the French coastline, we knew the moment for which we had trained for three months had finally arrived. Clouds covered the moon and the only sound was the swoosh of air over the wings of the six Horsa gliders carrying myself and 180 other glider-borne commandos on our mission, the success of which was essential for the invasion of Europe. We had been practising night and day to capture the Pegasus Bridge, which spanned the Caen Canal and the bridge over the River Orne a quarter of a mile away. We had even spent two weeks' training in Exeter, where there are two bridges in similar proximity. Everything depended on split-second timing if we were to capture the bridges with maximum speed and surprise and it was essential to land as close as possible to storm the German defences. Then we had to hold them until the Allied forces landed at the Normandy beaches a few miles away and came to reinforce us.

'I had joined the unit after seeing a notice asking for volunteers. We were under Major John Howard, an amiable, softly-spoken man who was a first-class soldier. The mission was so secret that even he did not know exactly what we were training for until the night before. The preparation very intensive and I was surprised when I eventually saw the huge gliders in which we would be flying. They held 30 men and were extremely precarious, with two wheels in the middle and a skid plate that came down between them. There was no question of picking a spot and landing them properly - you just had to let them run as far as they could and eventually they would stop. They were made out of the flimsiest plywood and there were several accidents during training. I was involved in one when a glider became twisted in its tow rope and nose-dived into the airfield. I got out by putting a foot through the side of the glider - they were that thin. Quite a few of the lads were injured and I was a bit shaken up, though I wasn't frightened - when you're young being injured or dying is the last thing on your mind. However, things began to look pretty scary as we glided in over France with the ground rising up to meet us.

27-year old Sergeant Charles 'Wagger' Thornton, Ox and Bucks Light Infantry, who in the glider on the way across had been singing 'Cow Cow Boogie' and had joined in with everyone else singing 'Abie my boy' and 'We're lucky fellers, we've got

no propellers. So cheer up my lads. Bless 'em all.'; **like almost everyone else on the gliders, he had chain smoked Players cigarettes.**

'We were driven straight to the runway. We discarded our equipment and wandered round the other gliders chatting to friends. In my particular glider, the glider pilot was Staff Sergeant Oliver Boland, the co-pilot was Staff Sergeant Hobbs and I recall saying to Ollie Boland at this point, 'Do you think we'll make it all right?' And he said, 'You've got no worries. I can land on a sixpence.' He was very, very confident. He was concerned about the amount of equipment and stuff we were carrying because he was worried about overloading but he said the Halifax would pull us off the ground anyway. And we sat around talking and I think it was round about ten-ish when some kind RAF chap came over with a big dixie of tea and on tasting it I was delighted to detect that there was a good measure of rum in it. This helped considerably again. We didn't expect such luxuries at the last moment. It was great that. About half past ten we were ordered to board the Horsas. This again was a feat in itself because we had to climb up a ladder and we were so overloaded that it was a job to stagger in. I got in and I sat about four seats down, four places down, on the starboard side. David Wood sat by the door, about four places along, on the other side.

'We sat in the glider talking. There was still no sign of nervousness. A slight tenseness because none of us had ever done a night flight in a glider before, it had always been daylight flights. And about ten to eleven the planes started revving up, trying out their engines: they were Halifax bombers. At about that time John Howard also came round the gliders, wished us luck, thanked us for our past help and 'cooperation and you could detect the emotion in the chap's voice, you know. It was a very emotional moment for all of us. I felt sorry for him and I looked across at David Wood and I could see that David looked a bit tense because he'd got a hell of a lot on his mind that night. He was only a boy, like the rest of us. We were all in the twenty-one age group; there were one or two slightly older. Anyway, the doors were shut and we were sat there just waiting then.

'Suddenly we became airborne. We could barely see, it was quite dark, there were a few cigarettes going and there was obviously a tenseness and nervousness because there wasn't the usual idle chatter - nobody was singing and there was almost silence in the glider, but within about ten minutes, the usual round of conversation started, people began to sing, the tenseness evaporated and it became just another glider flight.

'We were on the ground in the gliders for quite a while before we took off and I was frightened to death - we all were. We thought we were literally on a suicide mission. Once the gliders were in the air all my fears about the operation ahead disappeared. I think I just accepted that you have a time to be born, a time to live and a time to die. When our friends got killed around us we just had to accept it and that was it.

'On the way over, we were sat in the gliders all singing our heads off. We were singing as loud as we could until we reached the French coast, when we had to keep quiet.'
19-year-old Private Denis Edwards, a sniper in 25 Platoon, 'D' Company, 2nd Battalion Ox and Bucks Light Infantry.

'We were singing every conceivable type of filthy and dirty Army song you could think of.'
21-year old Private Harry Clarke, 2nd Battalion Ox and Bucks Light Infantry. Harry was badly wounded later in the war and sent home, with every expectation that he would not survive. But eventually, after losing a hand, he married the night nurse who cared for him.

Handley Page Halifax/Glider towing Operations

'Working towards D-Day the training was concentrated on mass landings and take-offs as the tighter the 'trains' were going down the runway, the easier it was to keep close during flight. We often had four 'trains' going down the runway at one time.'
Captain Bernard Halsall MC, 'C' Squadron of the Glider Pilot Regiment at Tarrant Rushton.

'Mass Hamilcar lifts were carried out at dusk on the 13th May and again in the morning of the 14th. Eight combinations of tugs and glider lifts were achieved in the morning of the 15th and again in the evening of the same day. At dusk on the 18th, a mass take-off of 24 combinations of Halifaxes and Hamilcars took place. Half of these crews were from 644 and half from 298 Squadron... May 22nd, a mass Halifax-Hamilcar take-off, with 30 combinations taking part today, appeared to be a great success. It was once again a combined effort by both Tarrant Rushton squadron crews. The only mishap was an undershot approach by the last glider down. All combinations were off in 22 minutes. Not bad.'
Flight Sergeant H. Barr RCAF. Five days before D-Day the tug and glider crews were taken to an undisclosed location.

'We were shown a model layout of the landing area with every detail set in place; bridges, roads, towns, pubs, rivers, even hedgerows and farm buildings. Two bridges in particular, one over the Orne River and the other over a canal, were laid out. A motion picture was shown giving a graphic picture of a simulated glider approaching the target landing area. On our return to base we were confined to the station.'

For Operation 'Deadstick' six Halifaxes of 644 Squadron each towed a Horsa carrying the troops of 6th Airborne Division responsible for securing the two bridges, one over the Orne River and one over the Caen Canal. The force attacked shortly after midnight and the gliders were released at about 6,000 feet; they then flew for a determined number of seconds on one bearing and then another and so on until their targets came into view. Meanwhile the Halifaxes, three carrying small bomb loads, continued on their original course with two dropping their bombs on a large cement factory in Caen to mask their real purpose while the third, encountering cloud, was forced to bring its bombs back. Achieving complete surprise, the gliders landed on the approaches to the bridges where, after brief and bitter fighting, they were both captured intact, despite the fact that the Orne bridge force was one glider short. It had landed eight miles away on a bridge over the Dives River.

The main glider operations of the day involved a force of 350, the responsibility for towing them being divided equally between 38 and 46 Groups. For their part in Operation 'Tonga', the first major assault of the day, both Halifax squadrons provided an identical force of 17 aircraft to tow two Hamilcars and 15 Horsas. The Horsas carried mostly six-pounder guns and jeeps, their tug aircraft each carrying nine containers, while the Hamilcars carried 17-pounder guns and Morris tractors of a Royal Artillery anti-tank unit. The gliders and their tugs had been marshalled on the runway adjacent to that used by the coup de main force.

Weather conditions were bad with low cloud and heavy rain but began to moderate over the Channel and improved steadily as the force approached the French coast, even though patches of cloud were encountered well below the release height of 1,500 feet. 298 Squadron lost three of its gliders during the early stages with two landing in England and a third in the Channel. Heavy flak from the German coastal defences cost them a Halifax but the crew survived; C. Anderson, the pilot thought he had counted all the crew baling out and then made his own escape but the flight engineer was still in the Halifax when it crashed, fortunately on a fairly even keel and he only suffered a fractured pelvis. The rest of the crew returned safely to Tarrant Rushton. 644 Squadron lost only two Horsas, both of which landed in England. The remaining gliders all reached their correct landing zones despite one releasing three and a half miles short and another breaking loose six miles short.

Operation 'Mallard', scheduled to reinforce all of the troops dropped earlier, was the third and final phase of the day's airborne assault, the largest daylight operation ever attempted up to this time, the success of which vindicated the exponents of daylight tactics. A force of 256 gliders was used with 17 fighter squadrons flying escort, its principal aim being to reinforce all the airborne troops already in France. The composition of the gliders for this phase was reversed with each of the Halifax squadrons towing 15 Hamilcars and one Horsa. As with the earlier operations, the Halifaxes towing the Horsas each carried an additional load of nine containers to be released in the dropping zone. As for the earlier mass operation, the Halifaxes were assembled along each side of the main runway and one Halifax from each alternatively moved across, was hitched to its glider and immediately moved off; the long hours of training had paid off handsomely.

This time all of the gliders reached the dropping zone safely where a 100% release was achieved. However, enemy tanks were sufficiently close to hit the tugs and 298 Squadron lost a second Halifax that day.

Flight Sergeant H. Barr RCAF in 2P-Q gave an eyewitness account of the incident: 'We were fairly well in line astern formation heading for home, when I noticed a German tank... set up on the rise of a hill, so that its gun could be elevated to fire at our low flying tugs. The aircraft in front of us was hit and shortly smoke began to pour from the fuselage. The tank fired at us as well but never scored a hit. Following the smoking kite down towards the Channel, we observed the ditching. Following proper procedure, we circled the downed plane several times, at the same time turning on our distress call over the wireless and also firing off Very pistol colours of the day. We observed the crew exiting the plane and as it remained afloat, they stood on the wings and waved. After about 20 minutes of circling and distress call, we observed a small navy ship making a bee-line for the ditched aircraft. Assured that they would soon be picked up, we headed back to base, after cancelling our distress signal. It turned out to be a Canadian pilot, R. I. 'Chippy' Carpenter and crew of 298 Squadron in 8T H-How. They were all back at Tarrant Rushton in a few days.

'On return... Carpenter and crew reported that a single small cannon shell from a Tiger tank had ignited two wheel covers that were in the parachute well area of the fuselage. Wheel covers protected the brake shoes from the dripping oil and grease from the... engines and they had been thrown into the aircraft by the ground crew. This practice was certainly frowned upon. The crew, with their small fire fighting equipment, were unable to extinguish the fire and the only solution... was to ditch in the English Channel.'

Thus, neither squadron lost a single man during the invasion operations. Four days later both squadrons were again active over the invasion area with six Halifaxes from each carrying out resupply missions to the British airborne troops. Each aircraft carried in its bomb bay a jeep, a six-pounder gun and six containers, all being successfully dropped from 1,000 feet. Experiments with this unique type of load had begun almost exactly one year previously at Stapleton. The two Halifax squadrons maintained these resupply missions until 27 June, carrying out several specialist operations during the period. These included one by 298 Squadron on the 17th when four of its Halifaxes dropped a mixed force of paratroops, jeeps and containers to SAS troops in France.'

Handley Page Halifax: From Hell to Victory and Beyond by K. A. Merrick. [43]

Between 10.56 and 11.02 pm on the night of 5 June six combinations of Halifaxes and Horsa gliders took off and presently reached a height of between 4,000 and 5,000 feet. Here patchy cloud was encountered, but otherwise weather conditions were good. June 6th was nine minutes old when the first combination crossed the French coast, soon followed by four others, the height then having increased to between 5,000 and 6,000 feet. The sixth combination lost the way and made landfall about nine miles east of the River Dives. The gliders were all released the moment the coast was crossed, for it was necessary to cast off some distance away in order to make certain they would arrive at the bridges alone and unheralded, like thieves in the night.

The three destined to land near the bridge over the Caen Canal did so with complete success, glider No. PF800 touching down within forty-seven yards of the swing bridge. 'Even after crossing the coast,' says Howard, a passenger in it, 'everything was so quiet that it seemed we were merely carrying out an exercise in England. Our chief worry was whether the poles we had seen on the photographs would wreck the glider when it came in to land. We were ready to face this risk, but we knew it was serious. To guard against it as far as possible we all linked arms in the glider and braced ourselves and my most vivid memory is of the long time that elapsed between the moment of release and the moment of landing, though it was only seven minutes. In point of fact what we had thought to be poles proved to be holes dug by the Hun a few days before. He had not had time to set up the wooden uprights.'

The glider, piloted by 24 year old Staff Sergeant J. H. 'Jim' Wallwork and Staff Sergeant John Ainsworth MM landed heavily, but safely.

* * *

'When we levelled out a bit at a thousand feet we opened the doors of the glider. One of them was straight in front of me. Sitting on my left was Lieutenant Brotheridge, my leading platoon commander and he undid his safety belt, I held his equipment one side and his platoon sergeant the other side and he leant forward very precariously and opened the door which lifted up into the roof. At the same time this was happening the back door was opened the same way by some of the men at the back. When Den Brotheridge slumped back into his seat and put his safety belt on again I looked out at the fields of France and it had an amazing tranquillising effect on me and on those near to me who could see. There you had the magnificent stock, horses and cattle, grazing

43 (Chevron Publishing Ltd 2009).

very, very quietly. It was so quiet; it was like being on an exercise in England. And the tranquillising effect went right throughout the glider because we were all quite silent by that time. But there wasn't much time to think about that because the glider suddenly did a right-hand turn, because we'd gone a way inland towards Caen and then another right-hand turn, so that we were coming into the landing zone from the south, losing height all the way. And as we did that turn I could see the River Orne and the Caen Canal, reflected in the half-moon, running down towards Caen. And we came to what we knew was going to be the toughest moment of the lot: the crash land.

'I was behind Staff Sergeant Ainsworth but could see Jim Wallwork in profile and could see the beads of perspiration on his forehead and face as he struggled to maintain control of that damned great monster he was driving. I knew that the arrester parachute in the tail would operate any moment now to help slow down the glider as it hurtled in to touch down at anything around 100 mph. Everybody had automatically carried out the landing drill soon after we had done our second turn. This was to link arms down each side of the glider with fingers locked into what was known as a butcher's grip. Legs up under your chin to avoid breakages when the floor disintegrated, as we expected it to on that bumpy field. Then all you could do was pray to God for a safe landing. My thoughts were many. Firstly the damned poles. Would collision with one of them cause just one of the many primed grenades we were all carrying to explode and everything else in the glider go up through sympathetic detonation - it had happened many times in Sicily! Were the enemy standing-to and perhaps reinforced with machine guns trained on the landing zone? Where would the other gliders land? It was all flashing through my mind as we experienced the first terrific bump! The glider seemed to take it well because we were momentarily airborne again - crash again but this time on skids because the wheels had gone - this was a lot noisier and damaging as the skids seared through the ground and sent up sparks as the metal skids hit flints and it looked like tracer fire flashing past the door causing inevitable thought of surprise lost. Airborne again and suddenly there was to be the last searing God Almighty crash amidst smashing plywood, dust and noise like hell let loose, followed by sudden silence as we came to a halt. The dazed silence did not seem to last long because we all came to our senses together on realising that there was NO firing. There WAS NO FIRING, it seemed quite unbelievable - but where were we?

'Everyone automatically released safety belts and felt their limbs for breakages. I realised that everything around me had gone very dark and my head was aching. My God I can't see! I clutched at my helmet and found that I must have hit the top of the glider during that last helluva crash and all that had happened was that my battle-bowler had come down over my eyes. What a relief! I quickly pushed it up and saw that the cockpit and door had telescoped and we would have to break our way out. I could hear the glider pilots moaning and knew that they must be hurt, but they seemed to be breaking out of the front and in any case the drill was to get the hell out of it before any machine guns had time to get into action. Everyone was doing the same and considering the situation, commendably quietly. I could hear the click of the safety belts being undone and I knew that men were getting out of the glider and people were pushing in front of me to get through the broken door. I did not know whether Den was out before or after me. All I can remember was as I stood clear of the mangled glider I saw the tower of the canal bridge no more than 50 yards away and the nose of the glider right through the enemy wire defences - precisely where I had asked the GPs to put it during briefing. I'd almost facetiously asked the glider pilot to put it so we would not have to use the Bangalore torpedoes, which every glider had brought with them for the purpose of breaking through the wire. And above all and this was the tremendous thing; there was NO enemy firing at all. In other words we had complete surprise; we really caught old Jerry with his pants down. The sense of complete exhilaration was quite overwhelming!'

Major John Howard in command of 'D' Company, Ox and Bucks Light Infantry, Coup-de-main group for Pegasus Bridge. Howard had left the regular army before the war and joined the Oxford police in 1939. Recalled to service, he rose rapidly and received a commission in 1940. He demanded the utmost in physical conditioning from his company - The Company could do 20 miles in 5½ hours, carrying all their gear which included mortars and Bren guns. Den Brotheridge had been a cadet in Howard's own training company and Howard himself had persuaded him to join the airborne forces. He knew that Brotheridge, like himself, had a young wife and that she was expecting a baby any day, but Brotheridge had no regrets and would never have thought of Howard as responsible for his fate. He had bet his CO fifty francs that he would be out of the door before him when the glider crashed and so lay claim to be the first Allied soldier to land in the invasion.

'Get your chaps moving,' Lieutenant Den Brotheridge called to Sergeant Jack Bailey and Bailey and his section took out the concrete pillbox with grenades. Then, 'Come on lads' and Brotheridge led the rest of his men across the bridge at the double. As Brotheridge ran across the bridge, a sentry on the far bank fired a flare in warning. The lieutenant put a full magazine from his Sten gun into the sentry and then threw a grenade into the machine-gun position to his right front. Behind him a Bren gunner, shooting from the hip, poured fire into another German machine gun. About that time Brotheridge took a round in the neck and went down, mortally wounded, but a burst from a Sten gun cut down the German and his men pushed on. A violent fire-fight erupted on the west side of the canal, but Brotheridge's men, supported by Sandy Smith's platoon, killed, drove off or captured all the German defenders and the bridge was taken within a quarter of an hour. While some dealt with the Germans in slit trenches nearby, the remainder made a defensive perimeter. Such of the German garrison as fought, NCOs for the most part, did so bravely, but the men of whom they were in charge ran off into the night towards the sea. Their choice of direction was unfortunate, for they soon met with our newly landed seaborne forces and were destroyed.

'We're here, piss off and do what you're paid to do.'

Staff Sergeant 'Ollie' Boland, Glider Pilot Regiment, who had just turned 23 and had found crossing the Channel an 'enormously emotional experience'. He found it difficult to believe that he was the 'spearhead of the most colossal army ever assembled' because he felt 'so insignificant'. Boland yanked his Horsa into a sharp turn to avoid Wallwork's glider. In the process, the tail broke away but Boland's troops were intact and ready.

'We heard the glider pilot shout, 'Casting Off!' and suddenly the roar of the aeroplane engine receded and we were in a silent world. It was like being trapped in a floating coffin in mid-space. Immediately the glider cast off, the singing, the talk, the conversation stopped. People realised what we were heading for. There was no going back now. We'd reached the point where we could only go forward.

'David Wood said, 'Forward' and with all his boyish enthusiasm - he was a great leader - he went gallantly into action and we all tore in like a pack of hounds after him. Suddenly I was brought to an abrupt halt, I was snagged on a load of barbed wire and a huge barb took a lump of flesh out of my right knee. Actually I cursed rather loudly and I can still recall David Wood saying to me, 'Shut up Clarke' - and this was in the middle of an attack. Anyway, we ran forward and there were at least two machine guns firing from the position we were about to attack. Charles Godbold and I were together and as we neared the trenches we could see from the flash there was a gun firing and Charlie said, 'We'd better sling a grenade.'

I said 'we'd better not sling a 36, let's sling a couple of these stun grenades, otherwise we'll kill our own blokes.' So we flung two stun grenades and we saw two people rise out of the trench and run towards the bank of the canal. Charlie let loose a long burst from his Sten gun but I think they got away: we found no bodies there the next day. And within probably about five minutes, a few skirmishes, there was a bit of firing, it all went quiet. We'd captured our objective. We moved up to the riverbank, my section and we passed a pillbox, there was smoke coming out of it and all was quiet on our side. There was a machine gun firing on the other side and a few bangs so they were obviously still engaged on the west bank of the canal. There were some jocular remarks from our chaps, like, 'Where the hell have you been?' I can recall those quite well. But it was all done in a happy sort of fashion because we were extremely glad to see them. We were getting a few counter-attacks coming in at that time.

'Certainly 7 Para must have been having a sticky time because by now the crescendo of firing was rising, it was getting very noisy and we weren't fully aware of what exactly was happening out there. We were in our own little unit clustered round the bridge but we had the feeling all the time that something nasty was happening. And as first light got underway, about half-past four, five o'clock, we suddenly found that we were pinned down by very heavy and very accurate sniper-firing.'

Private Harry Clarke, 24 Platoon, 'D' Company, 2nd Battalion, Oxfordshire and Buckinghamshire Light Infantry. Each glider carried 23 men of 2 Ox and Bucks and five Royal Engineers. In addition, each aircraft carried an assault boat, boxes of small-arms ammunition and a large quantity of rounds for the spring-loaded PIAT (Projector Infantry Anti-Tank) launcher. The pilots of the three Horsa gliders were required to navigate from their release point to the bridge, in pitch dark, without markers and using only a compass and stop watch to guide them. The second pilots concentrated on picking out their landmarks in the gloom. In a glider destined for the Orne Bridge, Peter Boyle picked up their critical mark, a wood called the Bois de Bavent. 'Turn to starboard,' he said. Barkway turned the Horsa and there it was, looming out of the darkness, the Orne River bridge. Piloting a glider headed for the Caen Canal, Ainsworth did not see the Bois de Bavent, but he and Wallwork turned at what they thought was the correct time on their original course. Their count turned out to be precise: Out of the night ahead of them they saw in the moonlight the twin lines of river and canal. Wallwork was on the ground first, at 16 minutes past midnight. The two other gliders, flown by Staff Sergeants Oliver 'Ollie' Boland and

Hobbs and Staff Sergeants Geoff Barkway and Peter Boyle, landed close behind and the troops in all three made haste to rush the bridge.

'It was only the second time they'd put a lot of gliders into an operation [the first was Sicily] and we didn't really know what our chances were, but we'd been given to understand that they weren't very high, that we were on a one-way trip really. We were taught to do certain things without question. As our regimental commander would say, 'You, if you want to ask a question, ask it when the war's over.'

'Some seventy-two hours before they'd shown us a sand table model and said, 'That's it.' It was a model of a bridge and then about twelve hours beforehand Major Howard spoke to us and he gave us the story. He said that it was vital that we took this bridge; the whole object was to stop the German armour coming in behind the seaborne troops once they'd landed. The airborne divisions would keep the Germans far back so that they couldn't shell the troops, but of course the problem is that an airborne division is so lightly armed when it lands, so unless it can be contacted fairly quickly, it's in trouble.'
Peter Boyle.

The glider pilots were ordered to unload the heavy weapons and to do so as quickly as possible, for the enemy were expected to counter-attack from Bénouville at any moment. 'That's a funny sort of make-up. You look like a Red Indian,' said Howard to Sergeant Jim Wallwork, the first pilot of his glider. 'Then I realized it was his blood, for he had been badly cut by splinters of perspex and wood.' The sergeant went on unloading the glider and then took his place in the defence. A PIAT was rushed forward to cover the approaches to the bridge and placed in position near the cafe where Monsieur Gondrée and his wife had by that time realized that they were witnessing the invasion of Europe. It opened fire and destroyed the first of three old French tanks sent in by the Germans as the vanguard of their expected counter-attack. The tank was set on fire and its ammunition continued to explode for more than an hour, so that men of the 7th Parachute Battalion now on the way to reinforce, were under the impression that a great battle was raging at the bridge.

'I don't think you had time to be fearful because there's never enough time to get ready for these things. At the last minute: 'Wouldn't it be better if we did this?' 'Wouldn't it be better if we did that?' 'Let's move that here.' 'You carry this in your glider. We'll carry that in ours.' 'Is there anything we've forgotten?' I remember various people came round and wished us good luck. Lots of putting names on the gliders: 'Adolf here we come' and that sort of business. Everybody was in pretty high spirits.'

Staff Sergeant Geoff Barkway, whose glider, landing third, hit hard, leaving one soldier dead and several injured and throwing Barkway and Peter Boyle into a pond just east of the canal. Dazed, both men struggled out and began to unload ammunition.

'Suddenly, we heard a swishing noise and saw a large, silent aircraft flying low towards the canal bridge. It crashed in a small field next to the bridge, only about 50 metres away. At first we thought it was a crippled bomber. We wondered whether to take a look at it or wake our sergeant. (One of our comrades had had a birthday the same night. They'd been drinking in the café until 10pm so they were all asleep!) We were moving forward cautiously when we heard what seemed to be the sound of running feet. Before we knew it, a bunch of about ten wild-looking men who were charging towards us confronted us. They were armed, but didn't shoot. I found out later this was because they were under strict orders to maintain silence as long as possible so that they had surprise on their side when they stormed the pillbox by the bridge. We were two boys alone and we ran. We could see that these menacing, warlike-looking men outnumbered us. But I still managed to fire off a signal flare to try to warn the rest of our garrison of about 20 men who were sleeping nearby.

'About 100 metres off, we plunged into some thick bushes by the track running alongside the canal. There were two more crashes. We knew that the British were landing in force. Firing had started all around the bridge and we could see tracer bullets whizzing in all directions. At first it was non-stop and then it died down to occasional bursts. It was clear that the British were rooting out the rest of our garrison from the bunkers around the bridge.

'We remained hidden throughout the night, scared to move in case we would be seen and shot. Sometime after noon next day, we heard and saw some more troops with a piper at their head moving from the direction of the beaches to cross the bridge. I found out later that they were Lord Lovat's Commando Brigade. We stayed under cover for the rest of the day and the next night. Then, hungry and thirsty, we decided to surrender. We plucked up our courage, put our hands in the air and walked out of the bushes. The British didn't fire at us. I'll always be grateful to them for that. We knew it was the end of the war for us and we were bloody glad of it.'

18-year olds Helmut Romer and Erwin Sauer, who were on sentry duty at the Canal de Caen bridge (subsequently renamed 'Pegasus Bridge') over the Caen Canal.

'Our primary objective, 23 Platoon, was to support the glider in front of us, Freddie Fox's glider and rush over the Orne Bridge through Freddie Fox's platoon and take up position on the other side. Freddie Fox's glider landed in fair shape. My glider - we landed about 300 yards short of the objective - landed perfectly, no problem with the landing and 'Tod' Sweeney was out and we did the usual thing we did when we jumped out of a glider: all round defence. In other words, a circle all round the glider. 'Tod' Sweeney sat in the centre and the first thing he did was to call an 0 group, which was an order group; that meant he called together the corporals and the sergeants and issued his orders. The next thing he had to do was find out where he was and he and the glider pilot in fact pinpointed the spot very well, actually and off we trotted down to a hedgerow.

'We probably travelled down this hedgerow 200, 250 yards, before we came out on the road which actually led to the bridge. We dashed on to the bridge, not shouting too loudly, but making plain to the other platoon on or near the bridge that we were in fact British: as we ran along the bridge we all shouted out, 'Easy! Easy! Easy!' That was our call sign. The call sign of the platoon on the bridge I think was 'Fox' and they shouted out 'Fox!' so that we recognised one another. Remember it was pitch black, we really couldn't see too far, so we had these call signs.

'So we dashed through the ranks of Freddie Fox's platoon, who were either lying on the bridge or were on the other side of the bridge in their gun position and we then attacked our objectives. I came upon this little farmhouse, it seemed to be more of a farmer's cottage than a farmhouse and banged on the door, big wooden door and it eventually opened. Then we used our ersatz French to the little old lady and the little old man who came to the door. Où est le Boche? They just didn't want to know. Not interested. They didn't know whether we were Germans or whether we were Polish; we could have been Czechs, we could have been Hungarians, we could have been anything. We just motioned to them to go indoors and there was very little we could do. It was a very small place and one of my men went in and just rooted around to make certain there were no Germans in there.

'Then we repaired to our positions. We didn't trouble to dig in. There didn't seem to be much point in digging in at this stage because my blokes were expert at finding well-concealed positions and if there did happen to be any fold in the ground where they could hide themselves they would do that. I took up a position in a little dip by the side of this farm cottage and I had with me Buck Read, one of my men and we decided we were going to have a smoke.'

Corporal Wilfred Robert Howard, 23 Platoon, 'D' Company, 2nd Battalion, Oxfordshire and Buckinghamshire Light Infantry.

While the Canal Bridge was thus falling into British hands, that across the River Orne, a few hundred yards to the east, was also being attacked. Here, too, success was immediate, one glider landing very close and the others 400 yards or so away. The attackers, under Lieutenant Dennis B. 'Freddie' Fox, closely followed by Lieutenant T. J. 'Tod' Sweeney MC and his platoon, seized the objective. Having crossed it, Sweeney found a small house on the other side in which 'there was a little old lady and a little old man.' In his best French he explained that he and his men had arrived pour la liberation de la France. The old couple were frightened; they thought at first that he was a German carrying out an exercise for the purpose of deceiving the French inhabitants, who might thus be induced to give themselves away and provide new victims for the Gestapo. Such German ruses as this were greatly feared throughout the invasion area and go far to explain the apparent indifference or covert hostility with which some of our troops were at first greeted. When dawn came and with it light on the situation, the little old lady, realizing what had happened, kissed Lieutenant Sweeney and made ready to rejoice. He, like Major Howard at the bridge over the canal, had been busy consolidating his bridge over the river. The sappers with both parties soon discovered that neither bridge had been prepared for demolition.

After a brush with a German patrol, the sound of grinding gears in the darkness seemed to betoken the presence of a tank, which, however, proved to be a German staff car with a motor cyclist behind it. The first burst of fire checked but did not stop the car and it roared over the bridge, only to be met with another and more accurate burst which sent it reeling into the ditch. Out of it was taken the German officer in command of the bridge defences, two empty wine bottles, a number of dirty plates and a quantity of rouge and face-powder. Declaring that he had lost his honour by his failure to maintain the defences of the bridge, the officer asked for death. 'I was a little worried,' says Major Howard, ' about the position on the bridge over the river, till I got on my wireless the code signal for victory.' 'Ham and jam;' said a voice, 'ham and bloody jam.' Then I blew the V-sign on my whistle.' Major Howard was reinforced by the arrival of Lieutenant Fox, fresh from his capture of the bridge at Ranville.

D-Day in a Stirling Flying Officer Gerry F. McMahon DFM

'The atmosphere at Fairford was electric. 620 Squadron had just been briefed that we (33 Stirlings in No 38 Group) were to spearhead the main force of the D-Day attack, which was to take place the following day. Our first task was to drop (north of the village of Ranville) a force of paratroopers (of the 7th Light Infantry Battalion, 5th Parachute Brigade, 6th Airborne Division) who were to hold one of the main bridges (the Orne River bridge), which would form part of the supply route for the defending German forces. (The paratroopers were to reinforce the coup de main party of the 2nd Battalion of the Oxfordshire & Buckinghamshire Light Infantry and a detachment of Royal Engineers, all under the command of Major R. J. Howard, who had landed earlier in six gliders to seize the Orne and Canal de Caen bridges). It was necessary to get this force into position before the Germans knew that the actual invasion was under way.

'We took off at 2230 hours on the night of 5 June with a full complement of paratroopers on board our Stirling IV, LJ849 E-Easy. Our pilot was Flight Lieutenant G. H. Thring, a Canadian. We had a quiet flight until we crossed the French coast, when we were hit by a considerable amount of light flak and suffered some minor injuries amongst the paratroopers. Shortly afterwards the flak thinned out and we were on an immaculate run to the dropping zone. All the paratroopers left the aircraft in their original order, including those who had suffered slight injury and who had refused to return to the UK with us for treatment. We learned later that they landed bang on target and held their position, as had been planned. (Fifty years later, in the Tower Hotel, London, my wife and I met Richard Todd. We were both guests of the News of the World and on our way to a reunion in Caen. In conversation it was discovered that I had actually flown Lieutenant Richard Todd, as he then was, the night before D-Day and dropped him and his paratroopers at Pegasus Bridge. Richard's comment was that our drop wasn't so close, as he had a long way to walk to the bridge. My comment was that you can't please everyone all the time and why had it taken him, 50 years to make the complaint! 'Several large whiskies resolved the situation.)

'We returned to England, being hit again by flak over the French coast and landed back at Fairford at 0145 hours on the morning of 6 June. It had been our intention to sleep before the next trip, but this proved impossible. The excitement that brewed when it was learned that it would be announced to the world that we had invaded the continent was a little too great. Later, our aircraft was in position, ready to head the 620 Squadron invasion fleet of glider-towers. The scene on the airfield was one that I shall always remember. On the grass beside the aircraft were several large gatherings of soldiers in camouflaged dress, armed to the teeth, all kneeling at their respective religious services, the padres in their white cassocks and regalia standing out very clearly amongst the men. Also intermingled with the soldiers were a great number of the aircrew.

'We took off in the afternoon. Although we had originally set off leading our squadron in what appeared to be clear sky, as we arrived at our rendezvous on time we soon became a little cog in a very big wheel and the surrounding air, in front, beside and behind us, was just a solid mass of aircraft and gliders. On crossing the English Channel, the sight in the air appeared to be reflected in the sea, in that as far as the eye could see shipping of all sizes was heading in the same direction. As we approached the coast of France we witnessed several lines of heavy naval ships bombarding the French coast.

'Our job was to drop the glider in an area between the French coast and the city of Caen. On the way to the dropping zone I noticed on our starboard some very accurate gunfire coming from a wood, which had picked off a number of aircraft and gliders as they were coming in. I gave the skipper a fix on this position with the intention of putting it out of action after we had dropped the glider.

'We duly released the glider in the dropping zone and headed for the wood at low level. Regrettably, the gun position saw us coming and hit us first. The first thing to blow was the petrol tank in the port wing, which blew up the wing and turned the aircraft on to its back. As rear gunner, my first indication that there was something wrong was when my ammunition came up out of the 'chutes and hit me in the face. Because of the 'G' pressure, we were in absolutely no position to do anything. However, my skipper had given up trying to fly the aircraft through normal elevators, etc and had his feet up on the dashboard pulling back on the stick in the fond hope that we would pull out of the dive. It was then that one of the miracles of the war happened. The aircraft came over off its back and we made a most beautiful belly-landing in a ploughed field that would have done justice to any pilot under normal conditions.

'The whole crew left the aircraft completely uninjured and we were able to run some 25 yards into a wheat field before the remainder of the aircraft exploded and burned furiously. Within minutes the aircraft was surrounded by German troops and, from the gist of their shouts, we realised that they thought we were still in the aircraft. We therefore stayed where we were in the wheat field for some time. Once all the Germans had left the scene, we had a crew conference as to what action we should now take, the position being, of course, that we had an invasion going on some miles behind us and odd pockets of paratroopers could be on either side of us. All we knew of our flight position was that after we had been hit we had about-turned and headed back over enemy territory and, from where we were, it was impossible to accurately pin-point our position.

'One of the crew felt that we should walk about unarmed and hope to find our own kith and kin. This I disagreed with. As a result he handed over to me his revolver and ammunition and this I placed in the top of my battledress, together with my escape kit and money wallet. It was then decided to wait until dark and walk in the general direction of the French coast. We hid out until dusk and just as the light was falling, along came two figures that at first glance appeared to be wearing American helmets.

'One of the crew in his excitement even thought the men were whistling 'Lili Marlene' and cried, 'The Americans are with us!' He leapt out to greet them. I think it was sheer reaction that made us stand up. By this time the two so-called 'Americans' had leapt off their bicycles and were covering us with machine-guns. They were German! Never has one felt so small. We were marched to a nearby German army camp where we were locked in a room, still wearing our guns, to await the arrival of a German officer. He very quickly put a stop to the nonsense and we were immediately disarmed of all visible weapons.

'As I was the only member of the crew wearing a decoration, they presumed I was the captain and I was called forward to meet the Army captain. He proudly announced that he was educated in England and that he would interrogate me in English, but he must first search me. As his hands were about to search, starting under my armpits, I reached into my battledress and withdrew my escape kit in its plastic container and wallet of foreign money and handed them to him quite openly. He said, 'What are these?' I replied that the escape kit was my ration for three days and the wallet of money contained personal papers to be opened only by the Gestapo, to which he replied, 'Ja, ja, I understand' and handed them back to me. I put these back into my battledress and was horrified to hear the clunk as the escape kit hit my hidden revolver. However, by this time I was already stepping backwards and the German captain did not appear to hear. He seemed satisfied with his search so I continued to walk backwards and Flight Lieutenant Thring stepped up as next in line to be searched. Each member of the crew adopted the same 'patter' as I did and we were all left with our escape kits and money.

'We were then ushered into another room and locked up until later that night. Time did not seem to mean very much, as we were all so desperately tired and hungry, having been up all the night before and throughout this day without a drink or a meal.

'Some time during the night the German army captain came to us with the news that he had been ordered to retreat to a position nearer Caen and that we were to accompany him. We started off, surrounded by what appeared to be a couple of hundred German soldiers and began to march. We then came across another small company of soldiers, some of whom had seen battle and one of whom had a badly broken leg with a protruding bone. Two of us were instructed to support him by crossing our hands so that he could sit on them. He was only about 16 years old. I was selected as one of the first 'chair bearers', an honour I did not appreciate at all.

'One of the German soldiers eventually found a stretcher that enabled the four of us to carry a corner apiece. In our weary state this lad weighed the proverbial ton and we resorted to a ruse whereby every few yards one of us took a turn to shout 'Holtz!' which not only stopped us but brought the whole company to a halt as well. Each time the captain had to return to our position to find out why the company had halted. En route we also watched, against the night sky, large fires in some town or other that was being bombed. The general consensus of opinion throughout the German company was that we should be tied to stakes and left to burn with it.

'On one of our stops, while sitting at the road side, I suggested to Gordon Thring that we might take advantage of the thick black night and make a run for it - some of us might get away. Gordon was of the opinion that two of the crew were not capable and that if others of us managed to escape those remaining would be shot. I agreed, seeing that the noise of battle all around us was making the Germans very touchy, but said that when I got the opportunity to escape without endangering the crew I was going to at least make an attempt.

'After a while we managed to find a motorcycle by the side of the road, which had been abandoned with no petrol, so we sat the wounded soldier on this and pushed him to the top of a hill. On reaching the top and seeing that there was a steep descent on the other side, we accidentally let go and the soldier disappeared into the dark. He was later found in a ditch at the bottom of the hill and his language was not appreciative of the help we had given him. The German captain then decided that it would be safer for him to look after his own wounded and we did not see the wounded man again after this.

'We marched all night and as dawn approached we arrived at a château that had obviously been used for some considerable time as a German headquarters. Listening to the conversation on arrival, we understood that all staff officers of the headquarters had withdrawn and now this was to be a fighting garrison. We were shown into a barn and a guard was placed at the door. I quickly removed the gun and ammunition from my battledress and hid it between some bales of straw. Although we were desperately tired, the skipper and I made a quick reconnaissance of the barn, finding that on the first floor there were wooden hayloft doors that, if pushed open, would give us access into the grounds. There was also a hoist and pulley and it was felt that we could probably swing over the château wall on to the road on the other side. Having agreed on this possibility, we gave up and fell asleep in a pile of hay.

'After I do not know how many hours, the German captain appeared with several bottles of champagne and some sauerkraut sausage and what appeared to be a type of brown bread. This was devoured with relish, even though the sauerkraut and bread had been 'off' for some time. The captain explained that the champagne was the only drink they had as the water was polluted. Later he brought a bottle of port and some cigarettes. Best of all was when an NCO brought us a pot of coffee!

'As night approached again, I began thinking of the hayloft doors and the possibility of escape. Two of our crew were not in good fettle and the skipper, quite rightly, decided against a mass escape. However, I said I proposed to go it alone and take my chance. As soon as it was dark I recovered my revolver and ammunition from the hay and climbed into the loft.

'I gently eased open the doors and noted with pleasure that there were no sentries in sight at this end of the barn. Also, there appeared to be just the right length of rope on the hoist and pulley for me to swing over the château wall, but I would have to take my chance on what was on the other side. I took hold of the hook and jumped for the wall, but instead of completing the swing I plunged violently downwards, ending up in a tangled mess at the base of the barn wall. After rubbing my various sore spots, I discovered that the reason was a simple one - the other end of the hoist rope had not been secured to the wall!

'I made a reconnaissance of the grounds and noted the positions of the German sentries, after which I headed back to the barn, securing the hoist rope to the wall and climbing back up and through the hayloft doors. All the crew were sound asleep, so I hid my revolver and ammunition back in the bales of hay and settled down. In the morning I explained to Gordon Thring that I had done a reconnaissance of the grounds and had decided against escaping. By this time there was a considerable amount of activity outside and on two occasions the Germans entered the barn to count that we were all still present.

'During the day the château suffered numerous rocket attacks by hedge-hopping Typhoon fighters and shells from the army. Gradually, it was being reduced from its three storeys in height to a load of ground rubble and the morale of the German troops was equally low. Talk between the soldiers indicated that they believed they were surrounded, but they no longer had R/T communication and, apart from the captain, no one to advise them as to what was the state of the war.

'Early the next morning Typhoon fighters again carried out rocket attacks backed up by mortars. The German soldiers moved out into a slit trench dug in the grounds. The captain asked us to leave the barn for our own safety. I collected my gun and ammunition and hid them again in my battledress and we then joined the Germans in the trenches. This was most fortuitous, because a few minutes later the barn was struck by two rockets and went up in a flash of fire and smoke. There was some talk amongst the Germans about sentries being killed during the night on the château wall opposite that from whence the invasion was coming and they were convinced that they were surrounded.

'One of the most amazing things to happen was that as we sat in the slit trench and as the Germans had to pass backwards and forwards, they would say 'Excuse British soldier!' and give a little bow, with old world courtesy. It got crazier and crazier, but we were pleased enough to share their protection.

'During the afternoon the German captain sent for me and for the skipper. We found him in a room in the basement of the château, admiring his stubbled face in a mirror. As we entered he turned around, obviously embarrassed and said, 'Me no English gentleman.' He then uttered the most surprising thing by saying, 'I wish to surrender to you myself and 40 men.' This came completely out of the blue as far as we were concerned because, although we had caused the rumours, we had no idea how far behind enemy lines we were. However, we decided to take a chance and said to the captain that we would only accept his surrender if he did so in the proper military fashion and marched with the men fully armed to give themselves up. He agreed and to show faith he handed me his own revolver.

'This was how a queer little party of armed Germans and ourselves set off from the château in the general direction of the coast. Just before we started, the German captain produced another bottle of champagne. He handed it to me measuring little sections of it with his finger and pointing around to the six of us. To make sure what he meant, he said, 'Too much for one drink' and rolled his eyes. The NCO shook hands with us all, with tears rolling down his face. I carried that bottle of champagne all the way back home to RAF Fairford.

'I also insisted that no matter what happened en route there was to be strict discipline and no talking in the ranks. This was also fortuitous in that on the march another 21 fully armed Germans joined us, thinking that we were going to reinforce the German front! These 21 were hand-picked snipers who had been left behind to cause havoc during the Allied advance. We marched for over 3 miles and were suddenly surrounded by Canadian soldiers. We shouted that the Germans were our prisoners and were coming in to surrender. After seeing them safely into a prisoner of war cage the army captain gave me a receipt for one German officer and 61 other ranks.

'The Canadians supplied us with jeeps to get us back to the coast and we had only one incident en route. We were stopped in one French village and told that a catholic priest and a girl were up in the belfry of the church sniping at our troops. They had sent for an 'artillery piece' and we watched the Canadians put this gun in place and take aim. Only one round was fired and it blew a hole right through the steeple, removing the opposition from inside.

'On arriving at the coast a beach marshal had us put aboard a ship, where we had our first meal for three days - and a safe passage home. Our encounter with the beach marshal was another strange coincidence, as he turned out to be a naval officer who not only came from the home town of our stalwart flight engineer Sergeant Bill Buchan of Galashiels, but also lived across the road from him! This strange reunion was conducted in Scottish and well beyond our multi-national comprehension. The amazing thing was that we were standing on a beach with the war going on all around us and we had two Scots passing the time of day as if they were on a peacetime day out to Berwick-upon-Tweed. We could not have asked to have been sent on our way home by a more friendly face.

'Our return to RAF Fairford caused quite a stir. Letters had been sent already by the commanding officer to our parents and families saying we were 'Missing, believed killed' because eye-witnesses of our crash thought the aircraft had blown up on hitting the ground. Over the next few days many VIPs came to talk to us and Gordon Thring was awarded the DFC for his crash-landing of the aircraft.

'We were all sent on seven days' leave and I headed for my home in Newcastle-upon-Tyne. As I opened the garden gate my mother and father were just coming to the front door and going to church for my requiem mass. My mother took one look at me and fainted. The original commanding officer's letter had not been cancelled and I was very lax in my own writing at any time and telephoning was just not a habit. My parents were not fully au fait with my flying habits as I told them very little about flying in those days so as not to worry them. All in all it was a colossal cock-up and the only one to blame was myself.

'On our return from leave we were despatched to be interrogated by MI9 in St John's Wood, London. I was not impressed by the quality of the interviews/interviewers, both of which reminded me of 'jobs for the boys'. After sitting for what seemed an endless time I was interviewed by a Squadron Leader 'penguin' who seemed to be a typical 'pen-pusher' - probably a very good administrator, but lacking any idea of what to do in actual war conditions. He accused me of endangering the lives of my crew members because I had tried to escape on my own. The interview was abruptly terminated when I told him what I thought of him!'

'I was to be in aircraft 33. We had very carefully worked out our load tables for the aircraft in terms of who should be in there first, who would have such and such weapons and who would have other things with them. On that particular night, first of all we were in a laager on Salisbury Plain, wired in for about a week, even our supplies and food were just dumped outside the wire gates and our own chaps went out and brought it in, because we weren't allowed to talk to anybody. We were being briefed, a week or so before D-Day, we knew where, when, how and everything about it. We had no communication at all with the outside world, except me one day, because I was Assistant Adjutant and I was sent to Southern Command Headquarters. I was terrified. I thought, 'Oh, my God, I hope I don't open my mouth'.

'We knew the whole thing, all the planning. We knew our own particular thing - we had sand-table models of the area we were dropping in and we knew every tree and every house intimately. We had maps galore and every day we had a fresh batch of aerial photographs for our intelligence officer to interpret.

'We were getting worried because we saw a lot of little holes being dug and we found out that it was posts being put in with wire between them as anti-glider defences. We also saw large areas flooded - we wondered if the whole thing had been blown.

'That night of D-Day, or the night before, at about 11 o'clock, we drove round the airfield perimeter, each stick of paratroopers in a three-ton truck and each truck stopped by its numbered aircraft. Mine stopped at aircraft number 33, as that was the one I was to be in - and I was going out first from the aircraft.

'The pilot and crew were lined up beside the aircraft - they shook hands and wished us luck and all the rest of it. The pilot was a very senior officer, an Air Commodore or something. He said to me, quite blithely, 'As I'm the senior officer going in tonight, I'm going in first, because we've got the gem crew'.

'I thought, 'Oh Christ - I'm going to be the first out of the first aircraft,' but I couldn't argue with them because he was senior to me and I couldn't say, 'Look, this will upset our load tables.' It wasn't the time. So I got in - and that actually saved my life. I'll tell you why in a minute. I think people thought I was very cool because I fell asleep on the way - but that's a thing of mine. If I'm very worried or really down about something, my tendency is to be like an old ostrich and put my head in the sand and go to sleep - and I was very worried and had lots of stress on me that night.

'I was wakened up - we lined up and hooked up. The old green light came on and out we went, with me in the lead. Incidentally, it was a very big hole in the bottom of the Stirling, with enough room for two men to straddle it and on the word 'go' pull their legs together and drop out through the hole. The man behind me had to hang on to me because the aircraft was jinking a bit. I could easily have fallen out - in fact a few people did fall out over the sea - because I hadn't a hand to hold on with as I had kit bags on each of my legs. One kit bag was full of a rubber dinghy and the other had picks and shovels for digging in. They were fixed to your legs - you pulled the rip-cord when you were out of the aircraft and they dropped 20 feet below you and then dangled below on a rope. I was having to hold these things to my leg. Out I went.

'We dropped from 400 feet, which didn't give you much time in the air about seven seconds. In the flurry of all this, I let the bloody kitbag on my right side slip instead of letting it out hand over hand. That gave me a very nasty burn all down my right hand. Then I thumped down.

'We had got in with the element of surprise. A certain amount of light flak came up and we could see tracer, floating by us. But nothing hit us - the big stuff hadn't really started and as I was getting out of my 'chute on the ground, looking up at the other aircraft, they started getting shot down. By that time, the ground defences had wakened up to what was happening and the ack-ack guns had gone into action. The aircraft round about the numbers 30 were the ones that all got shot down and it was just my luck that I went in first.'
Lieutenant Richard Todd, 7th Battalion, Parachute Regiment

While these six platoons of the Oxfordshire and Buckinghamshire Light Infantry were thus engaged in securing the two bridges, those who were to reinforce them, the 7th Light Infantry Battalion of the Parachute Regiment, arrived in the area. A wind stronger than had been expected was blowing; the battalion fell some distance from their chosen dropping zone and a number were killed in the air on the way down. On the orders of the commanding officer, Lieutenant-Colonel Pine-Coffin DSO MC who had landed with a bugler near the northern boundary, the regimental call was sounded at intervals. Its notes, piercing through the night, rallied many of the battalion and by three o'clock in the morning it had reached the canal bridge and established a defence perimeter, 'A' Company being in Bénouville, 'B' on a wooded escarpment farther inland and 'C' in the grounds of the local château. The situation was difficult and the immediate future uncertain, for Pine-Coffin had not more than 200 men with whom to protect the bridge.

They were required to hold on and they did so, with ever-increasing difficulty but with an unfaltering spirit, until the main army had got ashore and could come to their relief. 'A' Company was cut off in Bénouville, where it held out for seventeen hours, losing all its officers killed or wounded. During one of the numerous counter-attacks the enemy penetrated as far as the village and reached the Regimental Aid Post. Soon afterwards they were driven back and in the confused fighting the well-beloved chaplain of the battalion, George Parry, lost his life. 'B' Company, in the little hamlet of Le Port, passed an equally strenuous day. The place abounded in snipers, who fired from the top of the church tower till it was blown off by a shot from the PIAT served by Corporal Jim Killeen. 44 A counter-attack from Caen with tanks was beaten off largely by the efforts of Private McGee who destroyed a tank with a gammon bomb and in so doing won the DCM.

'Just before I jumped, I threw out a stuffed moose head which we'd purloined from a pub in Exeter and was planned to put the fear of God into any German it hit. Then out we went.'
Lieutenant Nick Archdale 7th Parachute Battalion

'By midday the battalion was in a pretty poor state. 'A' Company, which straddled the road coming up from Caen, had taken very heavy casualties earlier in the day, attacked by forward elements of 21 Panzer Division, tanks. They were saved by a corporal [sic] who got fed up with being shot at, got out of his foxhole, ran down the road firing from the hip and actually attacked a tank. Tanks don't like being sprayed by small arms fire because they have cracks, which they closed up and he got near enough to it to throw a Gammon bomb and, with a bit of luck, it blew a track off. That tank slewed across and blocked the road and that's what saved 'A' Company.

'Meanwhile we could hear the voice of the company commander encouraging chaps. What we didn't know was that he was lying in the window of a first-storey house in Bénouville with one leg mangled. It was his second-in-command, Jim Webber, who got through to us eventually to tell us the position and ask if he could have some reinforcements because they were hanging on by their teeth, they didn't know how long they could keep going. He had been shot in the lung but we didn't know it at the time because his webbing equipment covered all the blood and signs of wounding there. He insisted that there was no way of reaching 'A' Company except by the way he'd come and he insisted on going back with the relieving section. We sent an officer and a few chaps, ten or whatever it was back down to 'A' Company to help out and it was Jim Webber who led them back.

'B' Company was in Le Port. They were pinned down by quite well-ensconced Germans and movement was very difficult. They were just behind our headquarters position and they were really, really pinned down, particularly by snipers in the church tower. But we had this Corporal Killeen, an Irishman. Well, Corporal Killeen had a PIAT, a shoulder-firing anti-tank missile - very inaccurate, not very strong, very cumbersome, but quite effective if you happen to hit the right place. He mouse-holed

---

44 The PIAT (Projector Infantry Anti-Tank - a platoon-level British hand-held anti-tank weapon similar to the American Bazooka) had a penchant for jamming and was not much use at distances beyond 50 yards. It was not a popular weapon, but apart from the sticky-grenades called Gammon bombs, it was the only anti-tank defence available.

through cottages, got from one to another, till he got to within range of the church. Later he described all this to the great BBC war correspondent, Chester Wilmot: 'We were told to clear the church steeple but we couldn't get at it, so I took my PIAT into the upstairs bedroom of the house opposite, stuck it up on the window-sill and let fly with a bomb and I hit the church tower, knocked a bloody great hole in it. So I fired a few more times and each time I hit the tower and I made a real mess of that little church tower. I stood up and there was no firing. Later we found twelve dead Jerries up there. Some had been killed by our Stens and the PIAT had got the rest. I walked across to the church - I reckoned it was safe for me then - but, oh, God, I was sorry to see what I'd done to a wee house of God.'

'Absolutely true. He was a devout Irish Catholic boy. And there were twelve dead Germans in the tower. He'd killed the lot of them.'

Lieutenant Richard Todd, 7th Battalion, Parachute Regiment. Killeen's colonel, who was present, asked if the church had been badly damaged. Killeen, who was from Wigan, said 'No, we just knocked half the top off; we wouldn't have touched it if the snipers hadn't been there. And when I went in sir, I did take my hat off.'

On the canal itself, two gunboats, one coming from Ouistreham, the other from Caen, were dealt with. A fierce fight developed in the château grounds held by 'C' Company and a number of German Mark IV tanks were hit and set on fire. Between lulls the officer in command, Lieutenant Atkinson, conversed with the matron in charge of a number of civilian patients convalescing in the château. She was wearing trousers, seemed tired, but gave him all the information about the Germans that she possessed or could discover and then went back to bed. One or two snipers wearing civilian clothes were found, notably a man in a morning coat and grey flannel trousers. They were killed or captured. Towards evening the pressure on the battalion had become very difficult to withstand. It was then that the hard-pressed men, lifting their heads, beheld the gliders coming in with the remainder of the Division and some much-needed stores. Their hearts were greatly lightened at this sight, 'which,' said Private Owen 'was the happiest I ever saw.'

Certain moments are vivid in the minds of those who fought by the canal and the river from before dawn till after dusk on that long summer day. There was the sound of Major Howard's victory signal travelling over the night wind to the ears of the parachutists struggling to reach and reinforce the bridge. There was the large hole which gaped in the side of the water tower at Bénouville, hiding a nest of snipers. It had been punched by the first shot fired by a captured German anti-tank gun. There was Monsieur Gondrée in the little cafe by the swing bridge, tending the wounded and adding to the noise of battle a more convivial sound. He uncorked ninety-seven bottles of champagne, carefully hidden for just such a day as that: (the German occupying troops had been kept happy with a concoction made by his wife of rotting melons and half-fermented sugar, which they bought at twenty-five francs the glass and drank with avidity). There was Corporal Killeen reverently removing his steel helmet at the door of the church of which he had just smashed the sniper-infested tower. There were the red berets of General Gale and Brigadier Poett as they walked across the bridges about ten in the morning, 'for all the world like umpires at an exercise'. There were the gliders 'swaying and rustling' through the evening air, bringing reinforcements and supplies. And, above all, there was that moment when the straining ears of the airborne troops on and about the bridge heard at first afar off and then steadily nearer and nearer the shrill voice of bagpipes announcing the arrival of the 1st Special Service Brigade.

They had come in from the sea and fought their way inland, seeking to fulfil their promise that they would be at the Canal Bridge by noon. When the skirl of the pipes could be no longer doubted, the temptation to reply by a bugle call in accordance with the prearranged plan was very strong. To do so would mean that the way was clear; but it was not. The little hamlet of Le Port still harboured German snipers. Since they heard no bugle notes, the commandos, on nearing Le Port; went into action. They helped to clear Le Port and at two o'clock were heading for the bridge. On they came, Brigadier the Lord Lovat DSO MC at their head, with his piper behind him playing a shrill tune and behind the piper the commando soldiers marching in step. They reached the bridge and the green berets mingled with the red. Men of formations which had sustained the valour of British arms in the cold, clear fjords of Norway, in the dank jungles of Madagascar, in the stinging sands and stony hills of Africa, in the streets of Vasterival, in the tracer-lit docks of St. Nazaire, met with men who were performing for the first time a like office in the green fields of Normandy.

Index